SCREENSHOT TOKYO

A PHOTOGRAPHIC EXPLORATION

SCOTT SHAW

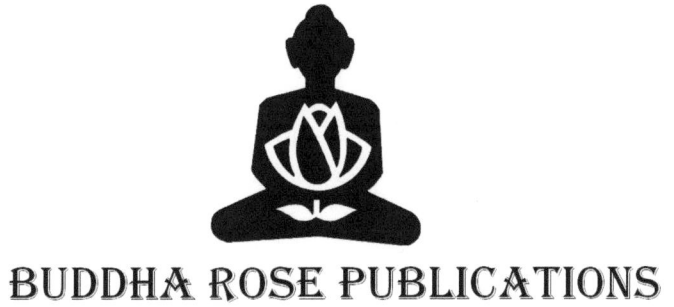

BUDDHA ROSE PUBLICATIONS

Screenshot Tokyo
A Photographic Exploration
Copyright © 2016 by Scott Shaw
All Rights Reserved
No part of this publication can be duplicated
in any manner without the expressed written
permission of the publisher.

First Edition 2016

ISBN: 1-877792-92-6
ISBN 13: 978-1-877792-92-2

Printed in the United States of America

10 9 8 7 6 5 4 3 2 1

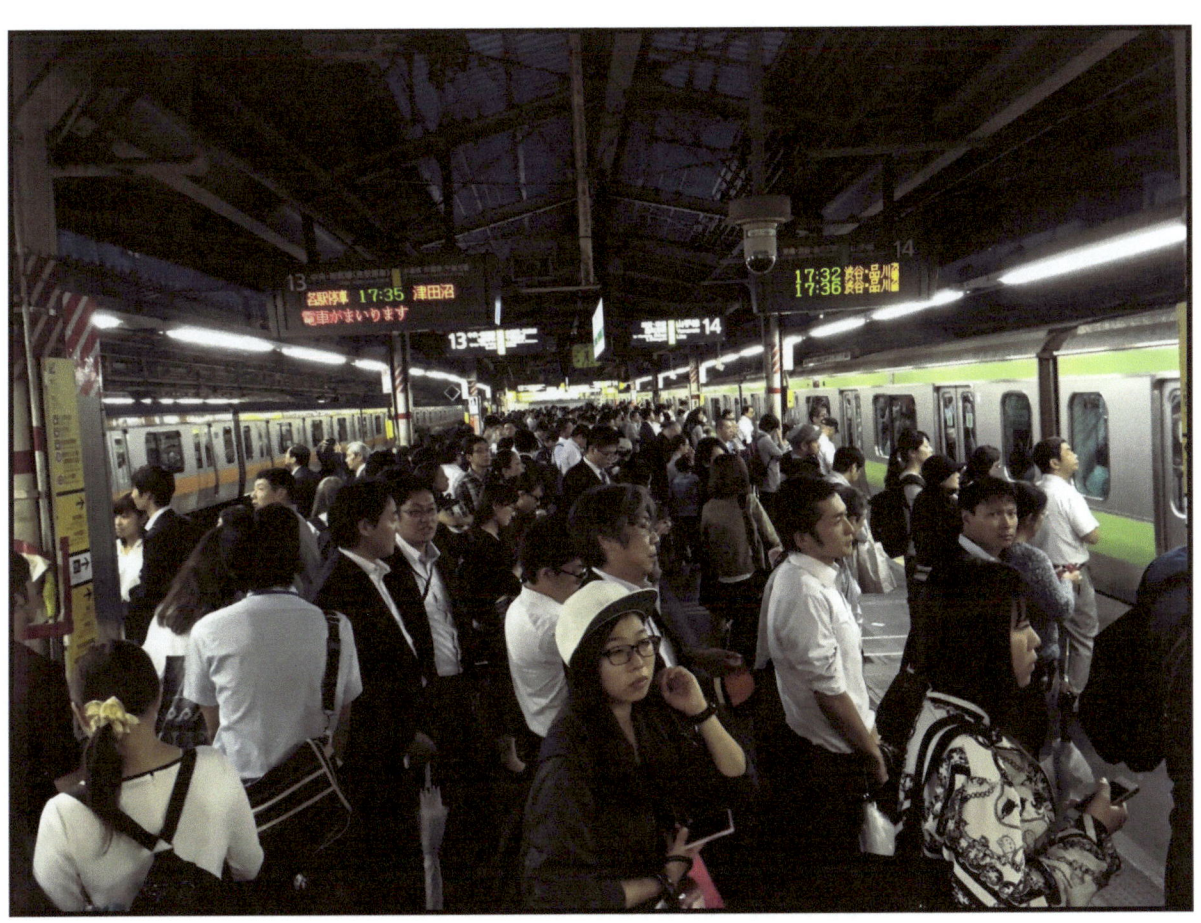

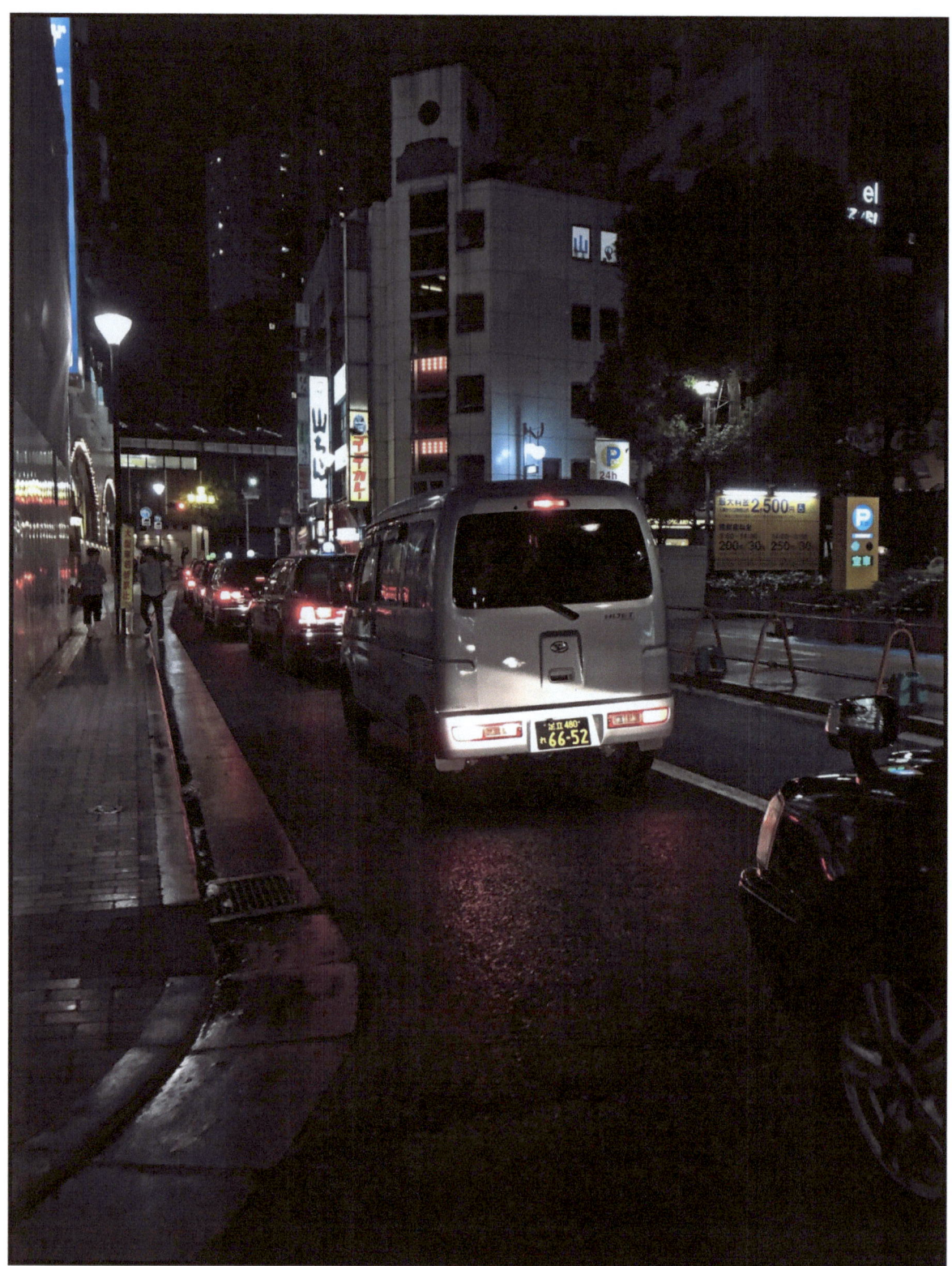

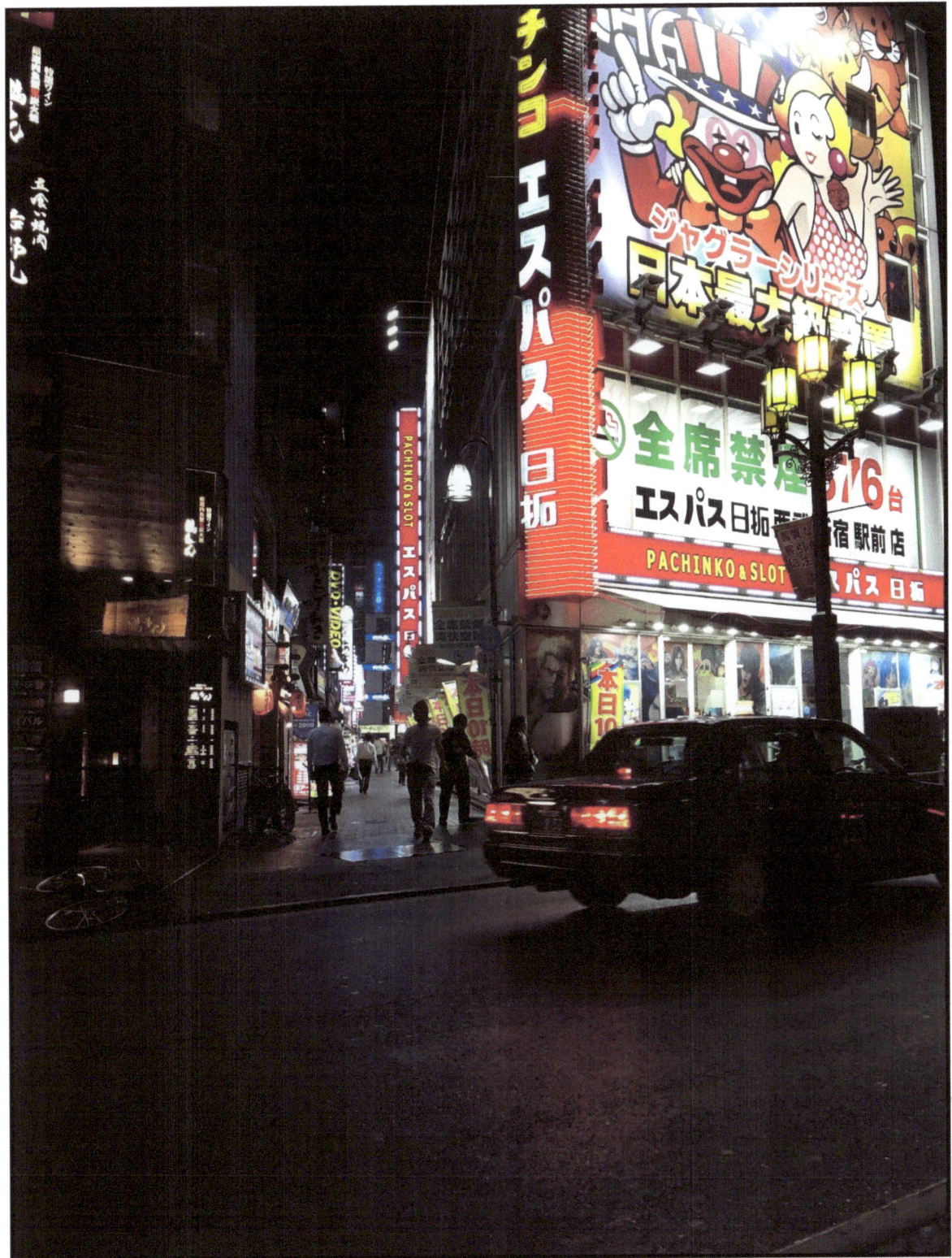

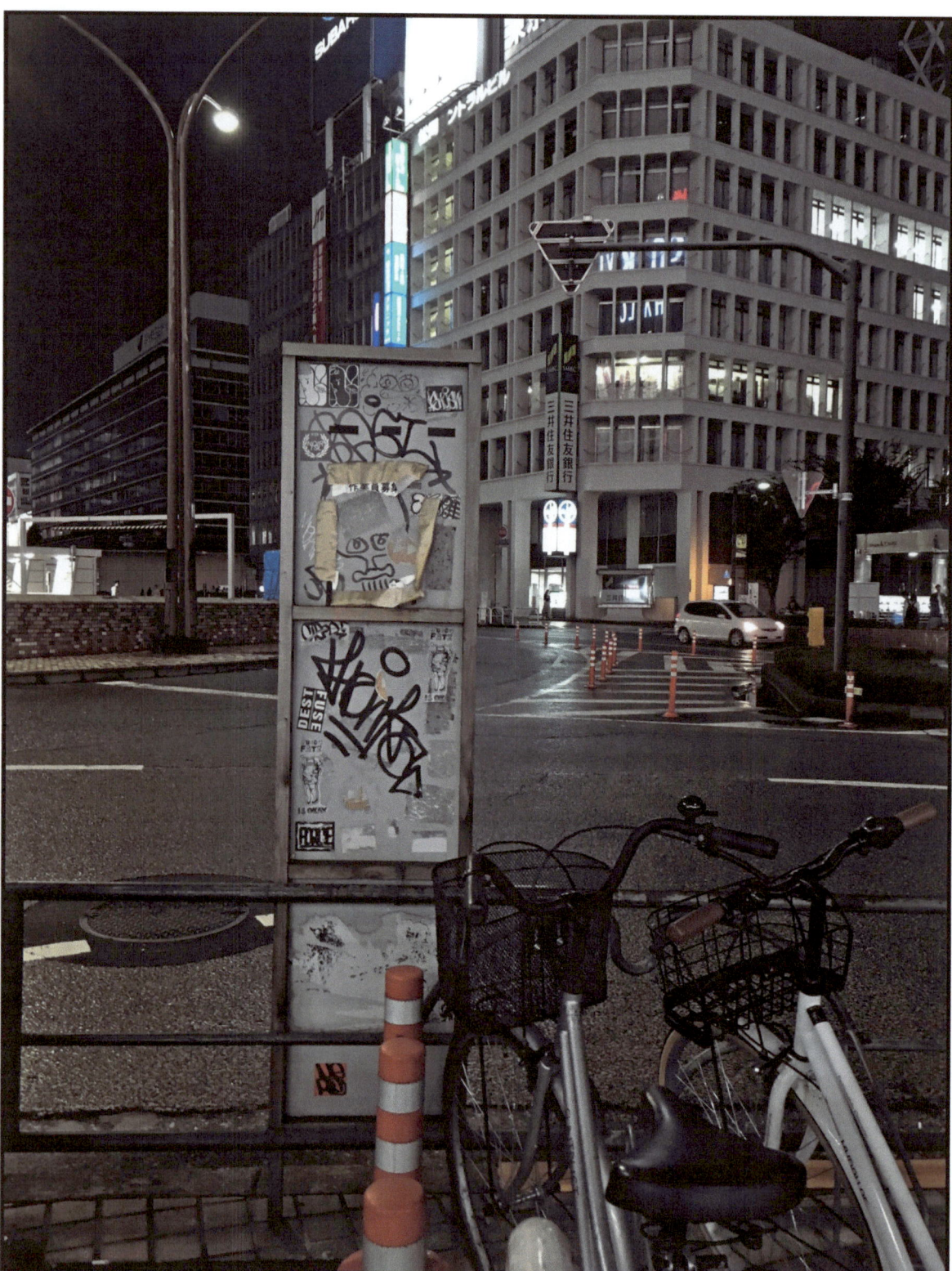

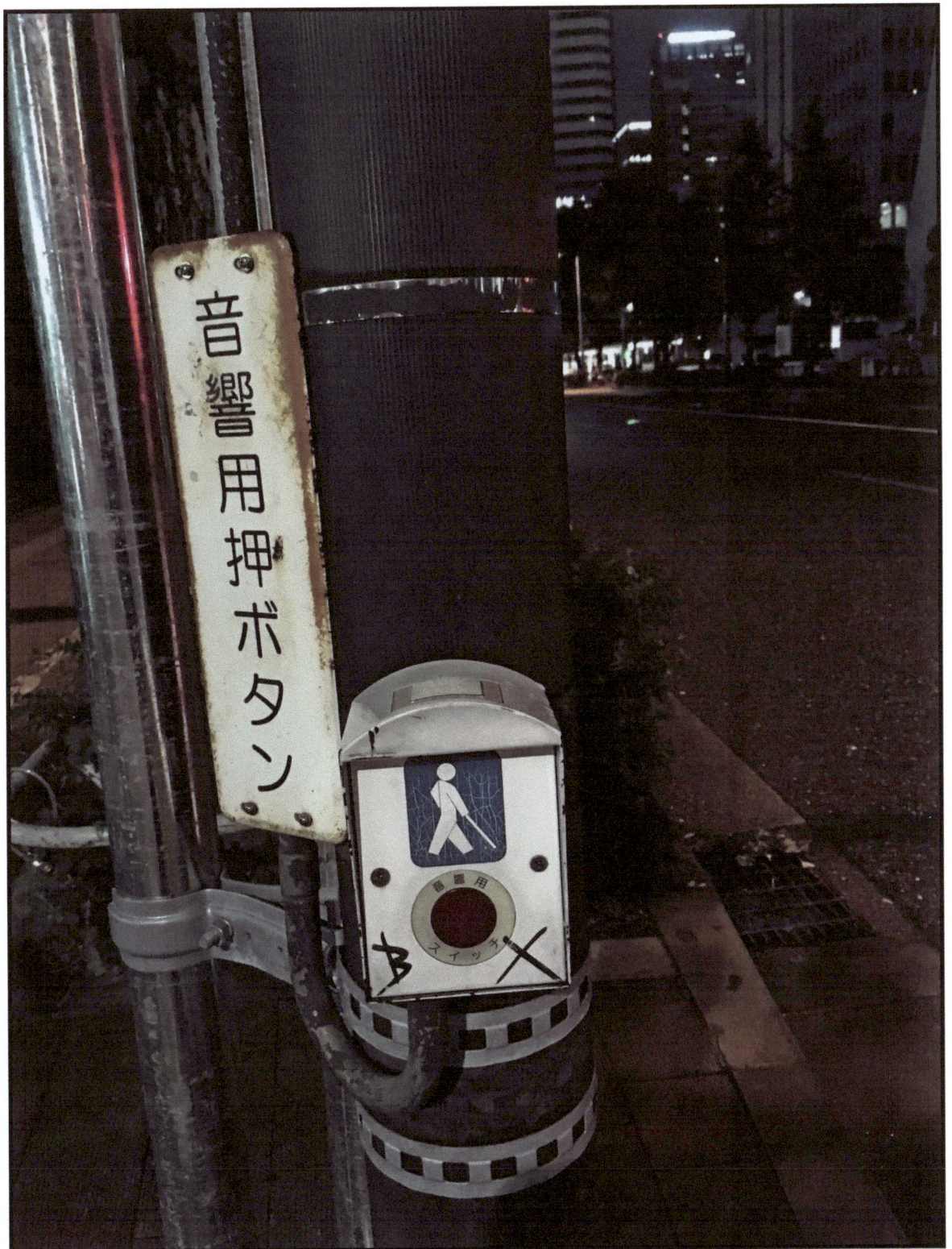

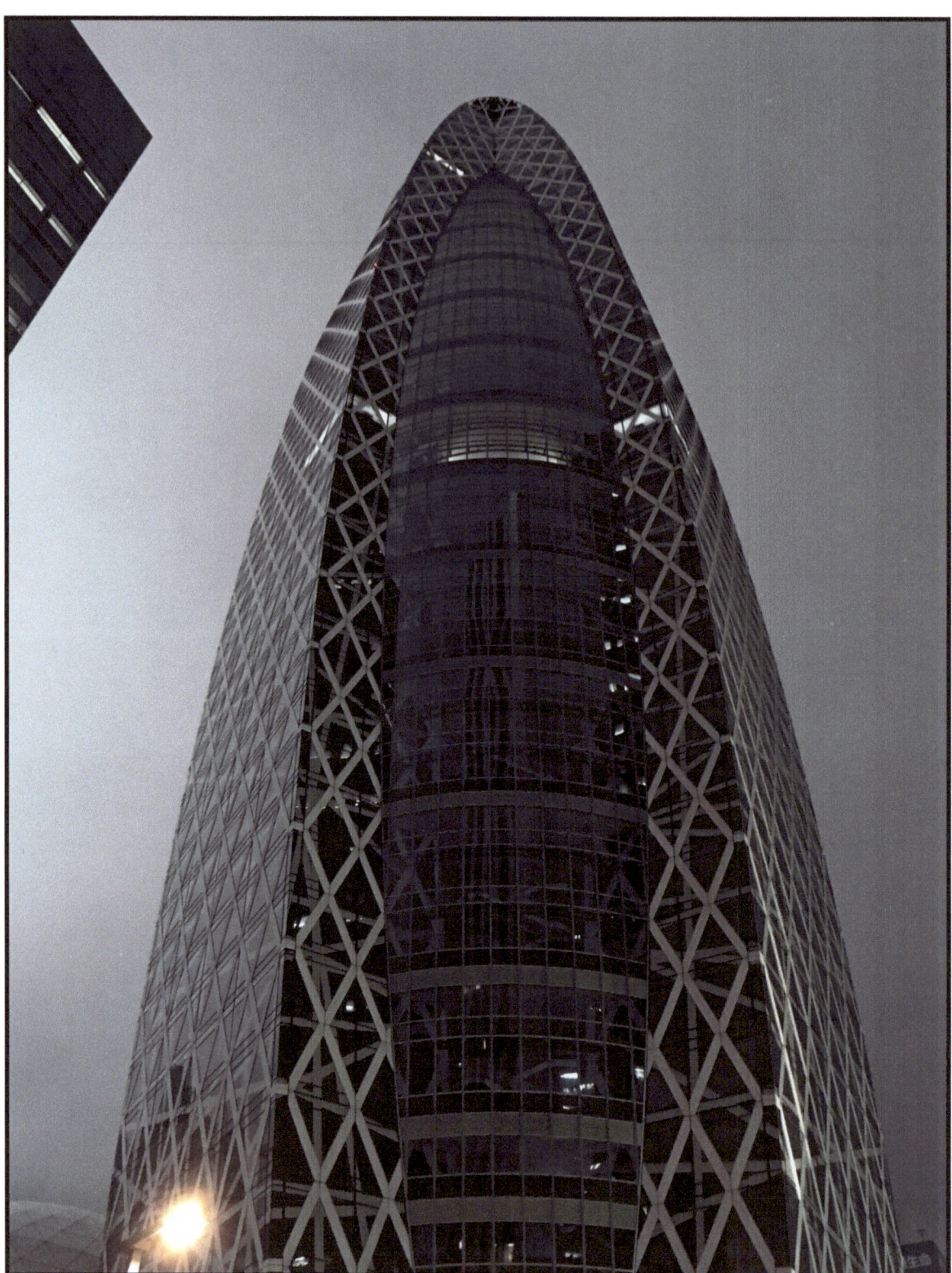

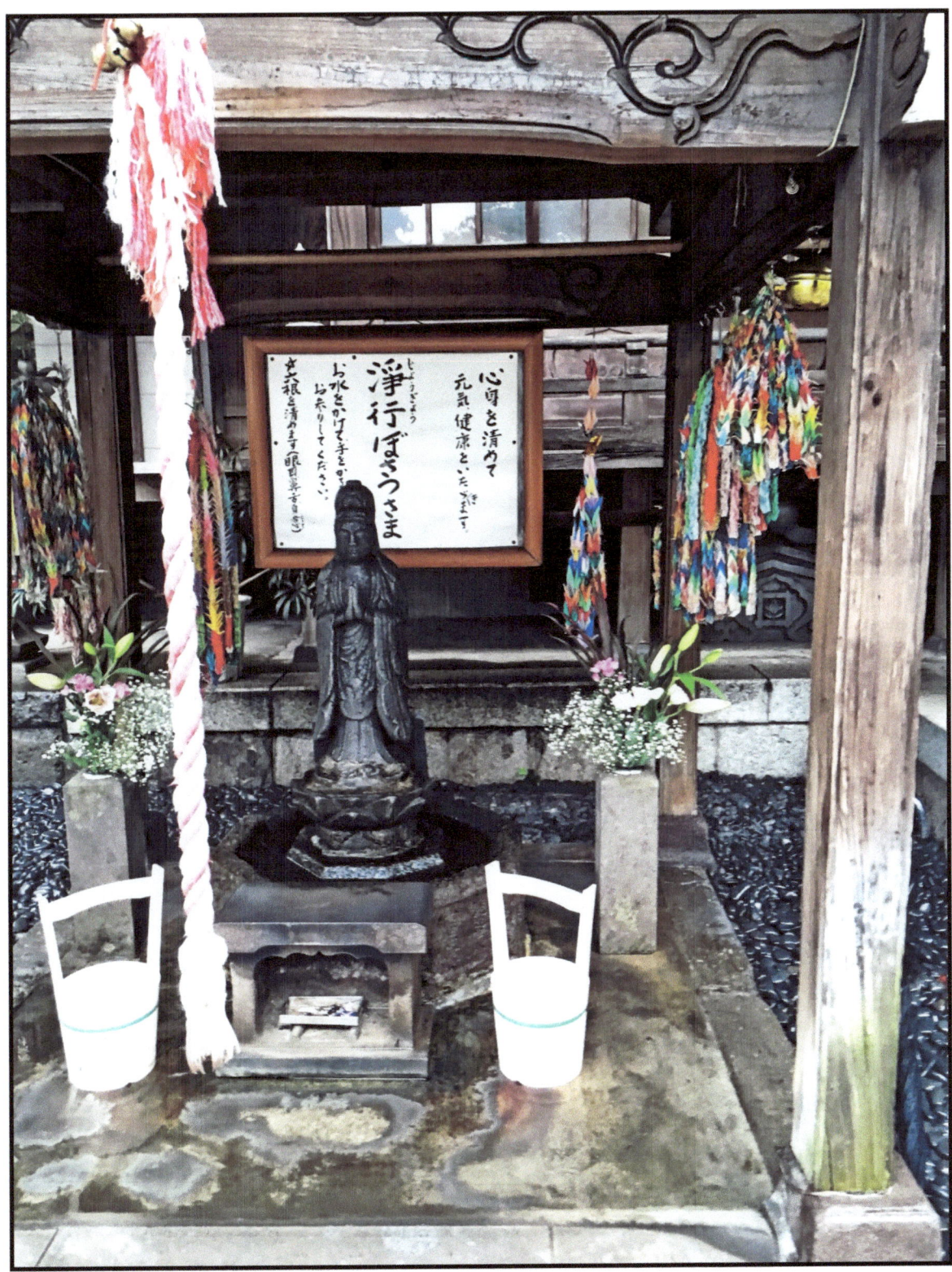

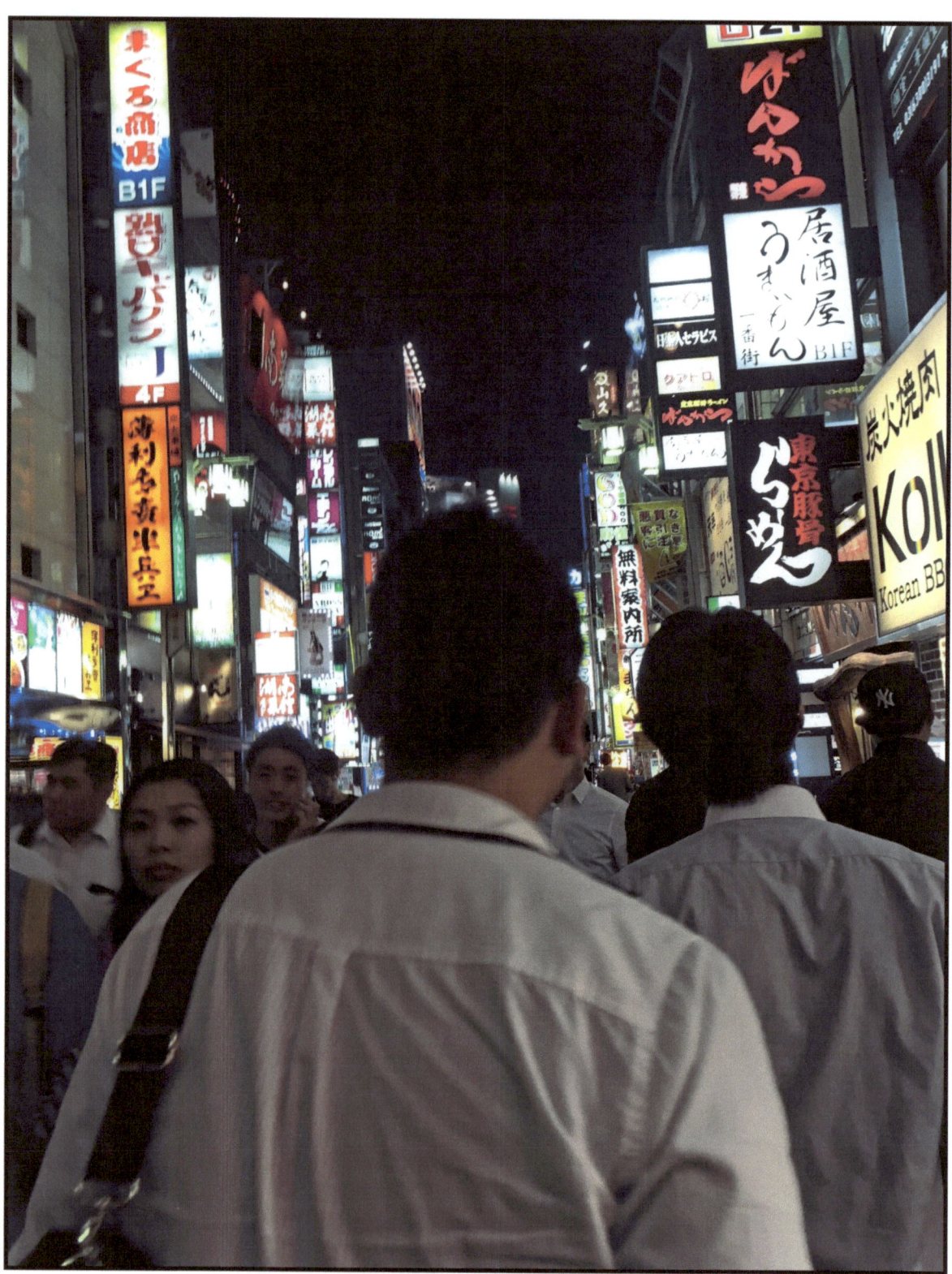

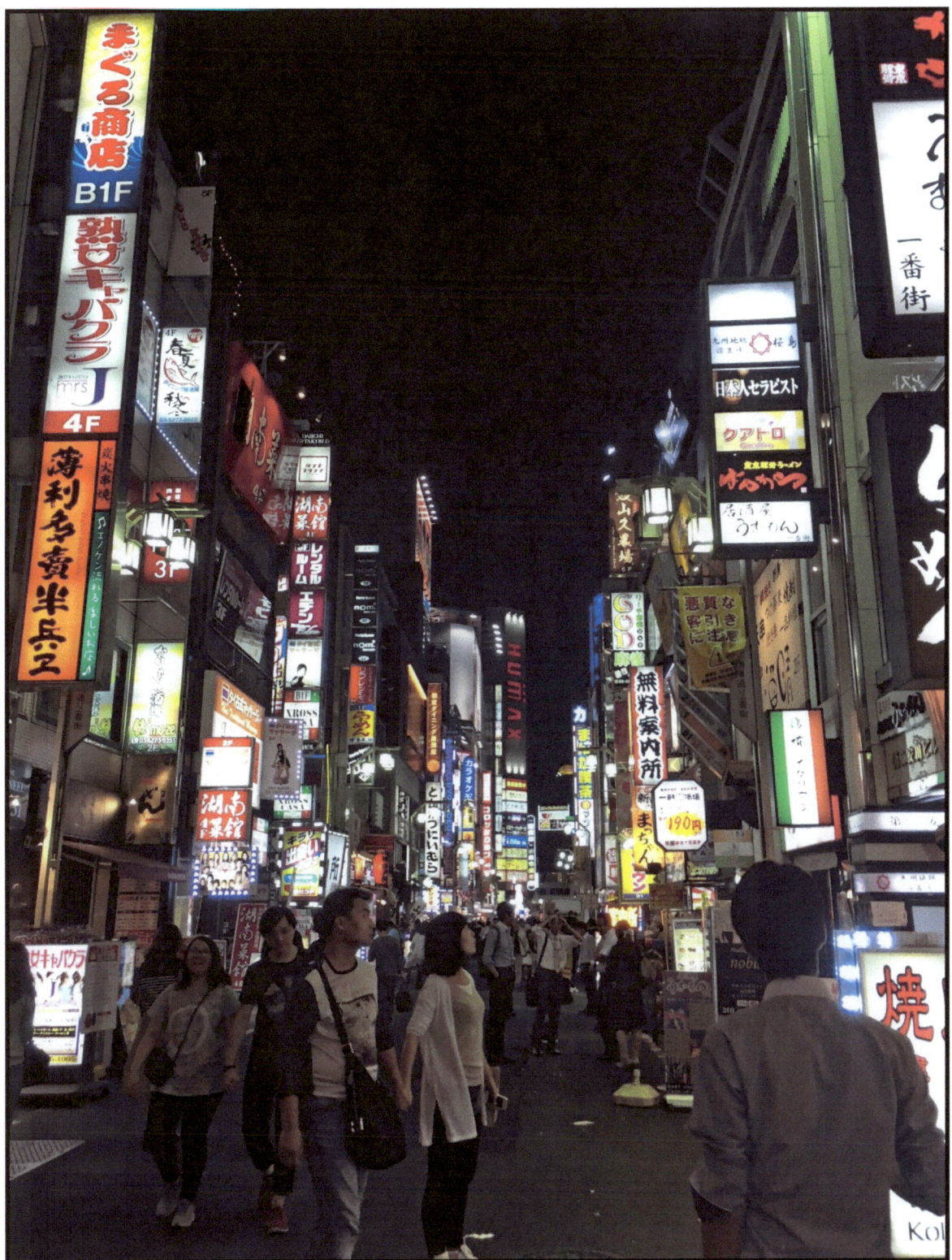

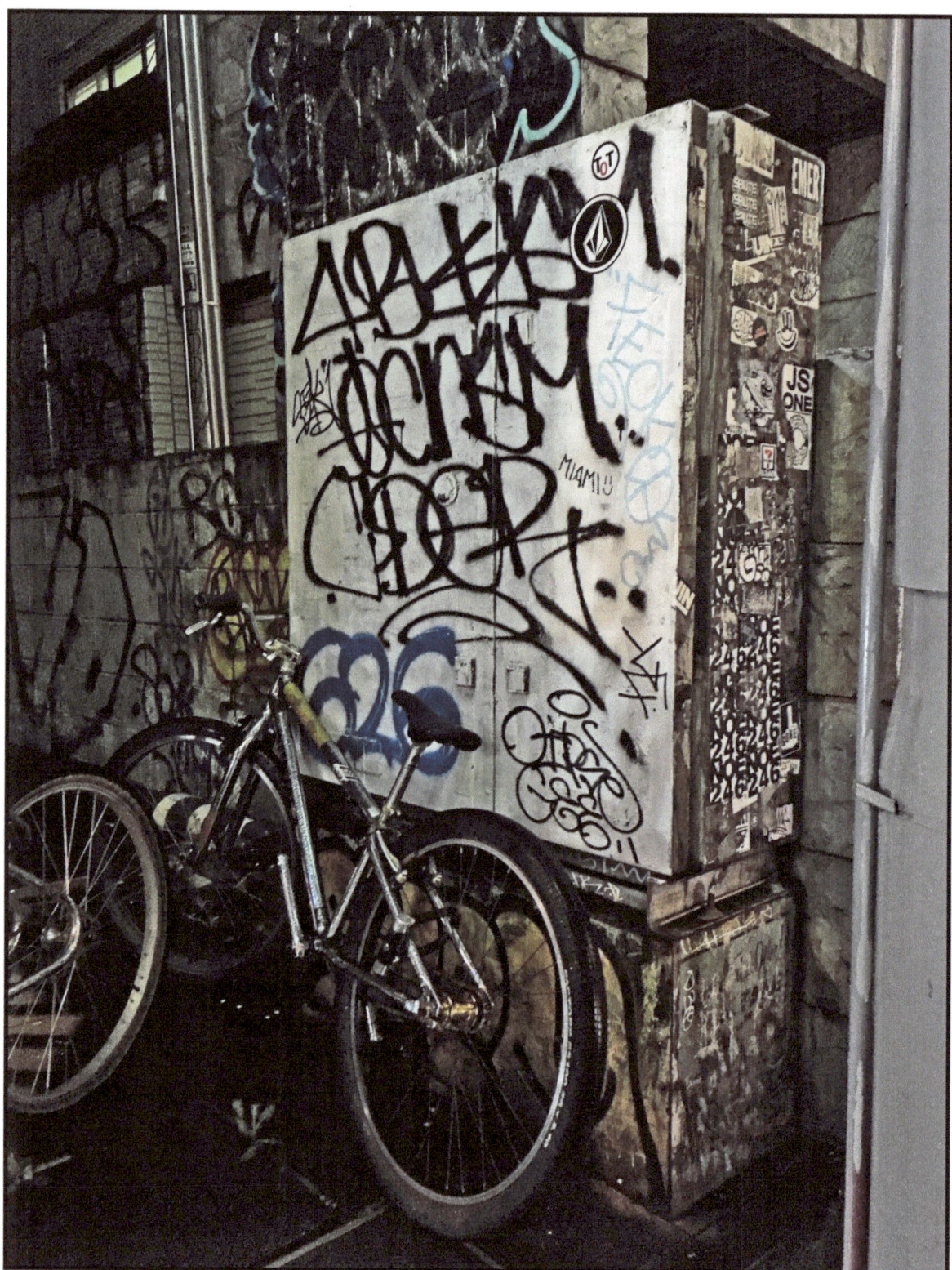

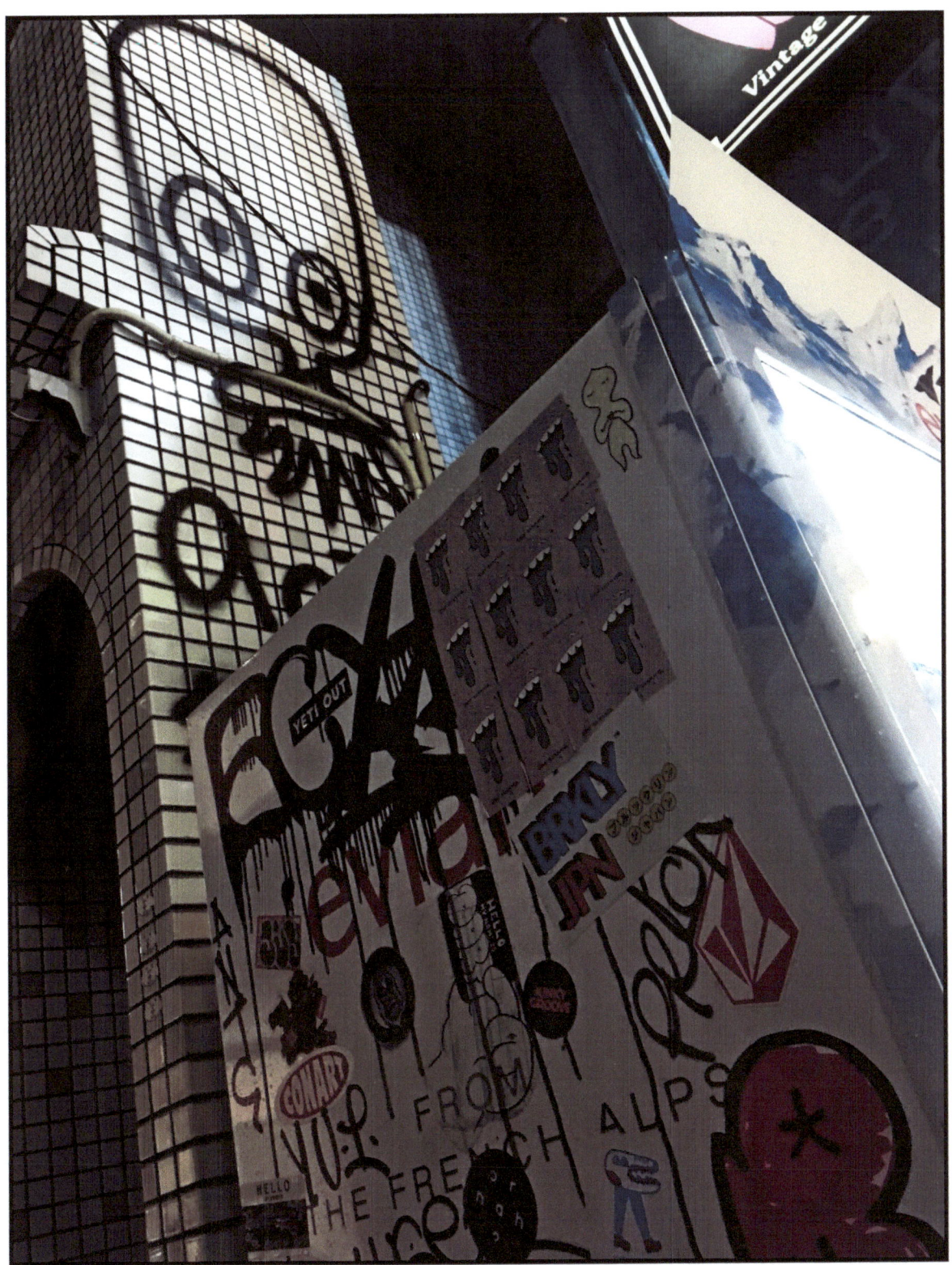

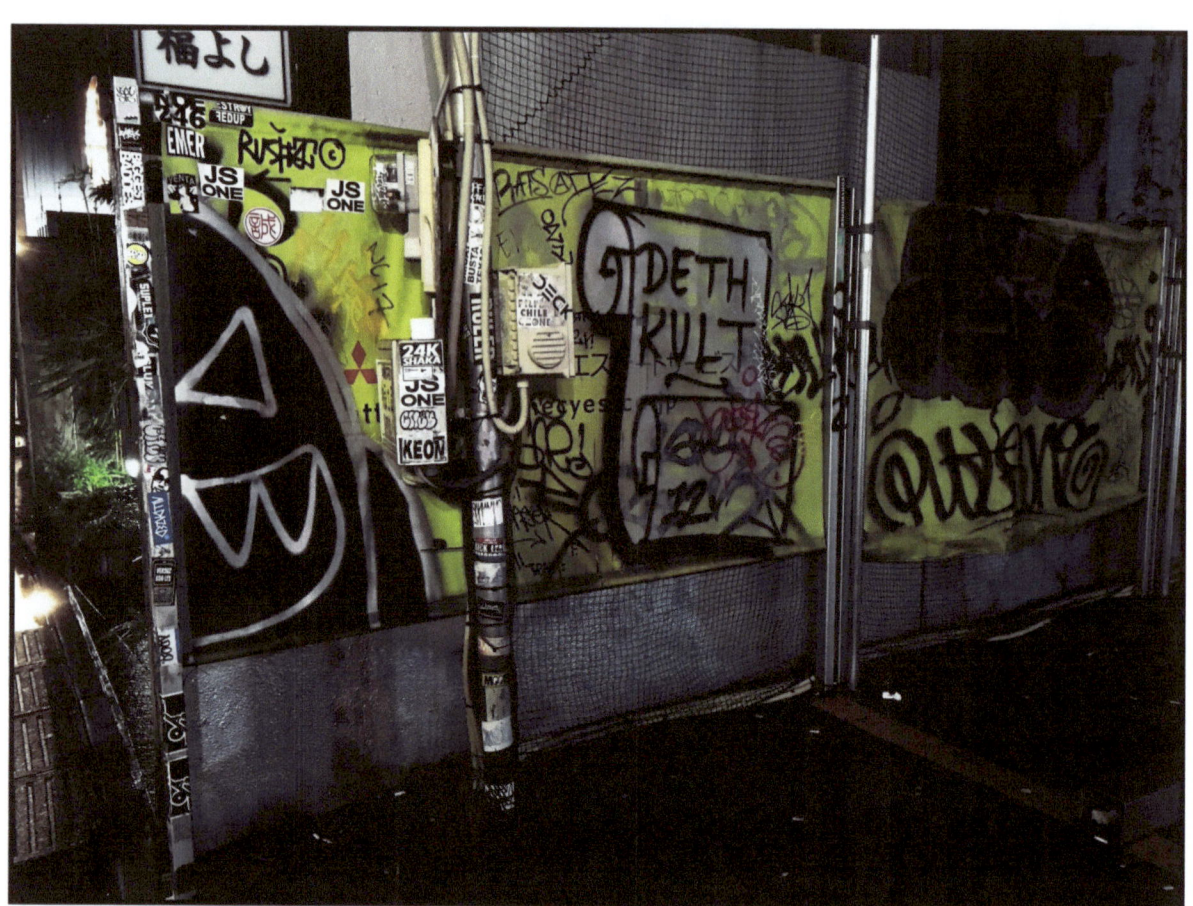

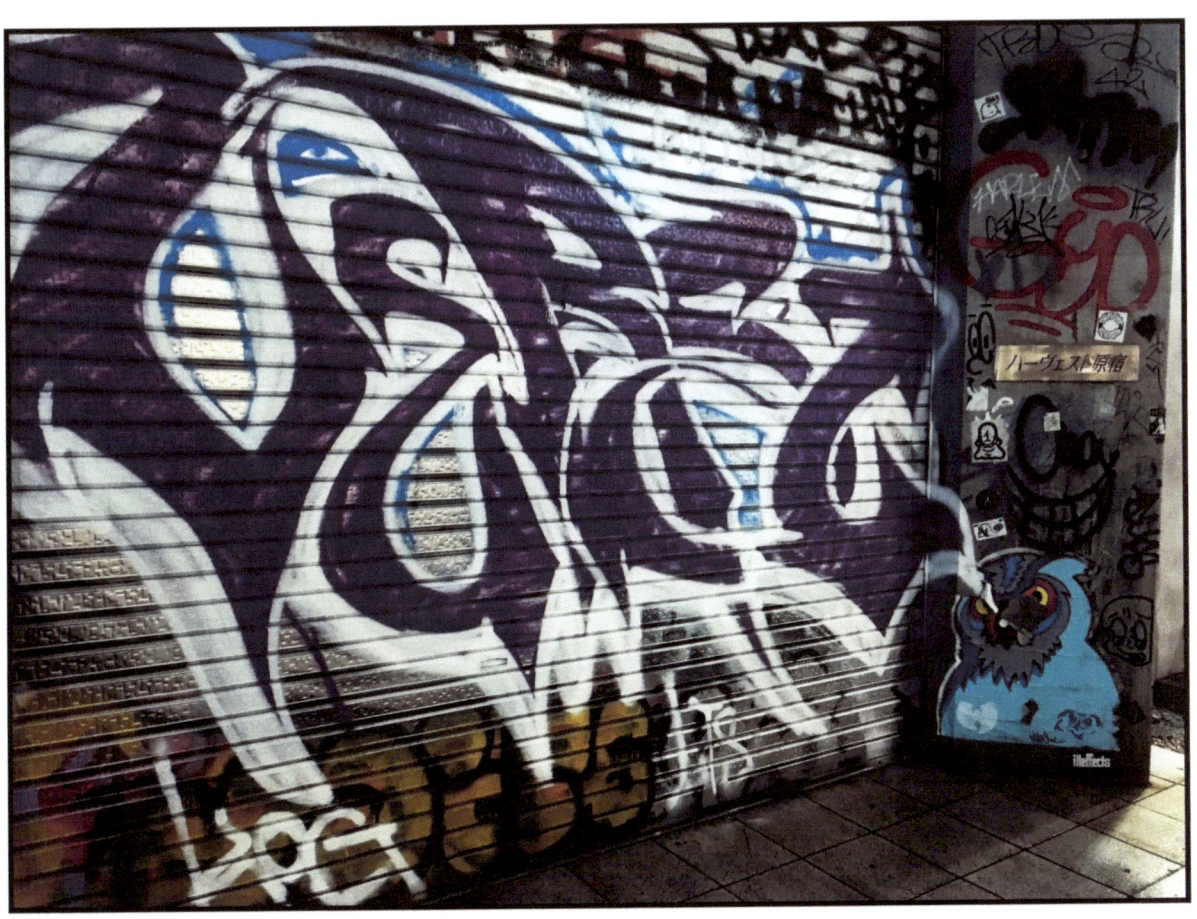

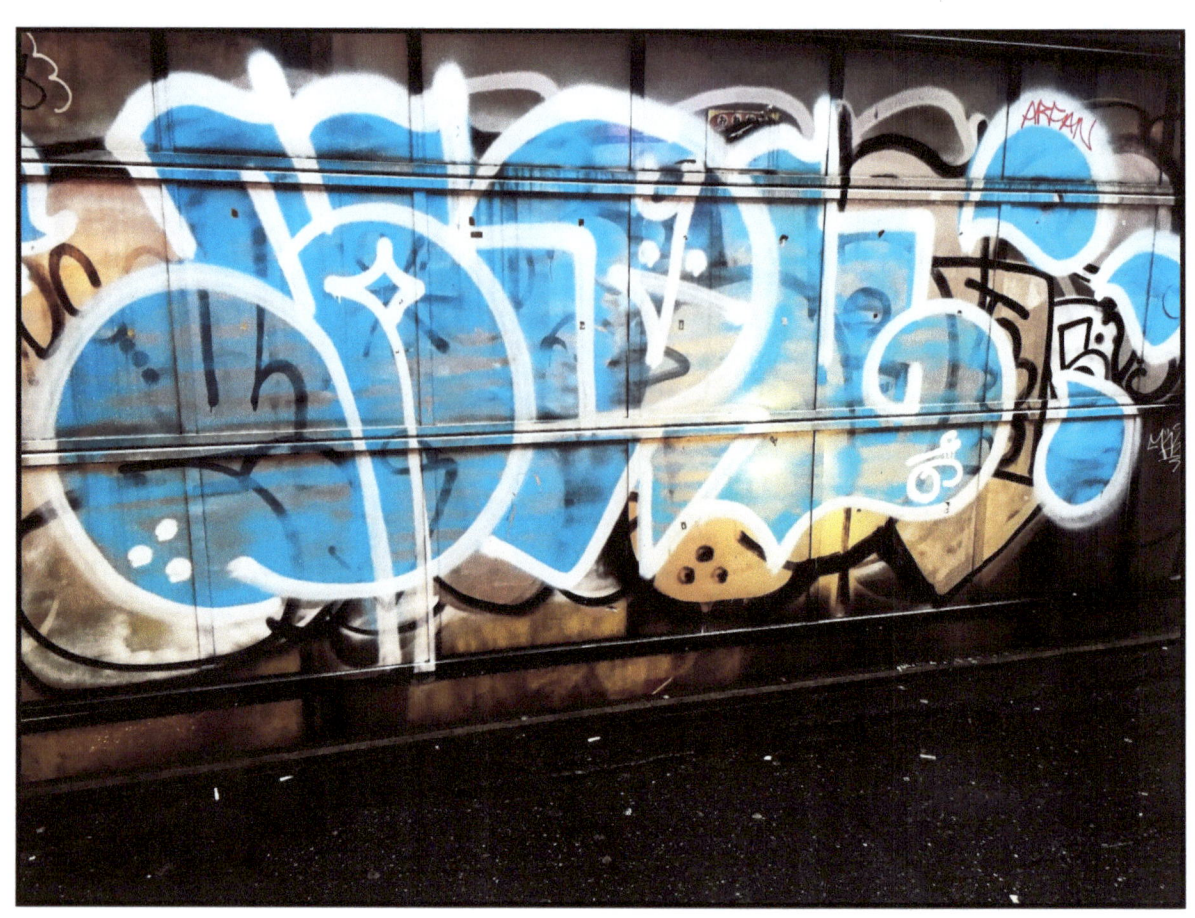

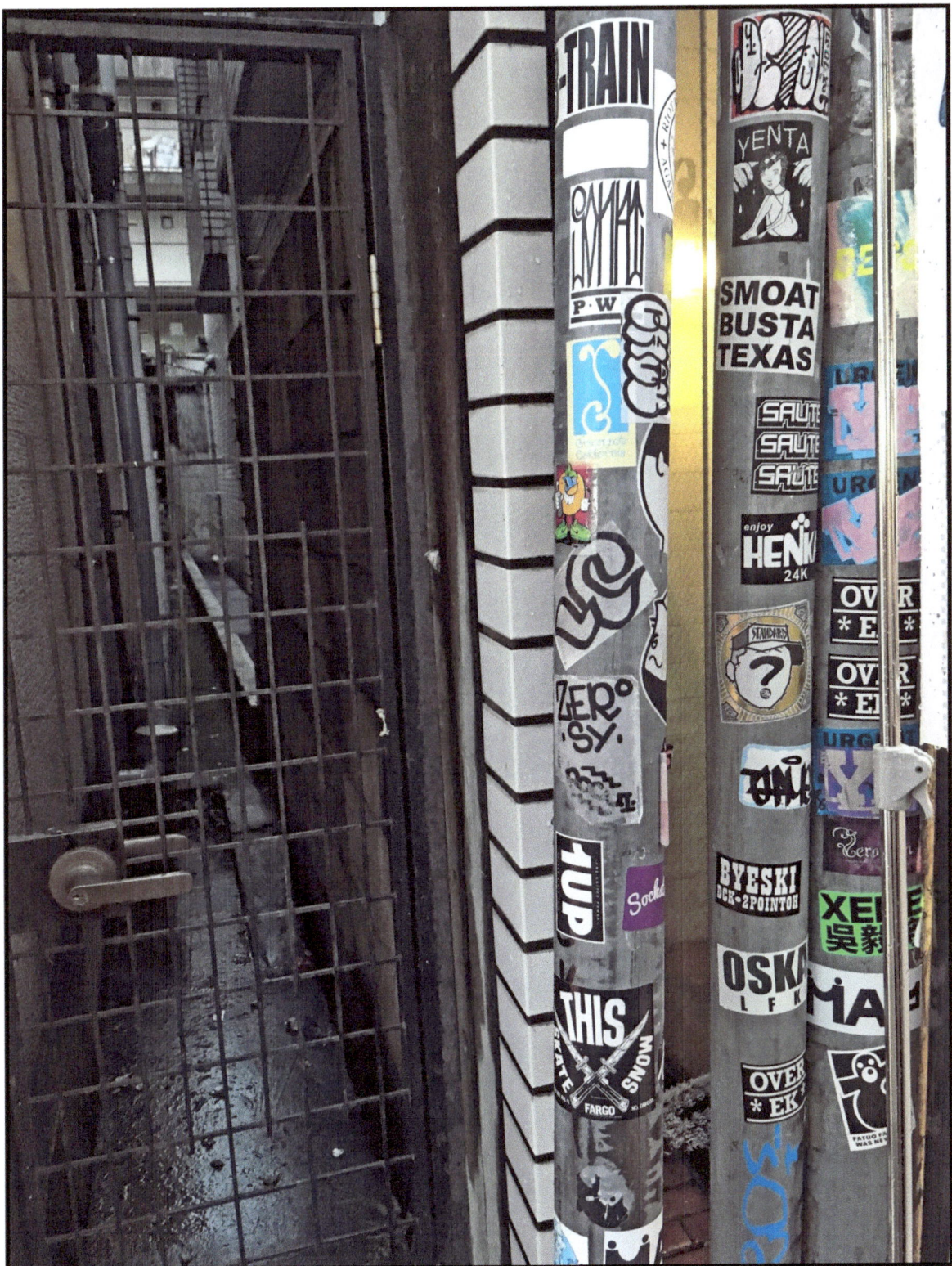

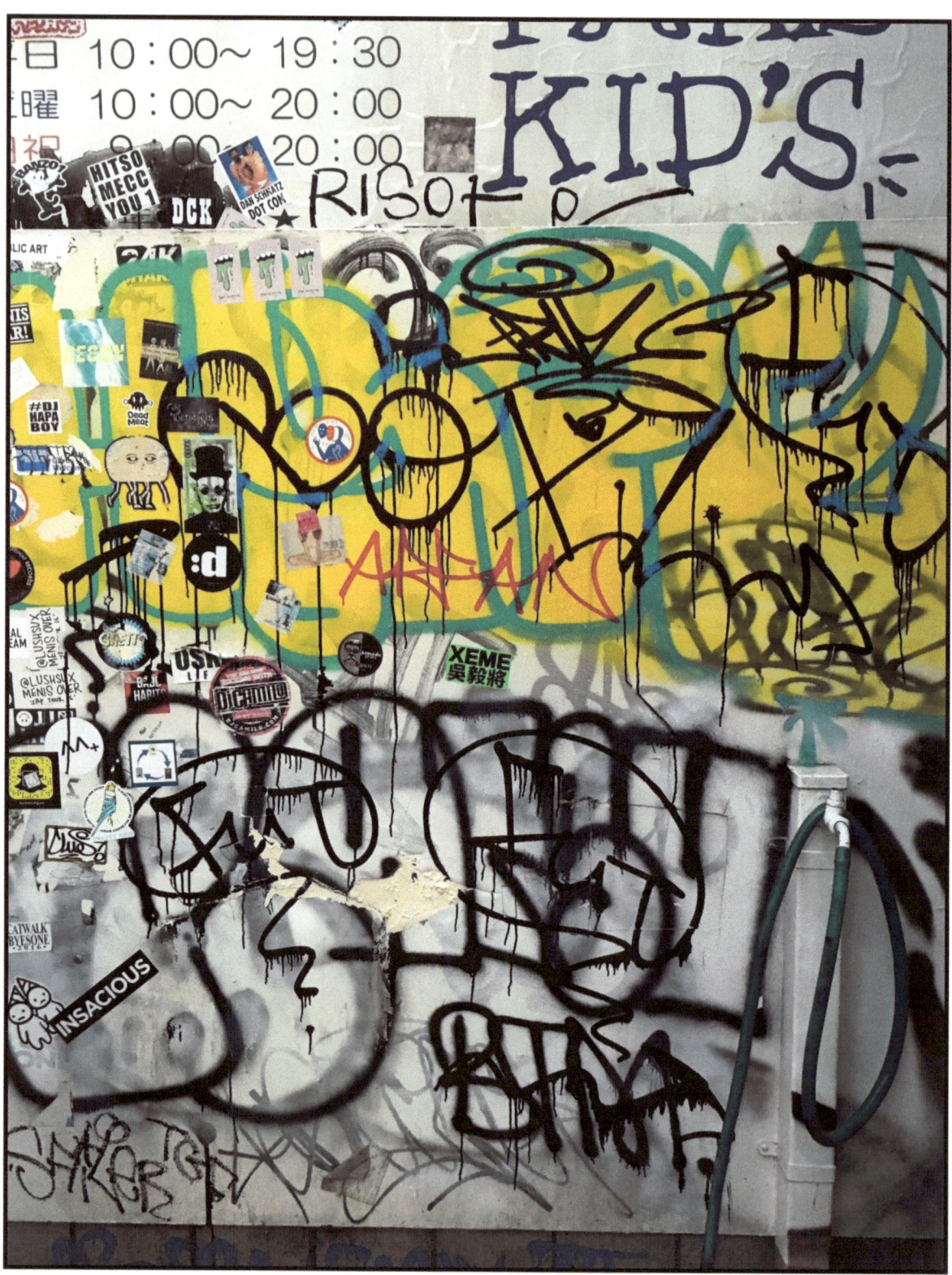

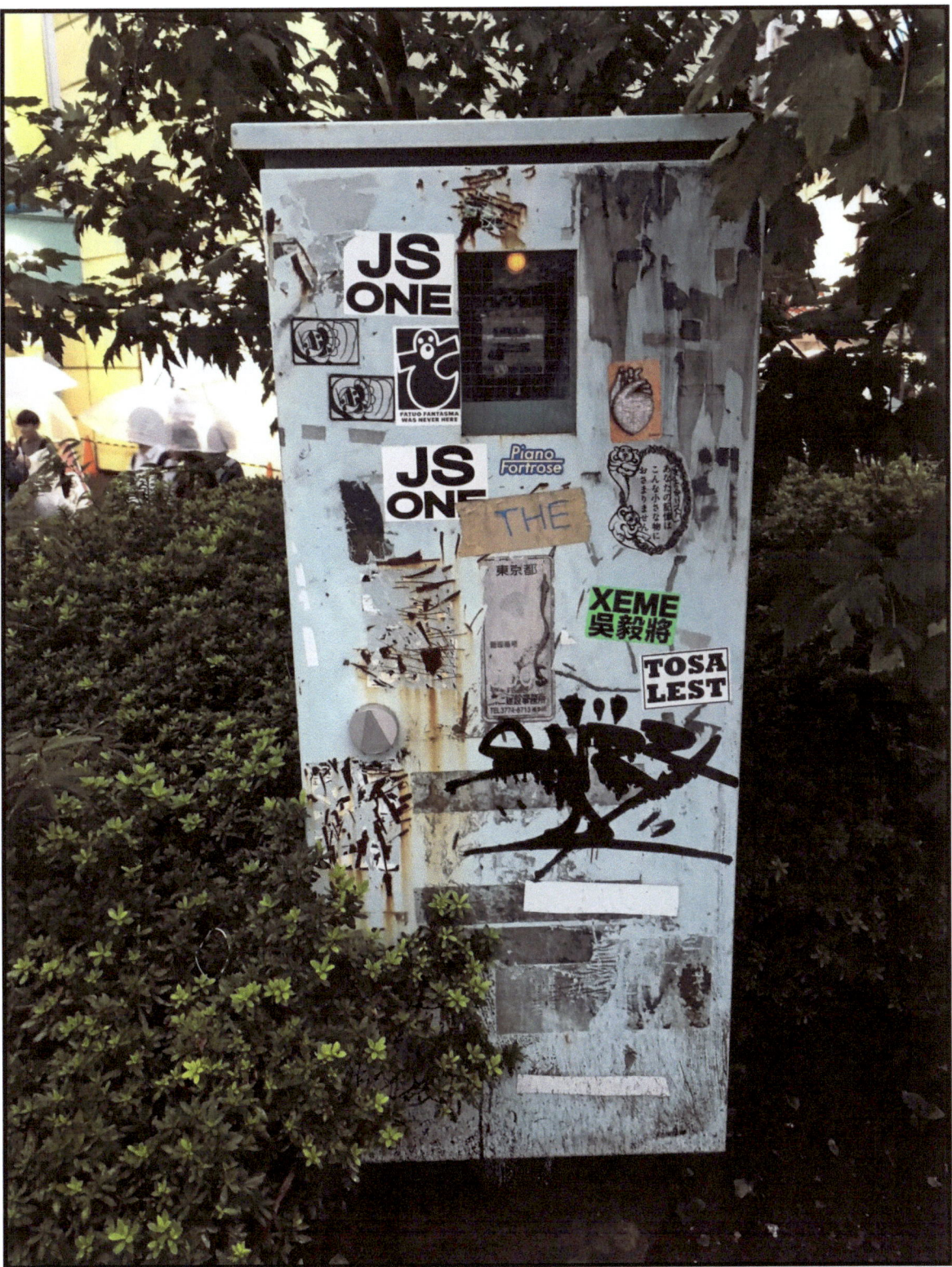

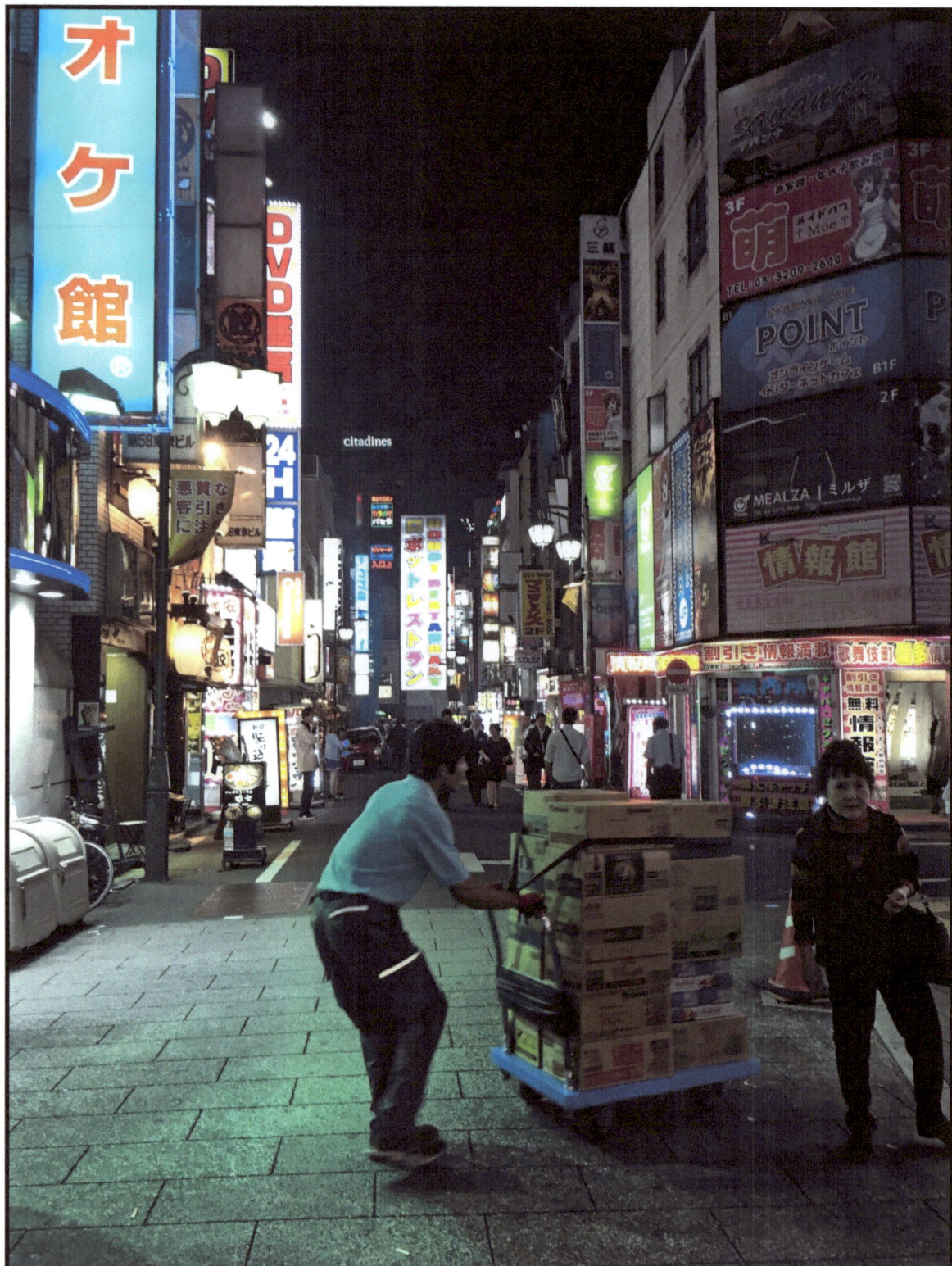

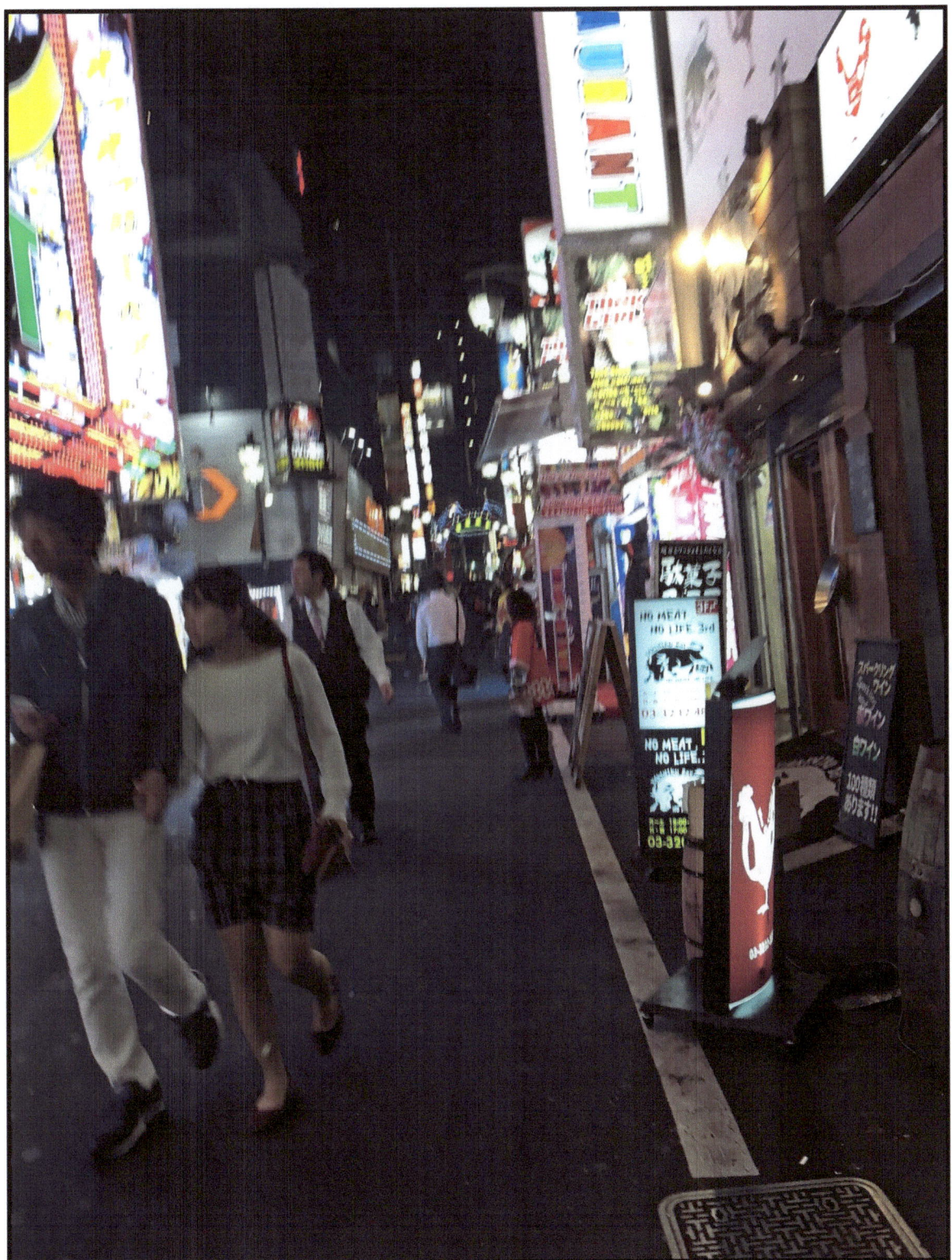

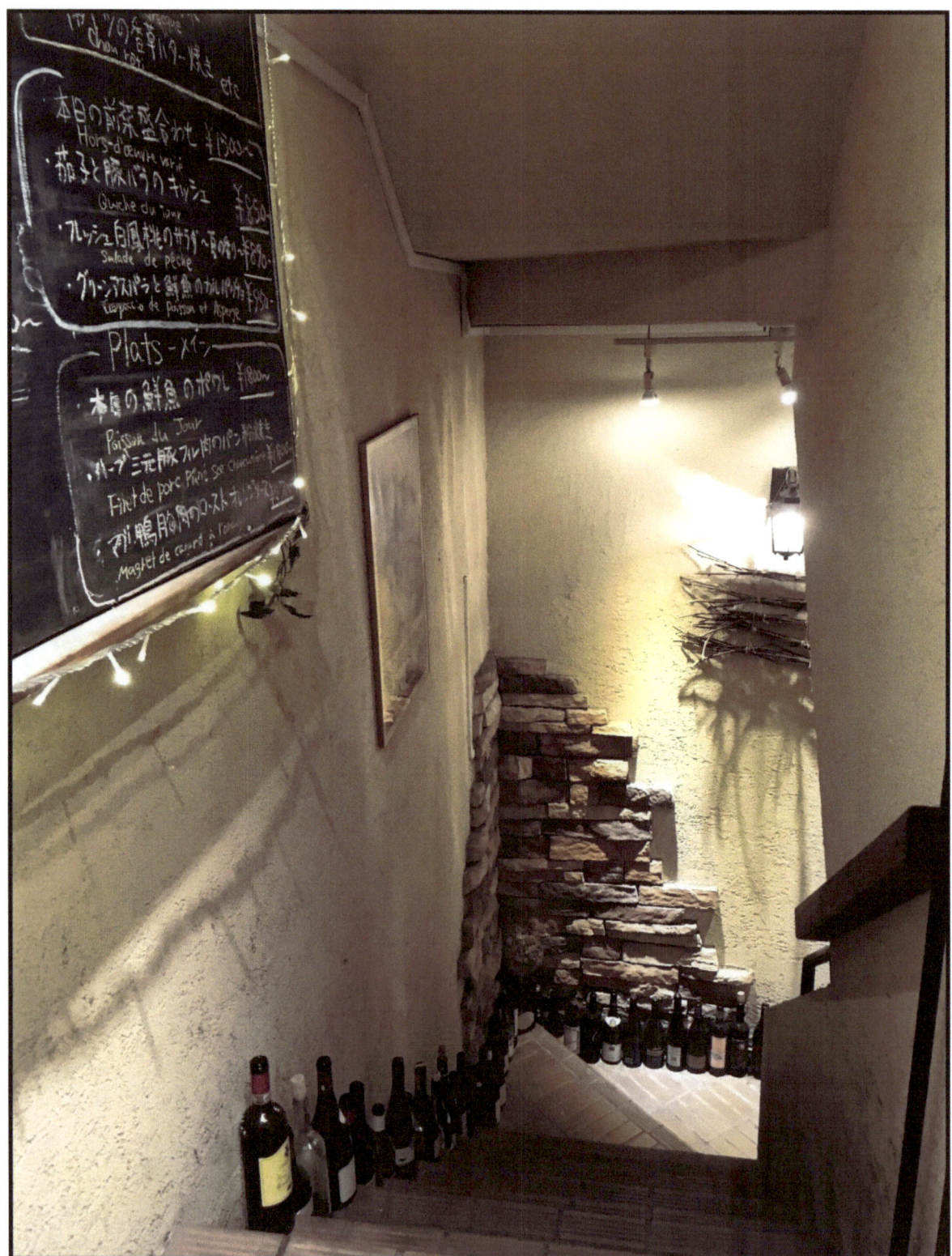

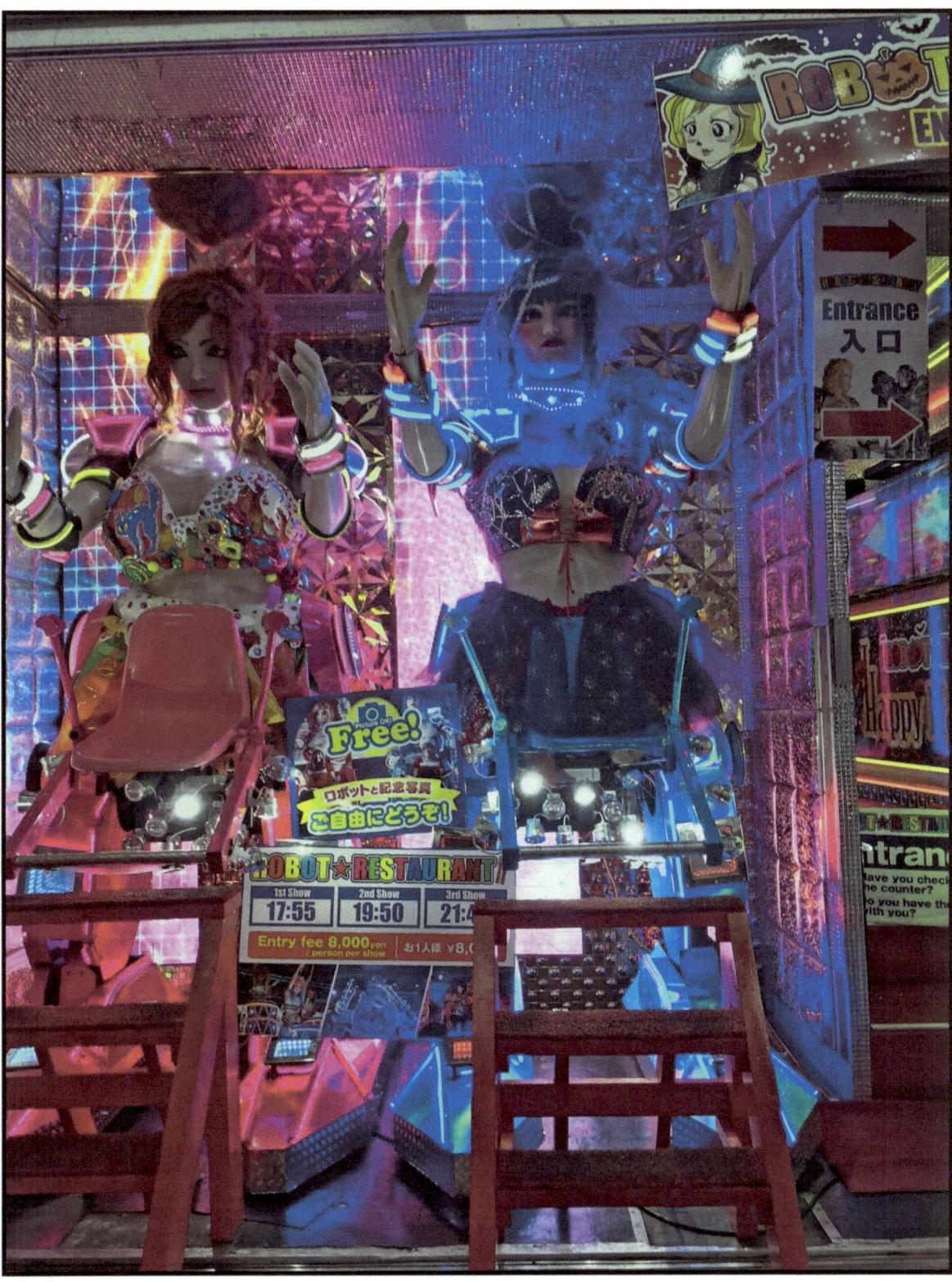

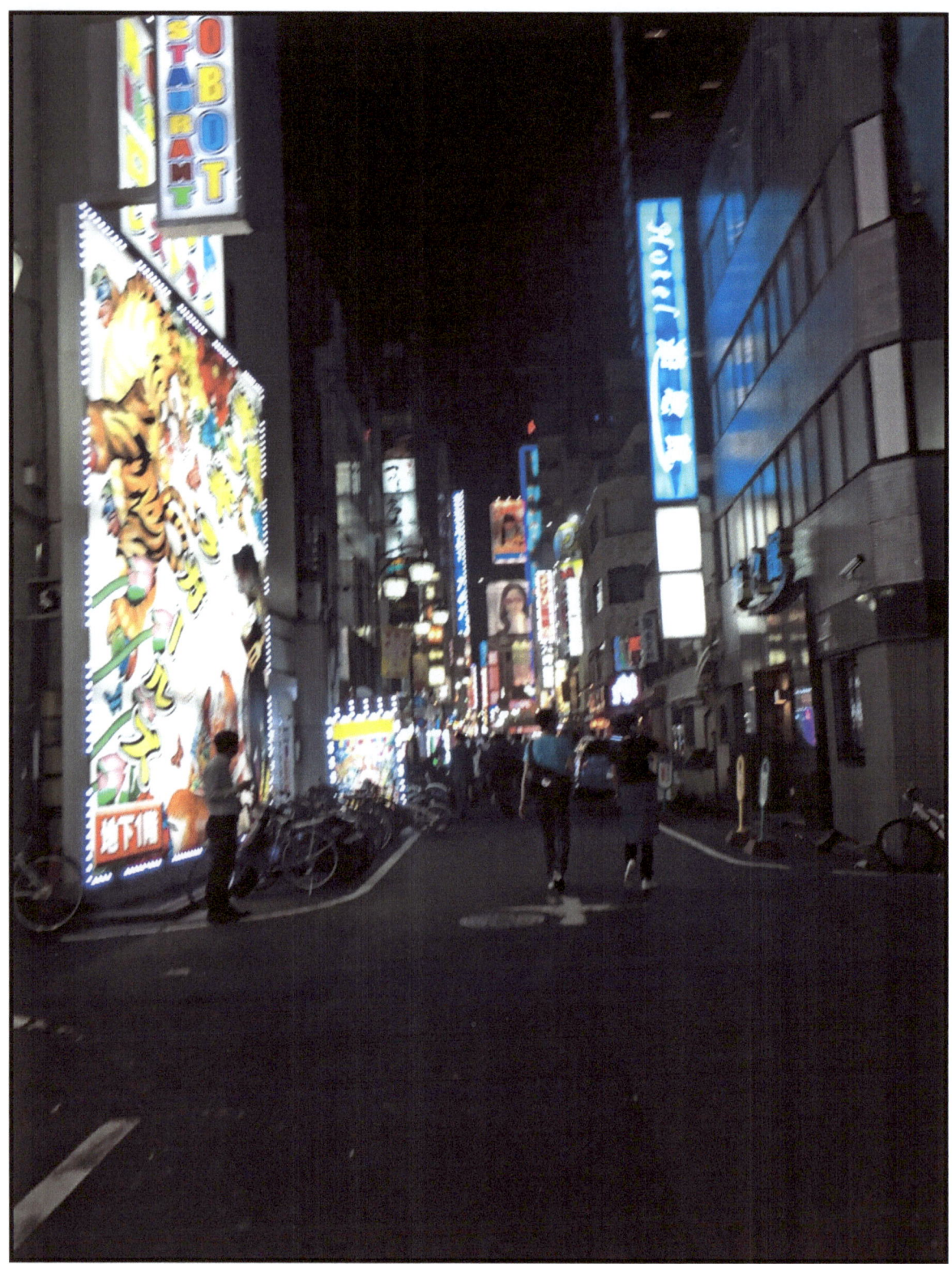

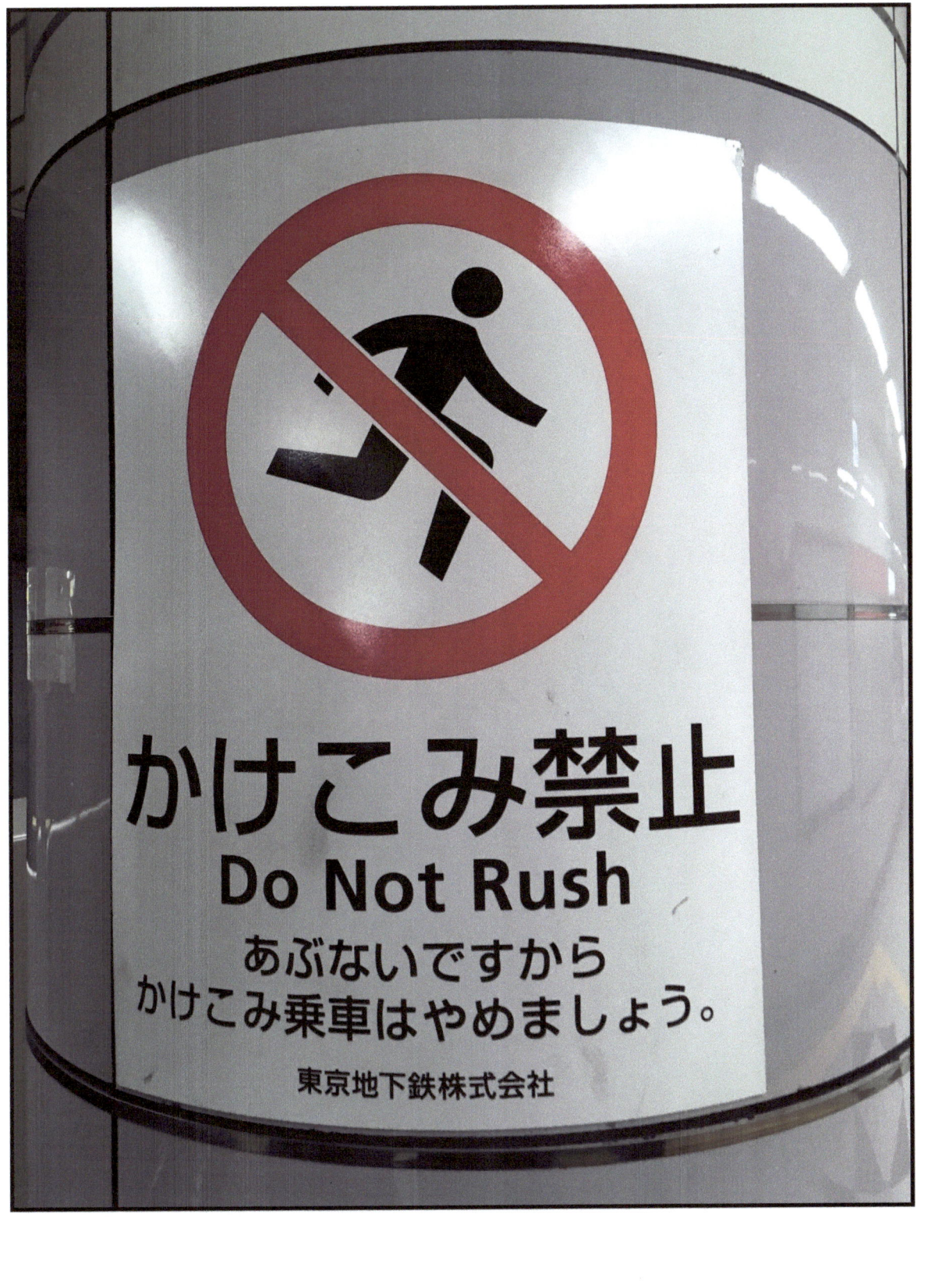

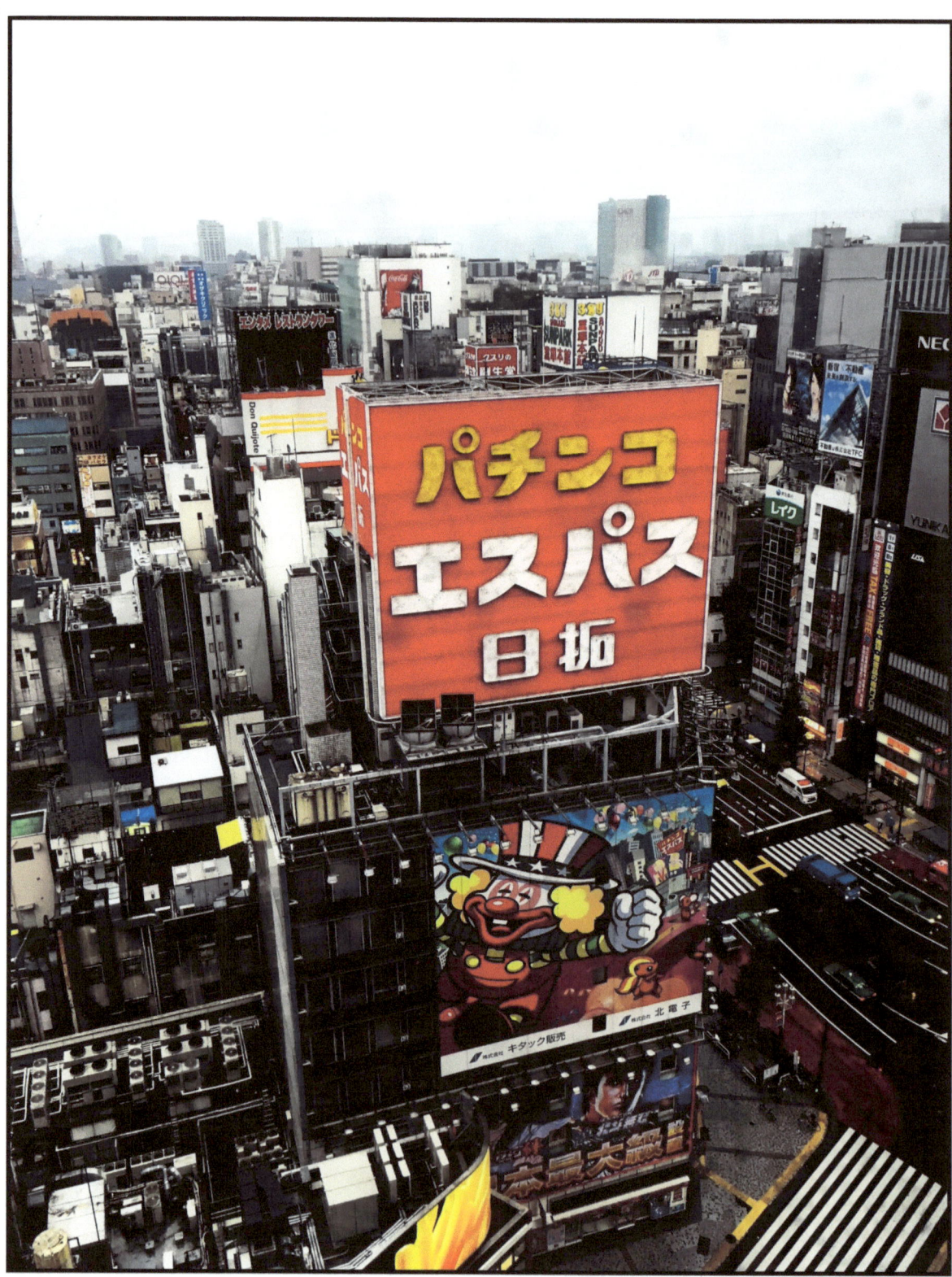

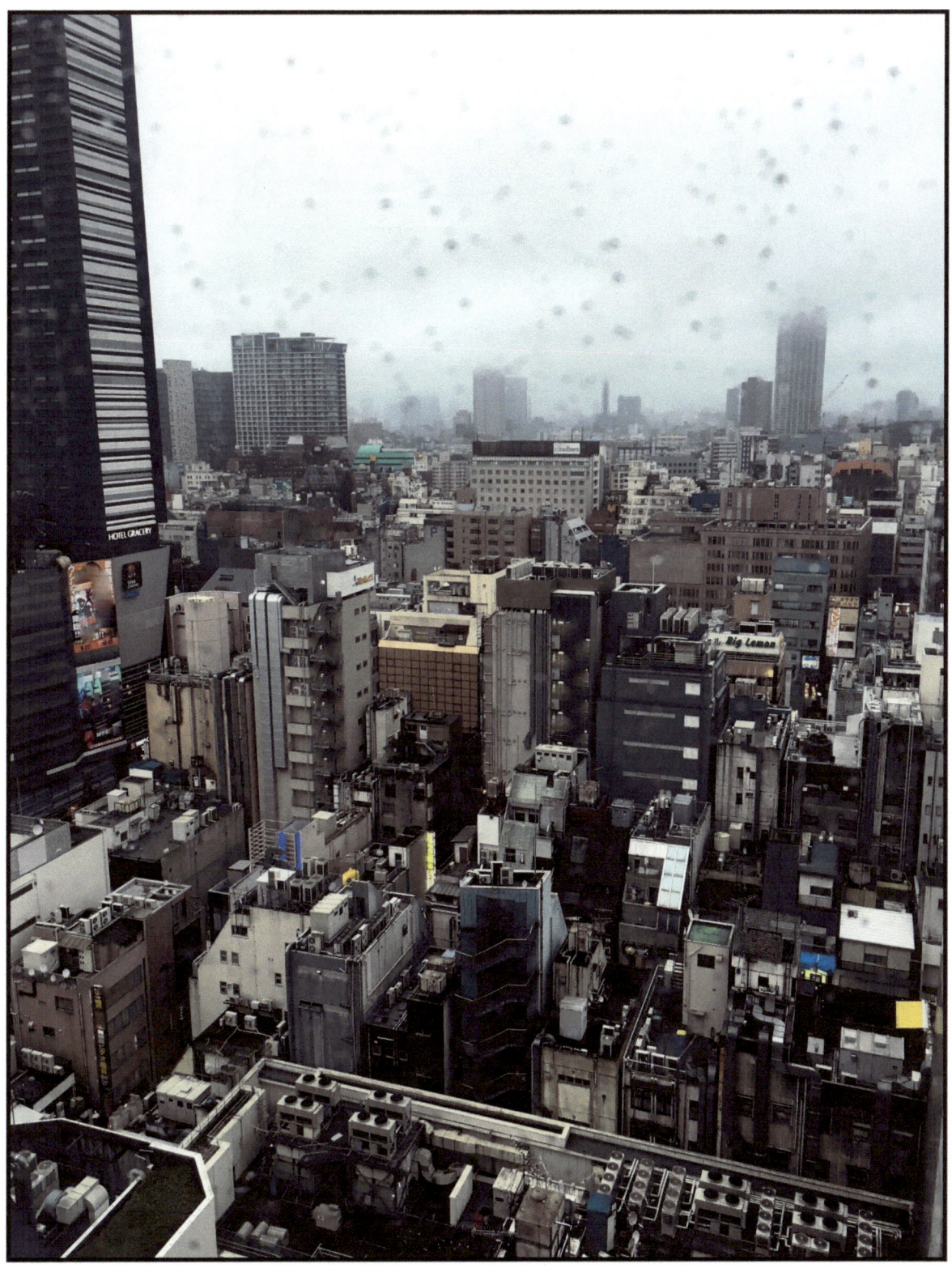

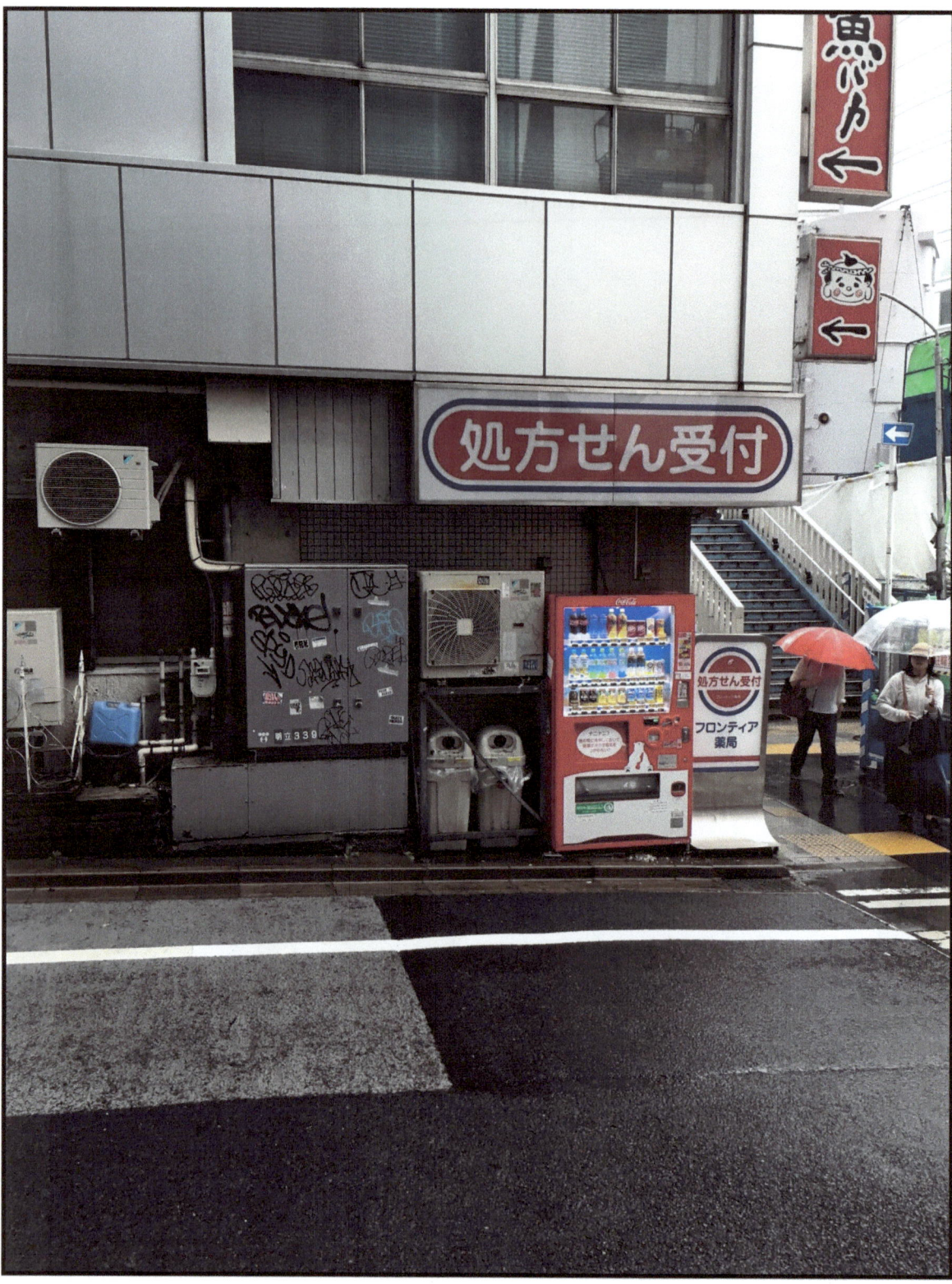

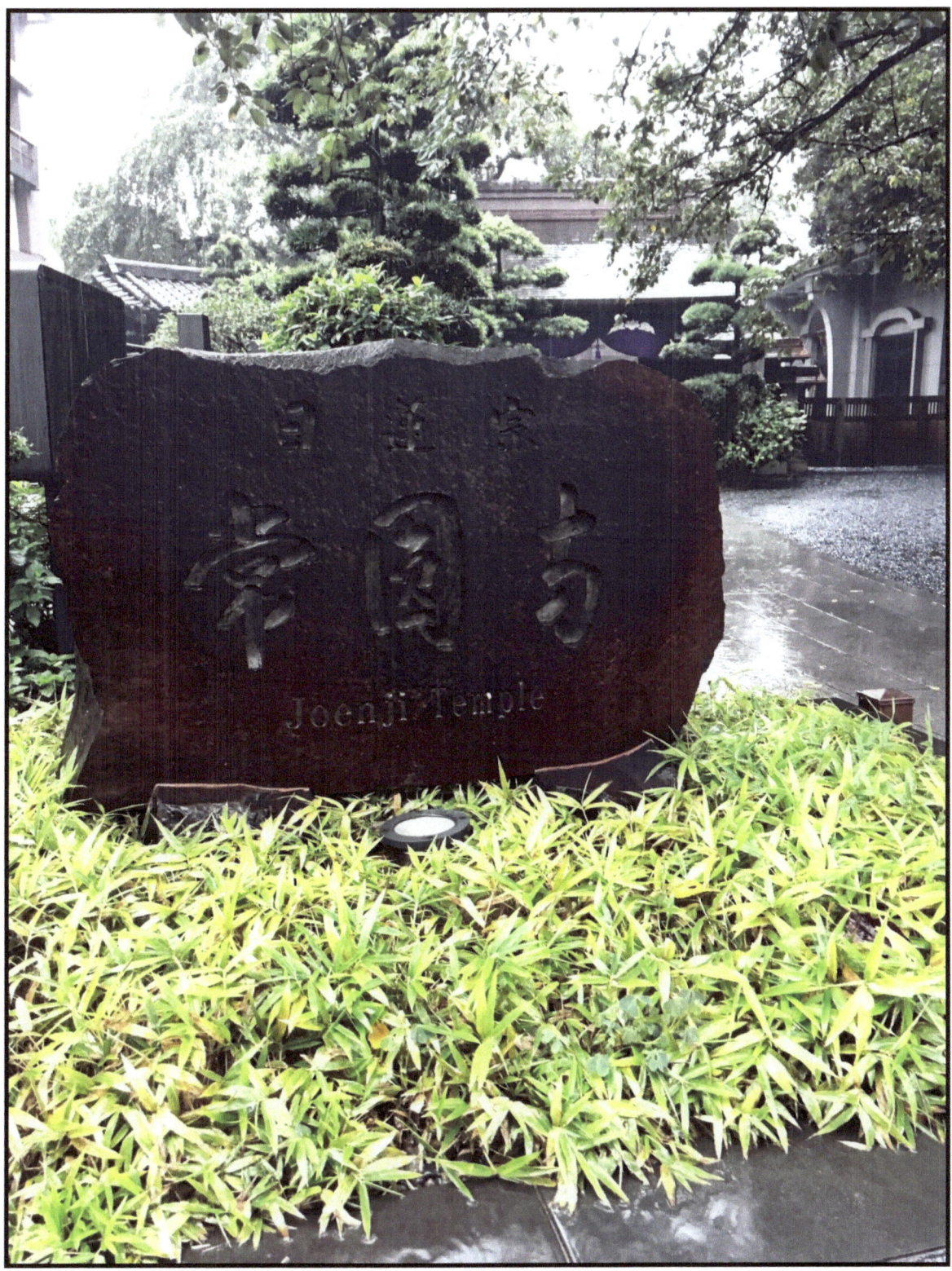

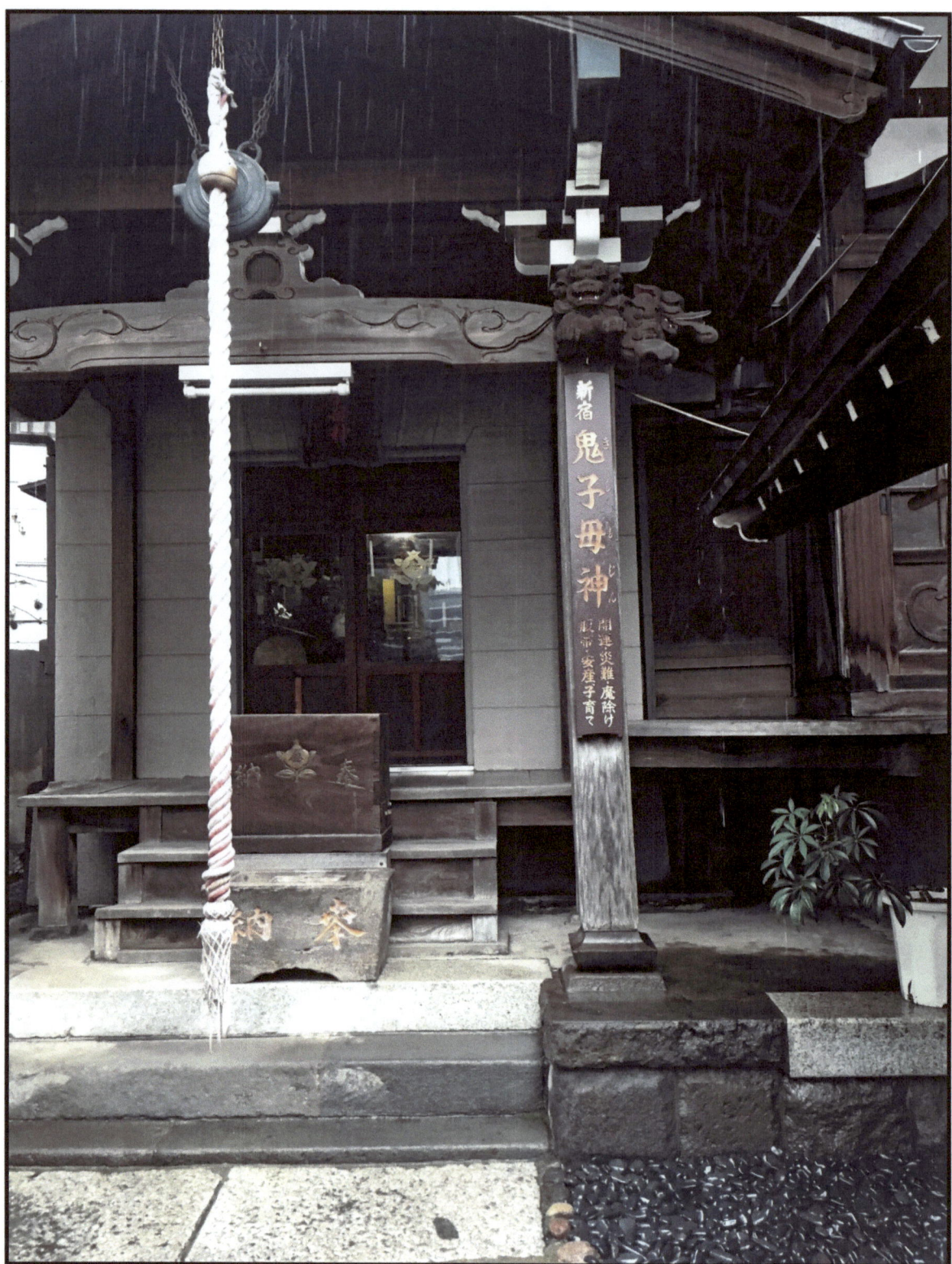

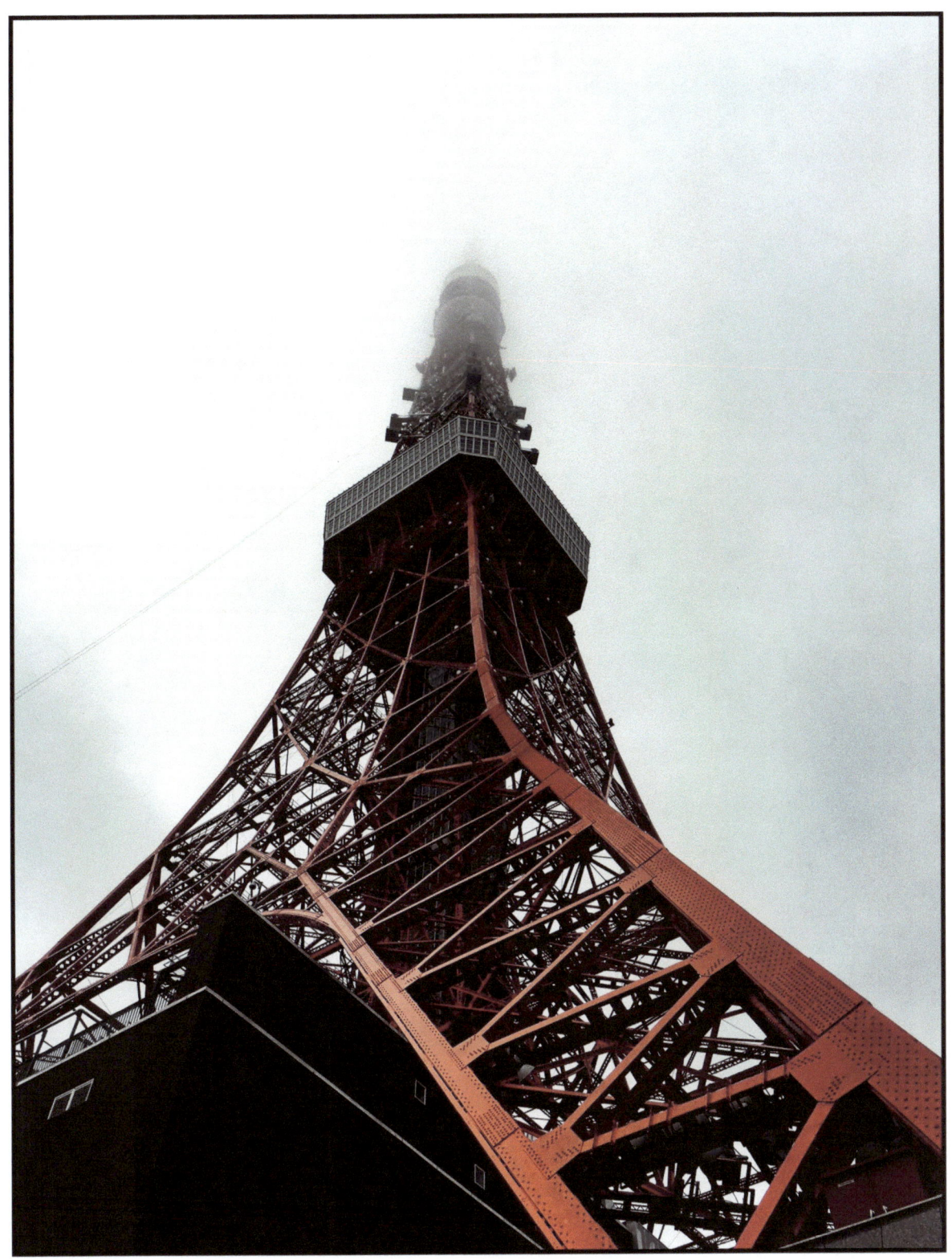

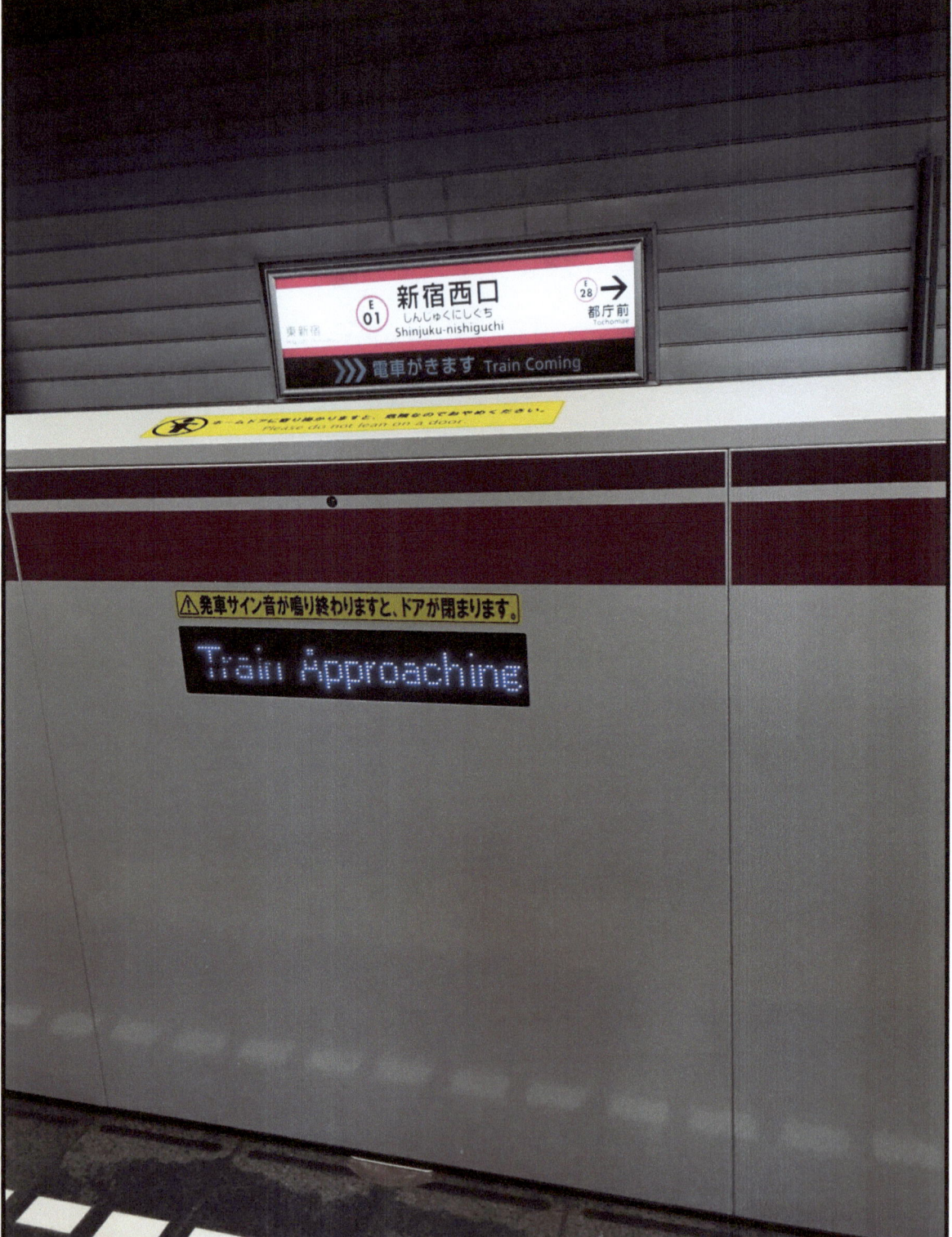

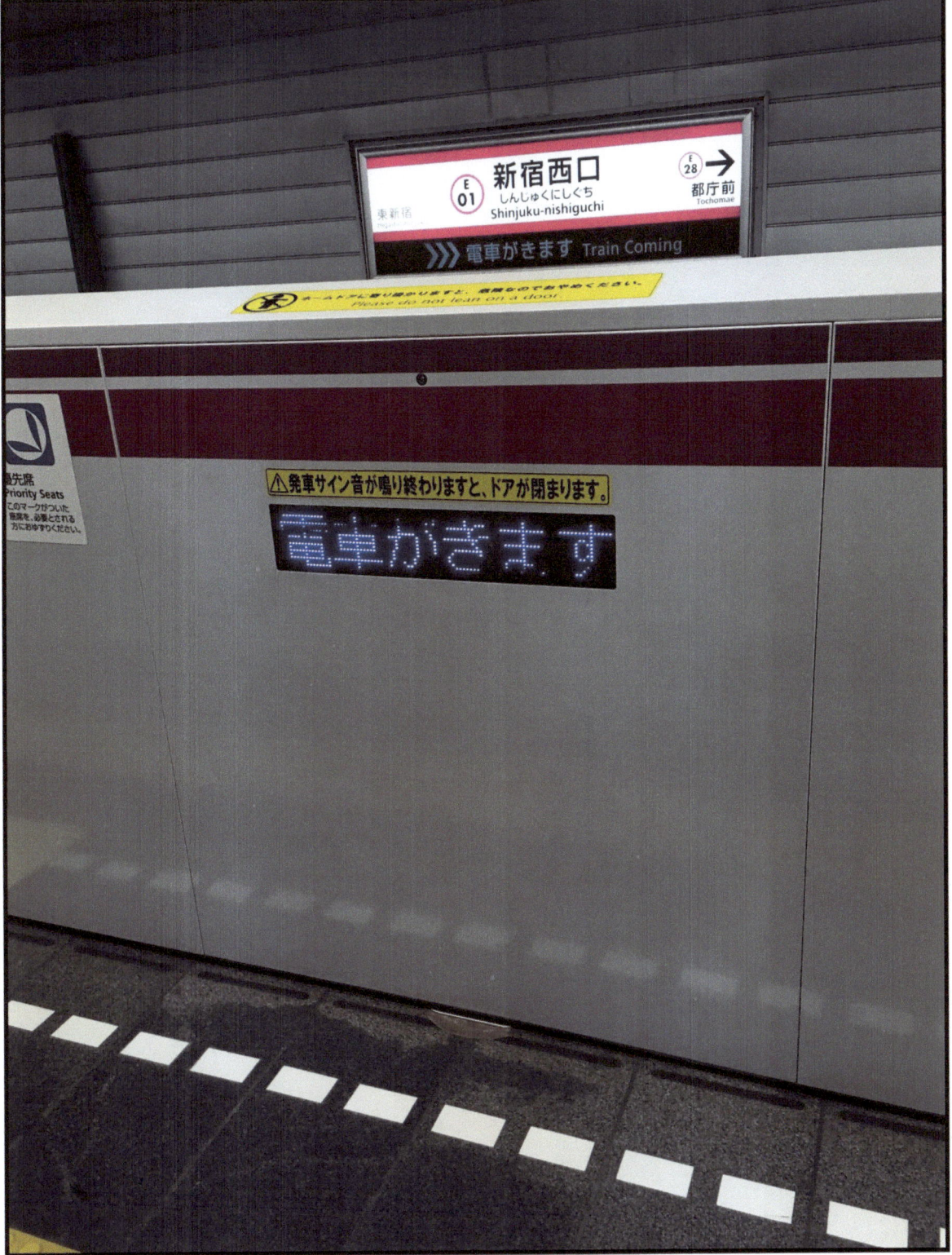

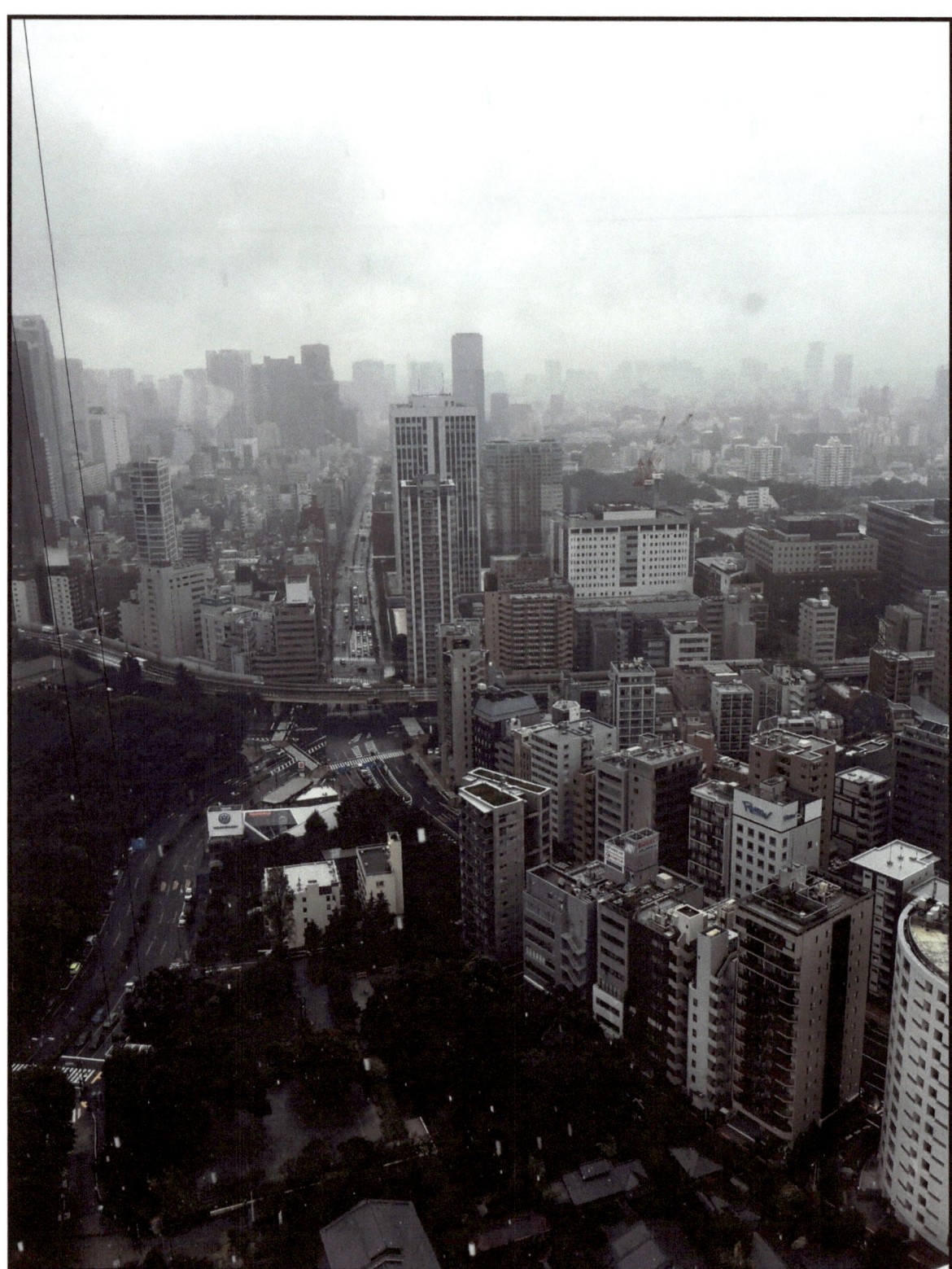

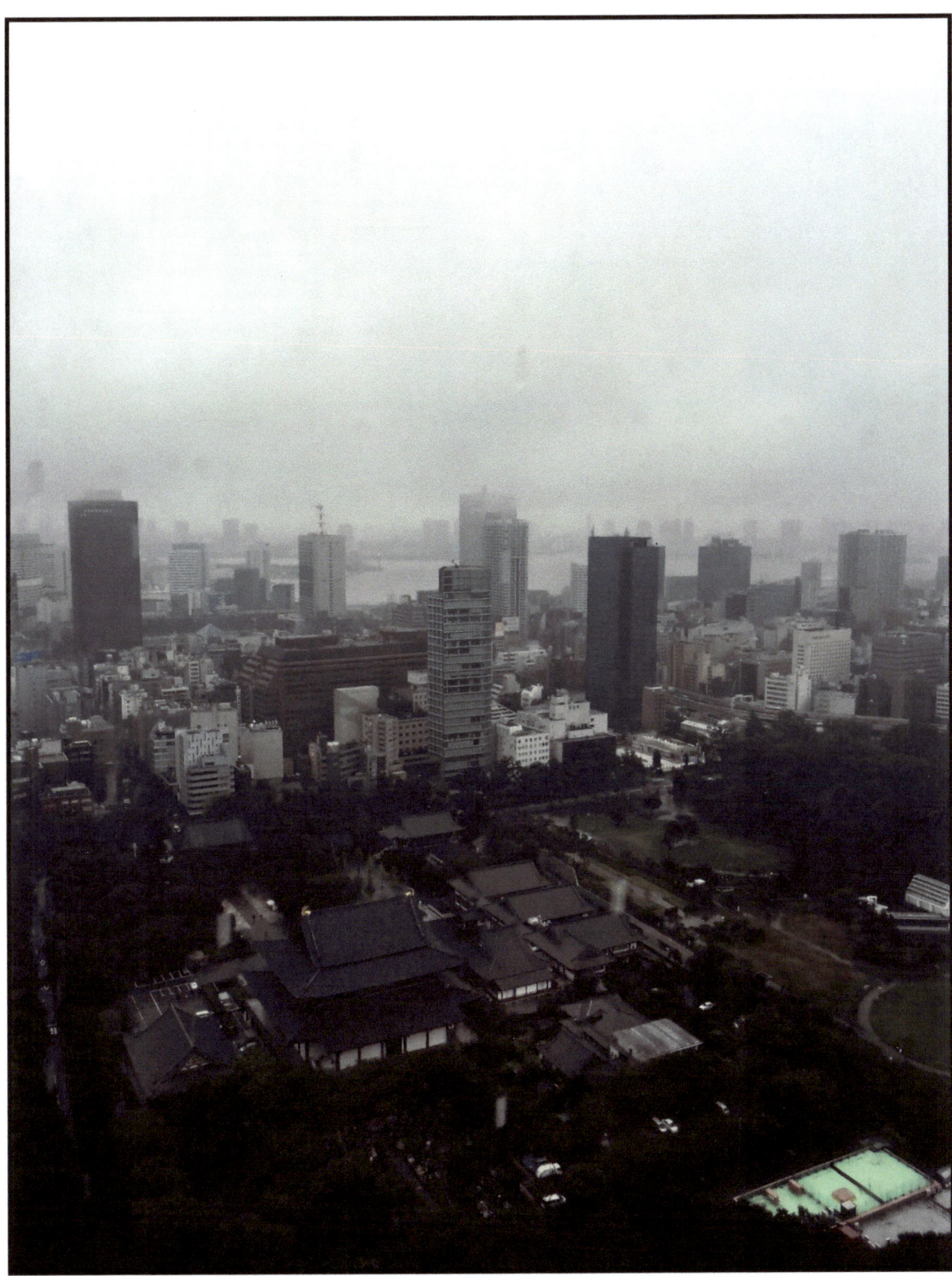

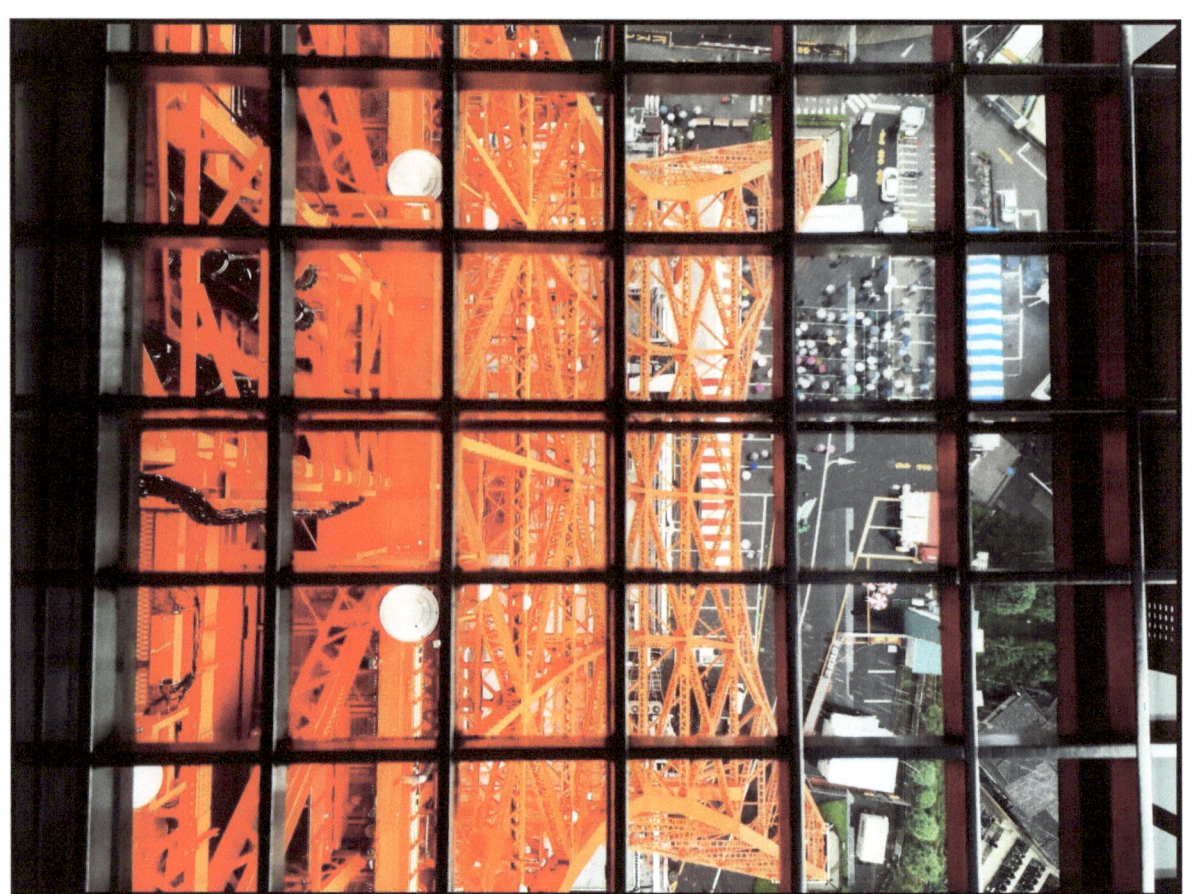

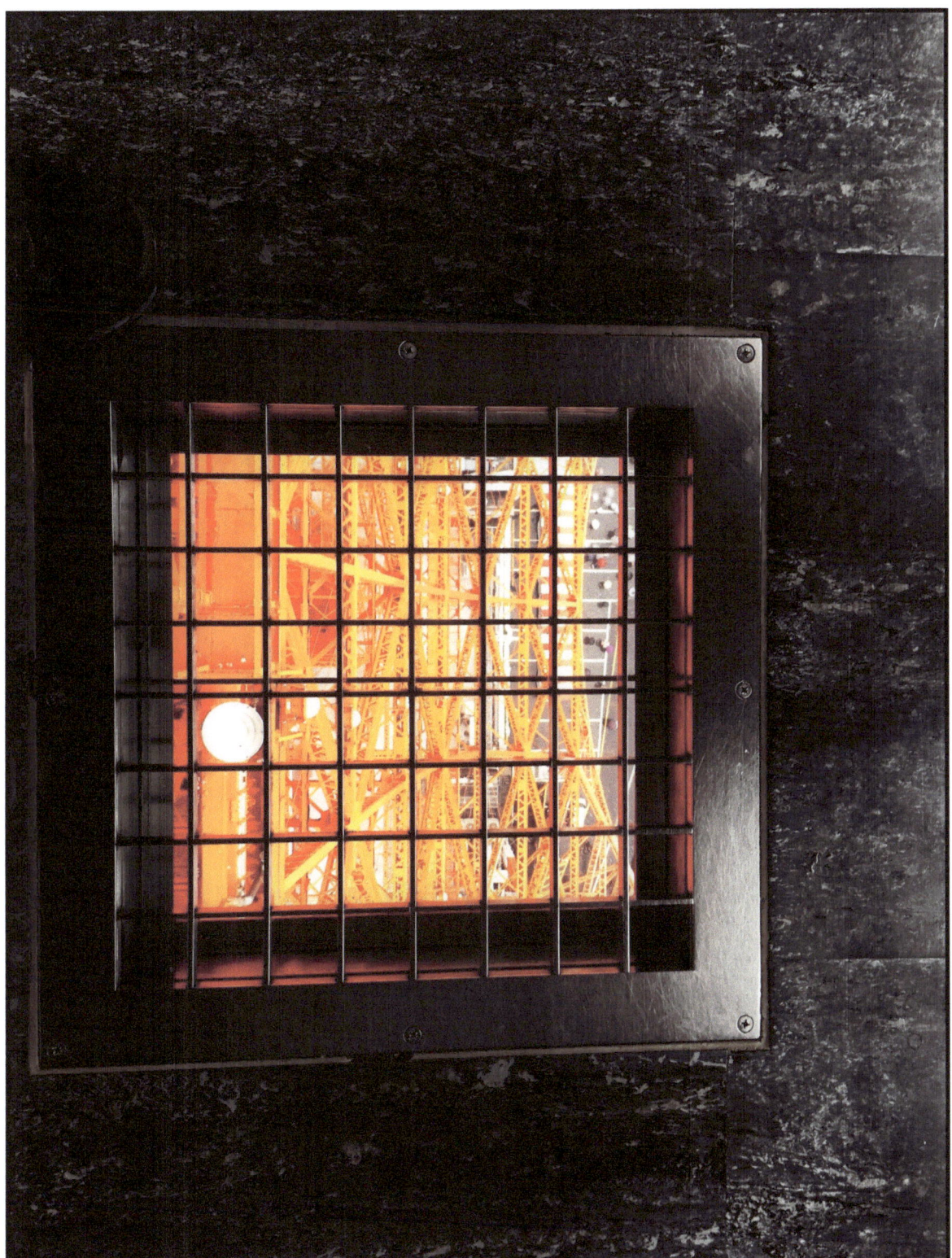

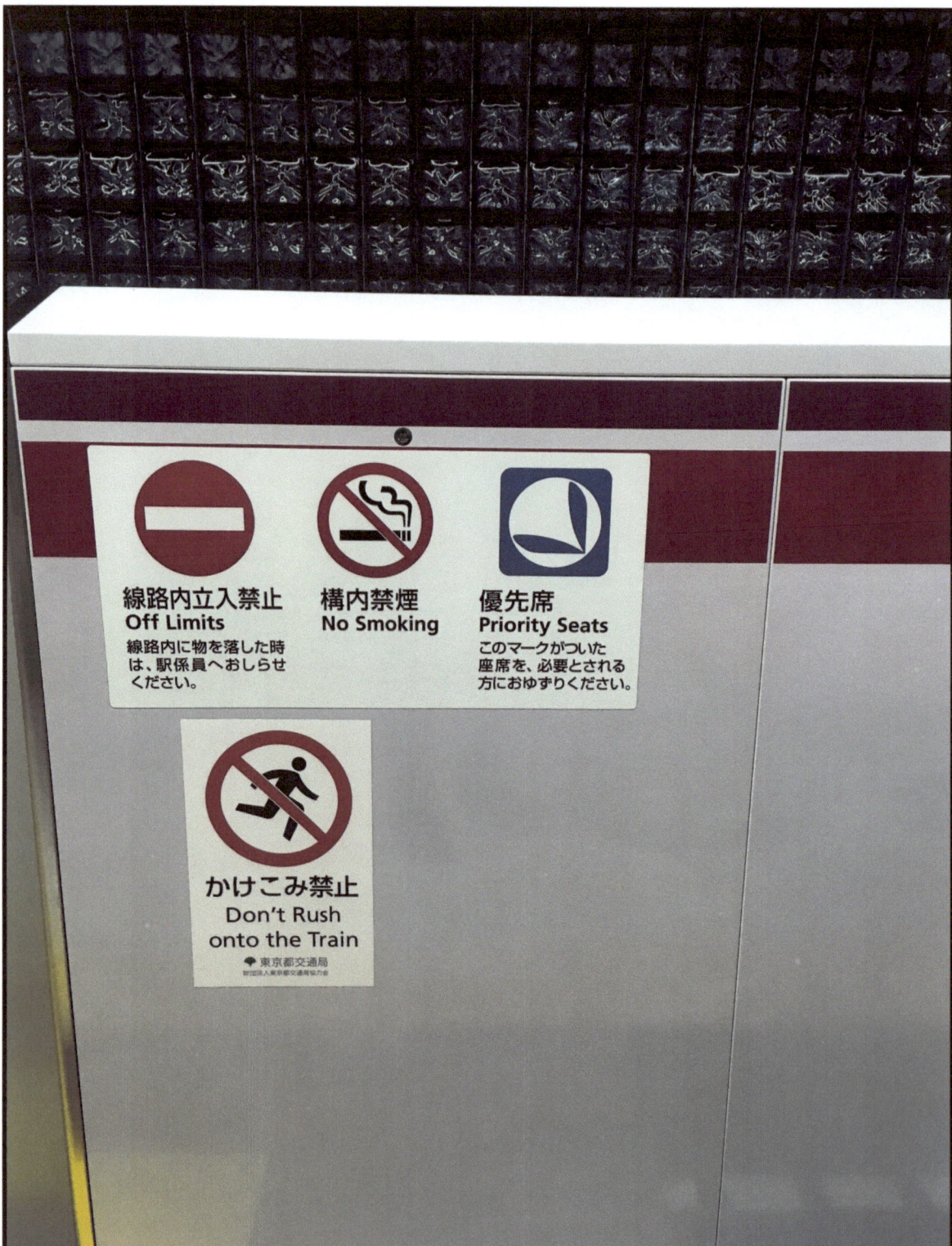

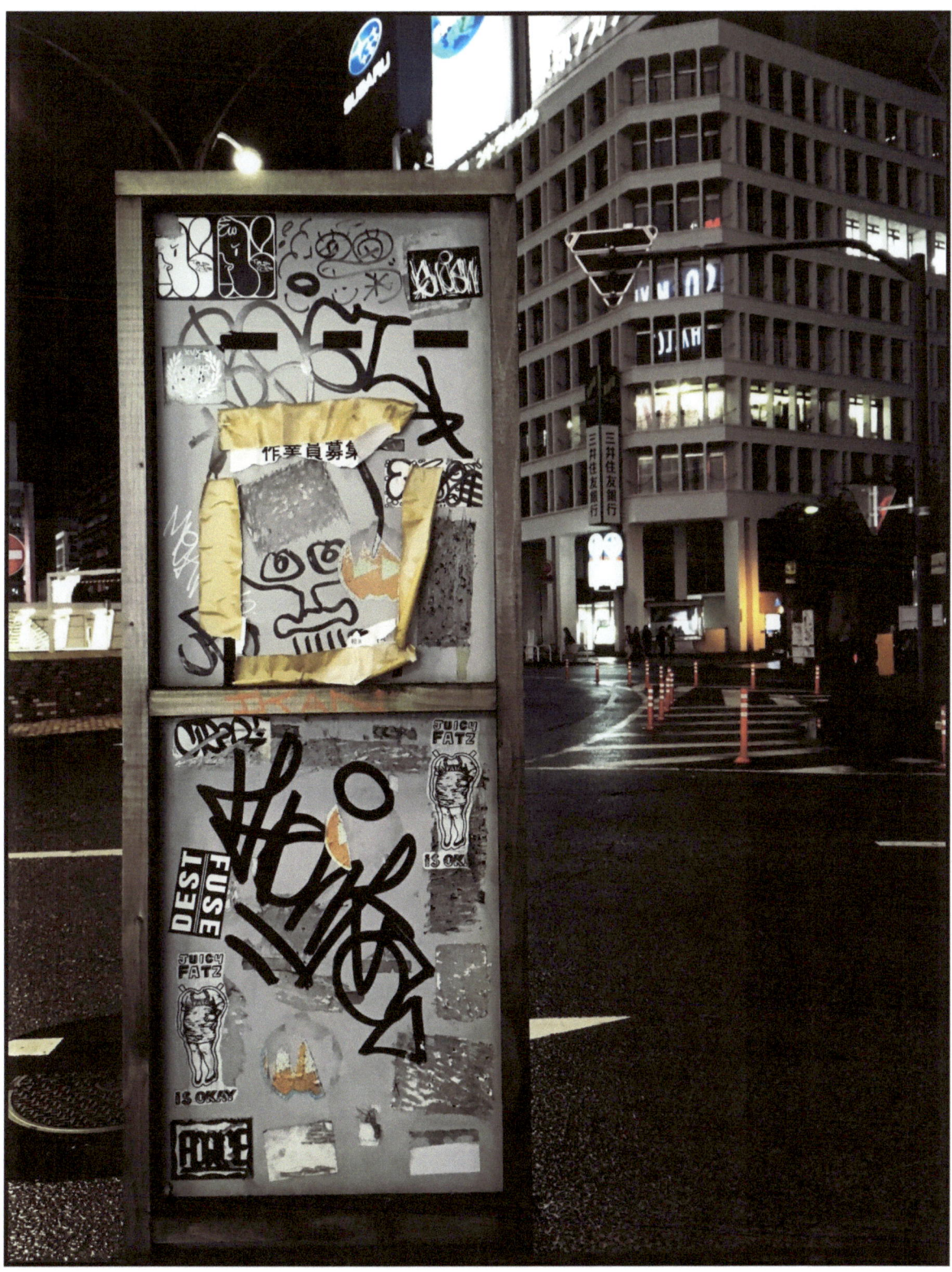

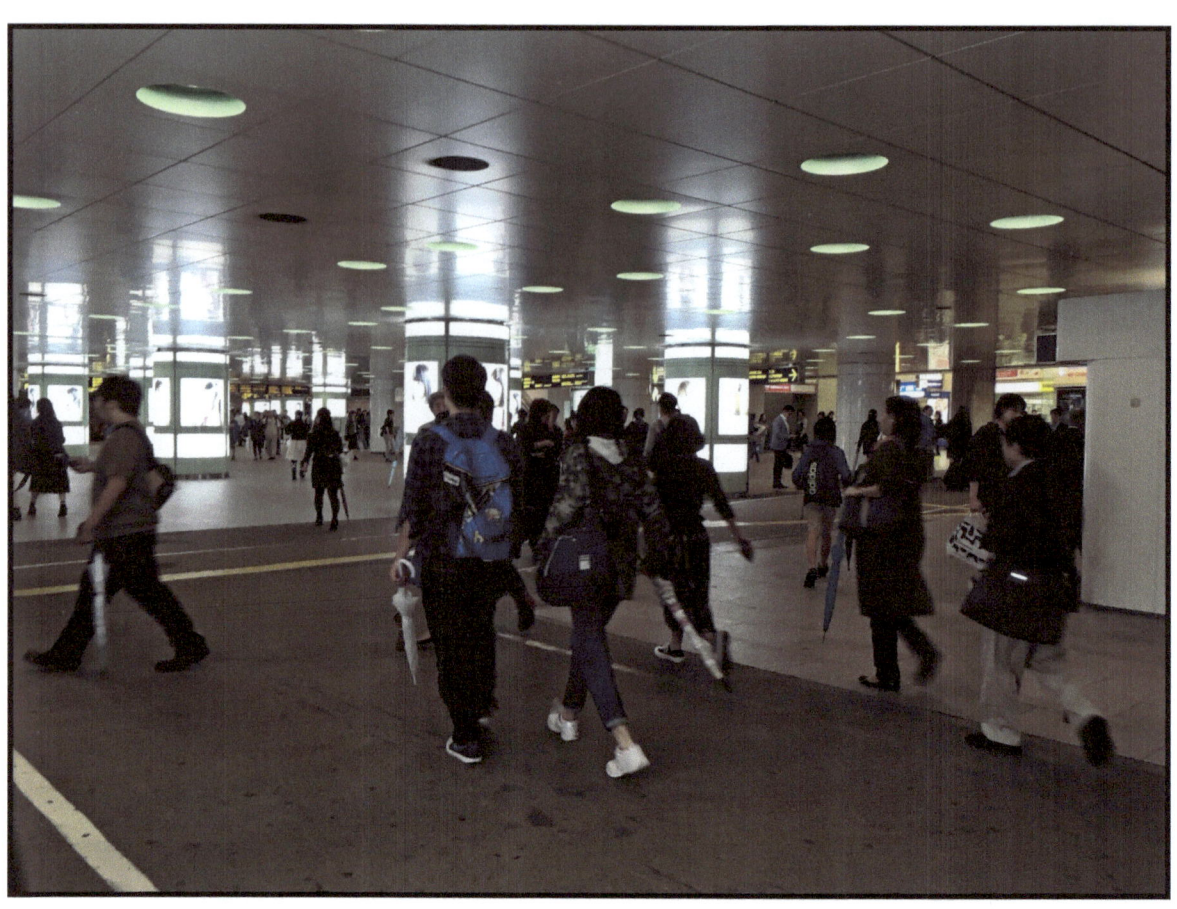

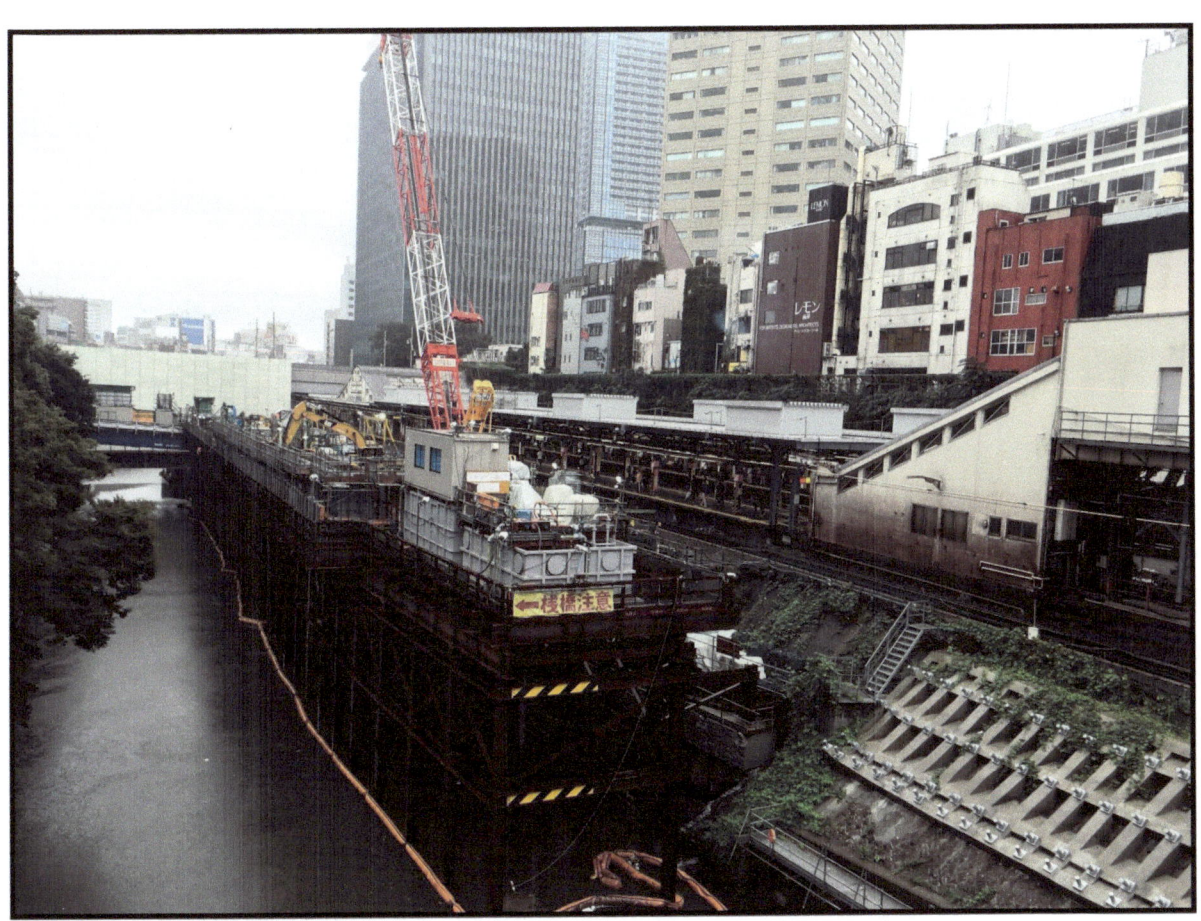

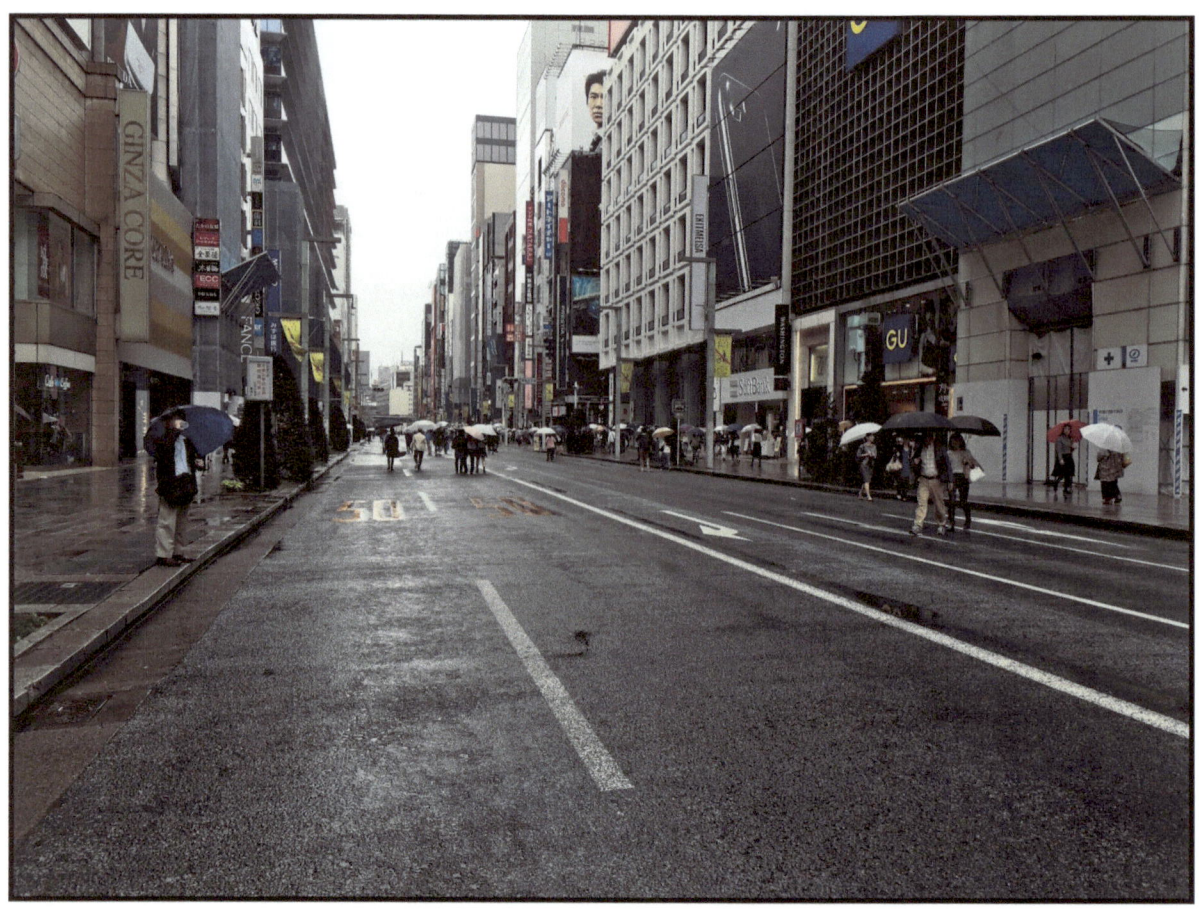

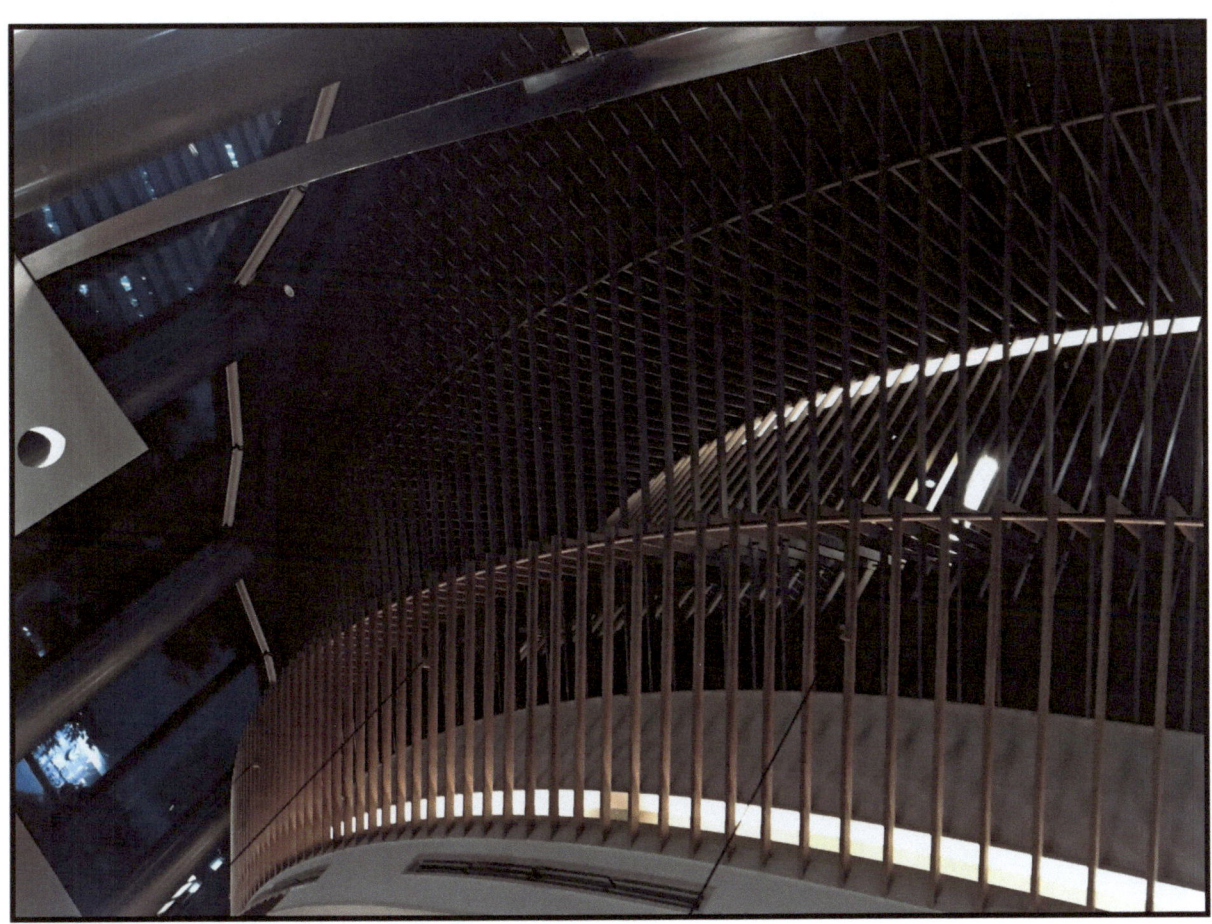

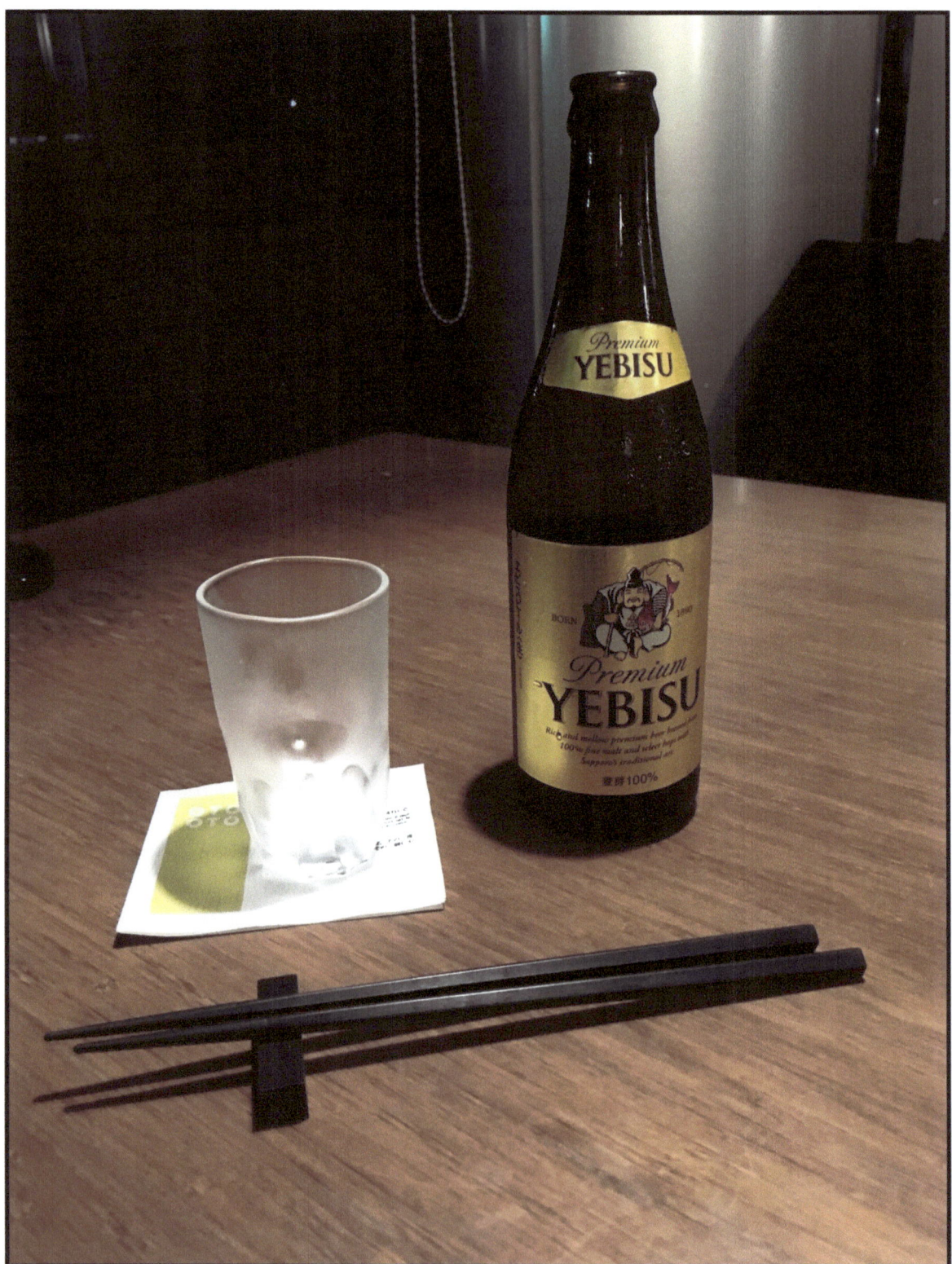

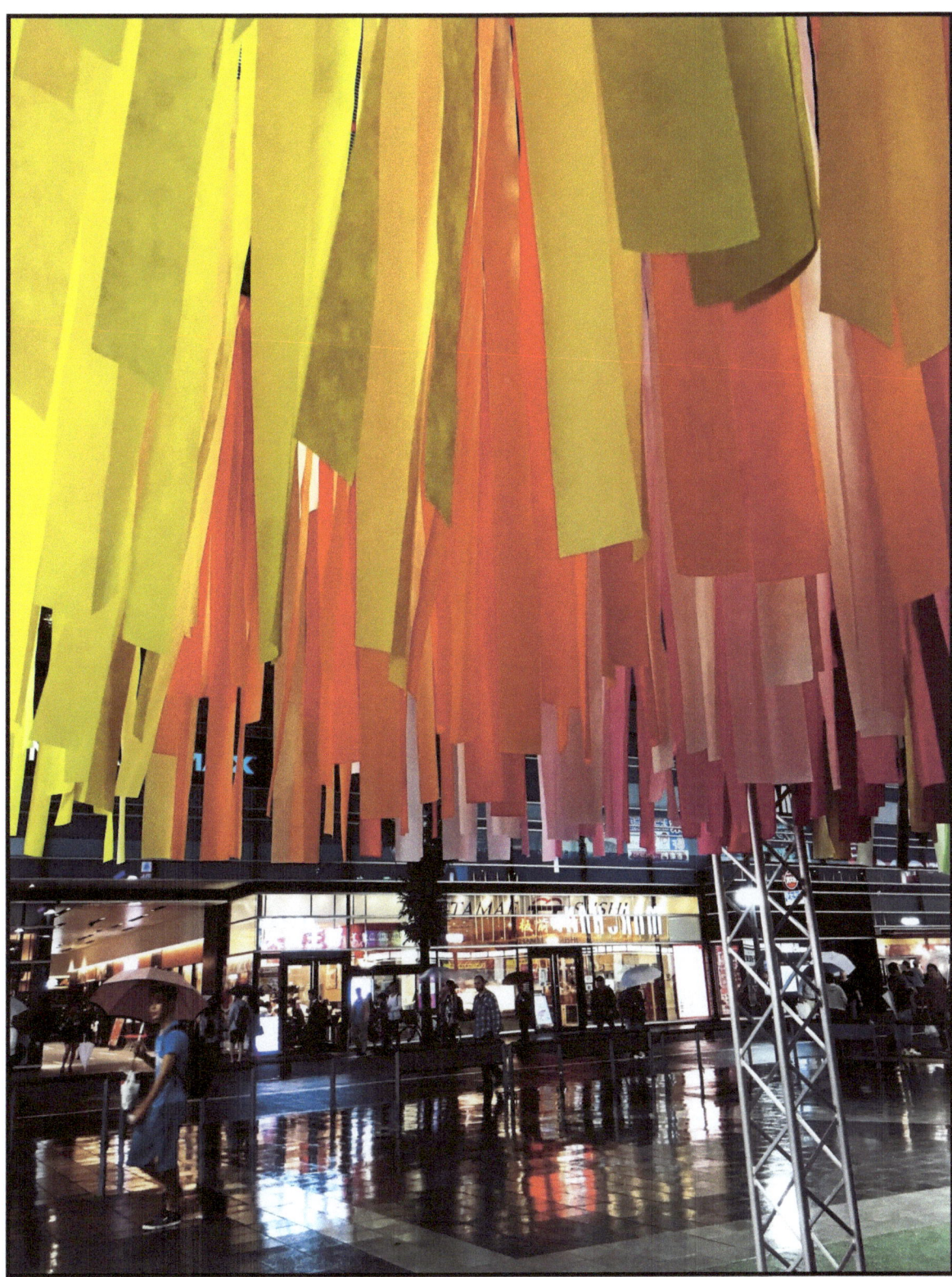

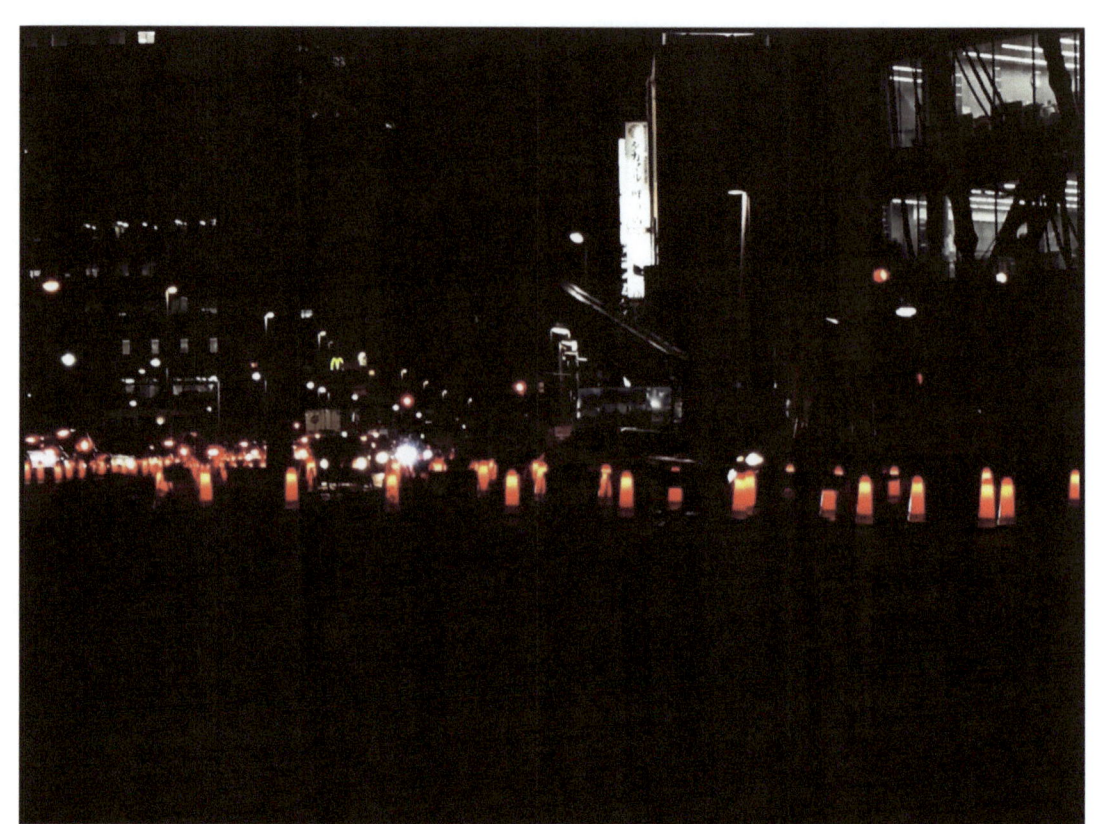

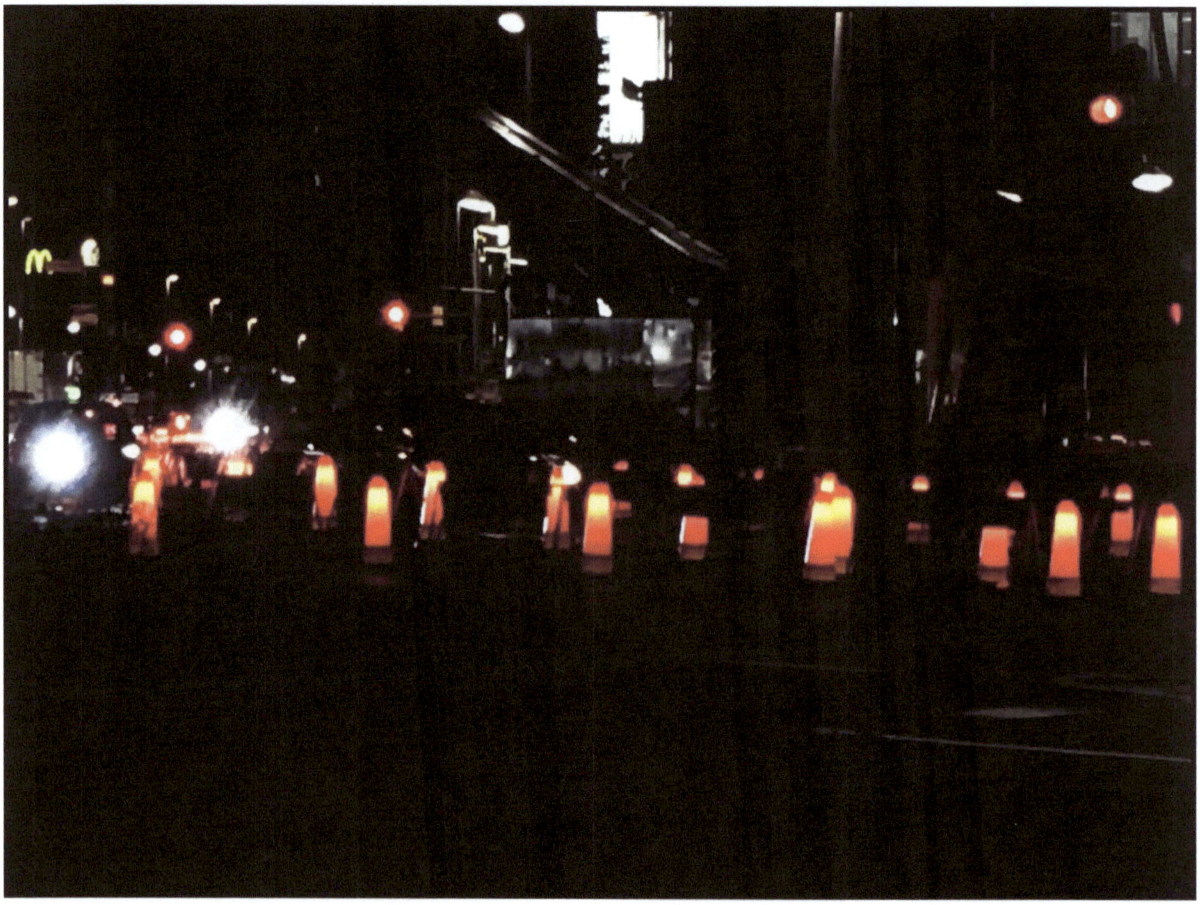

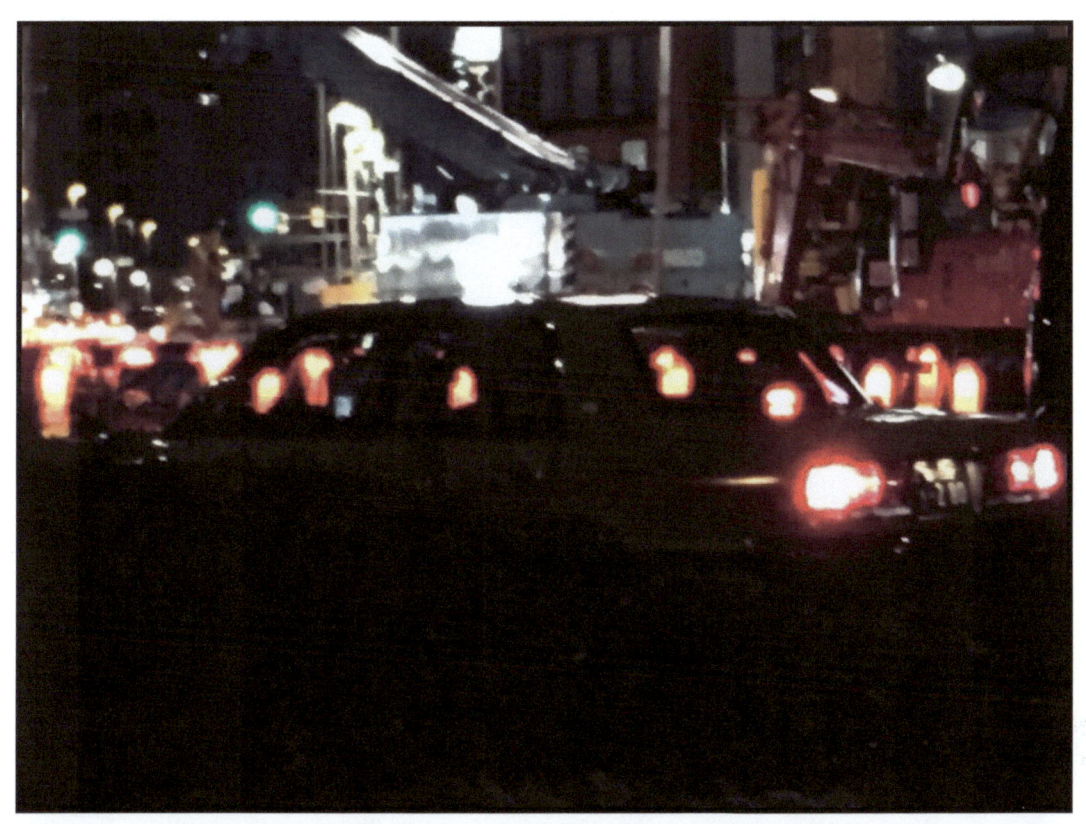

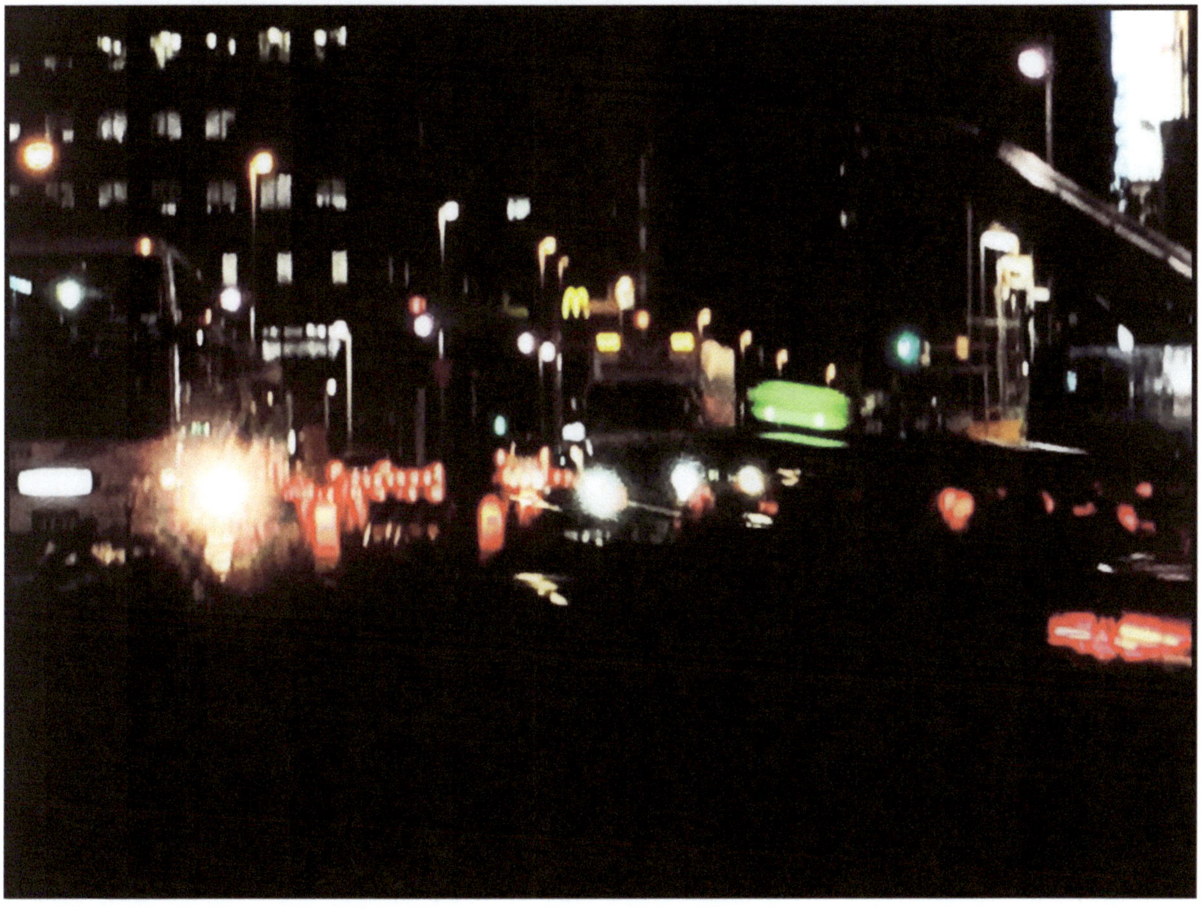

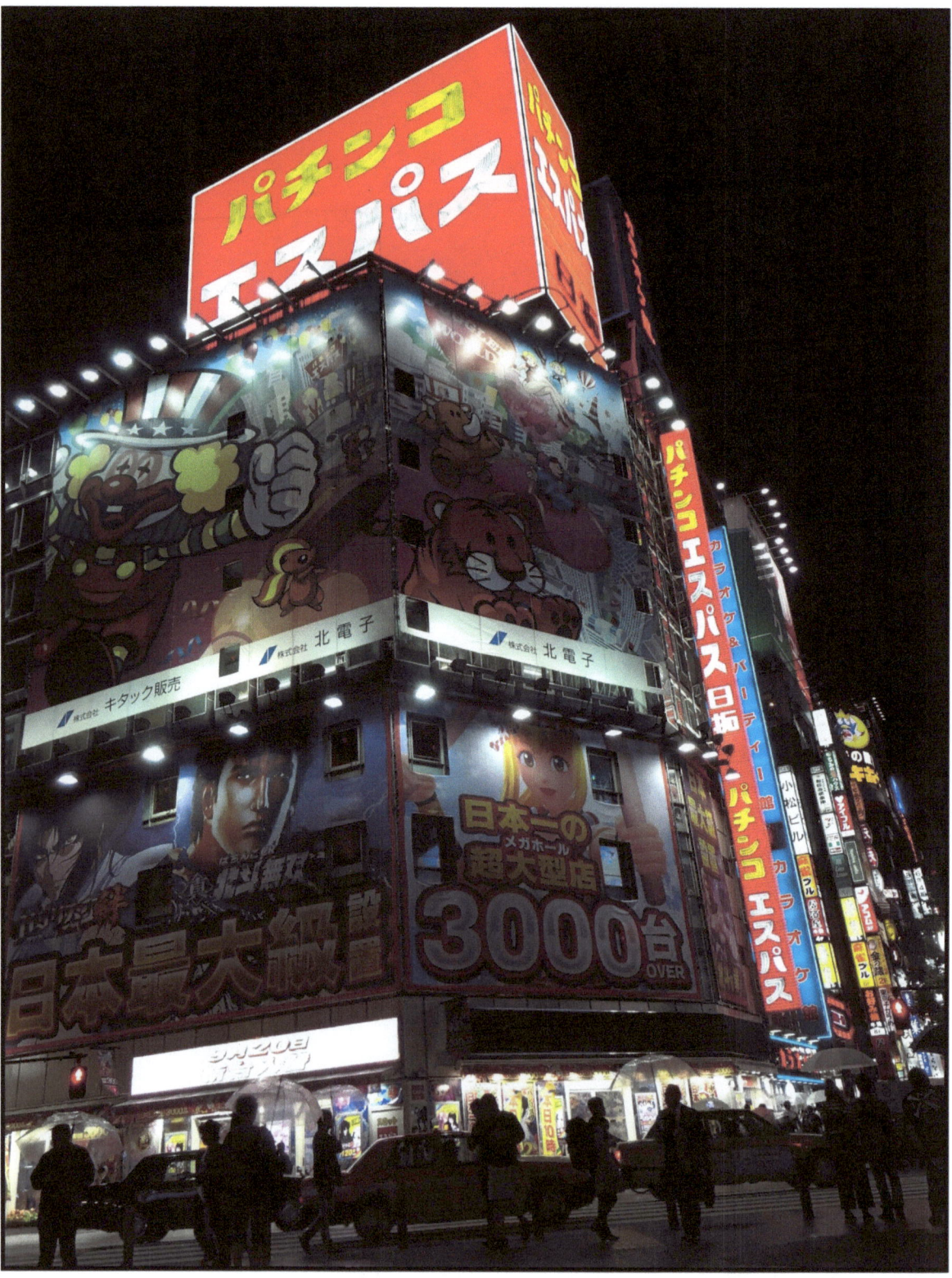

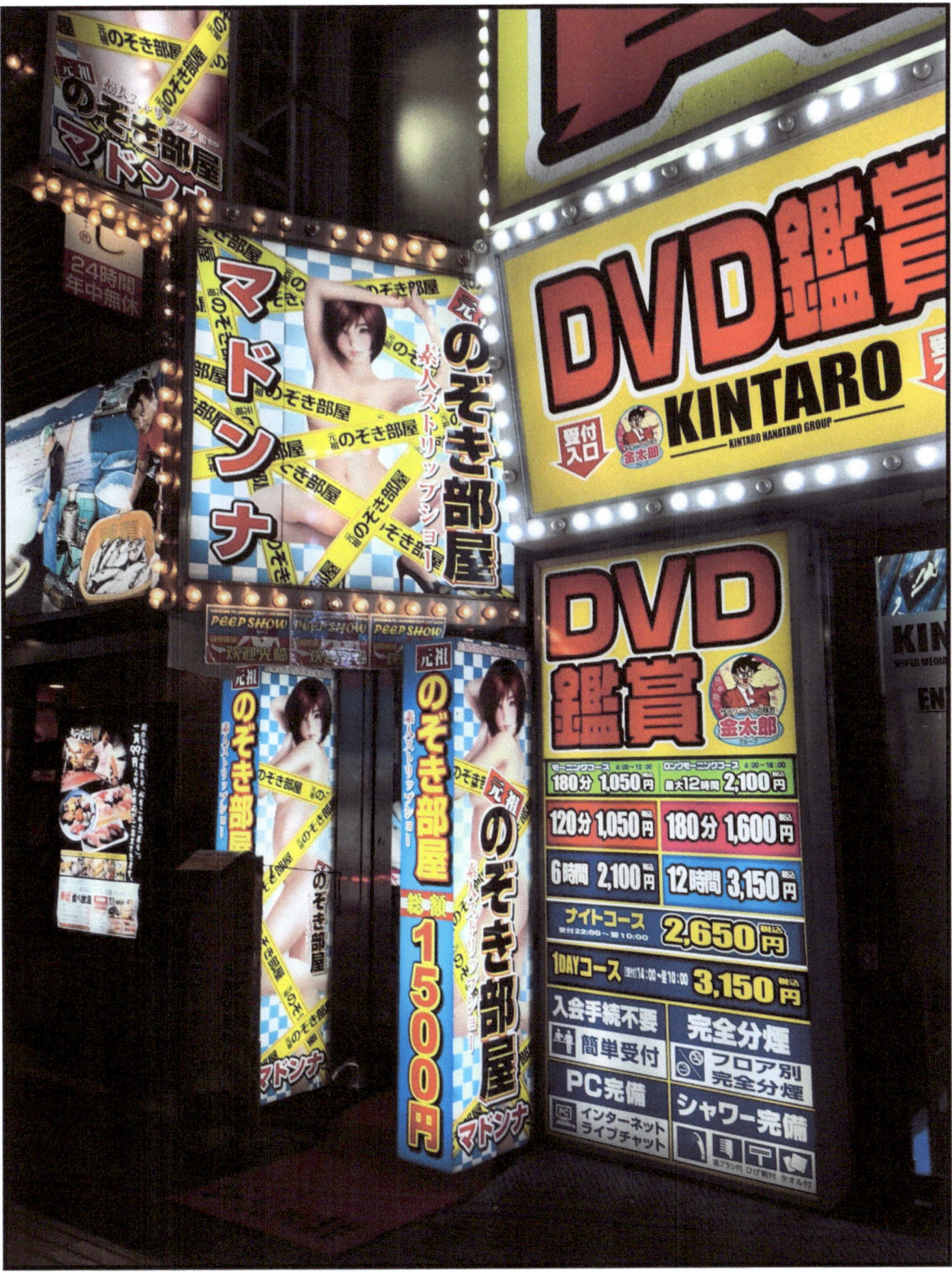

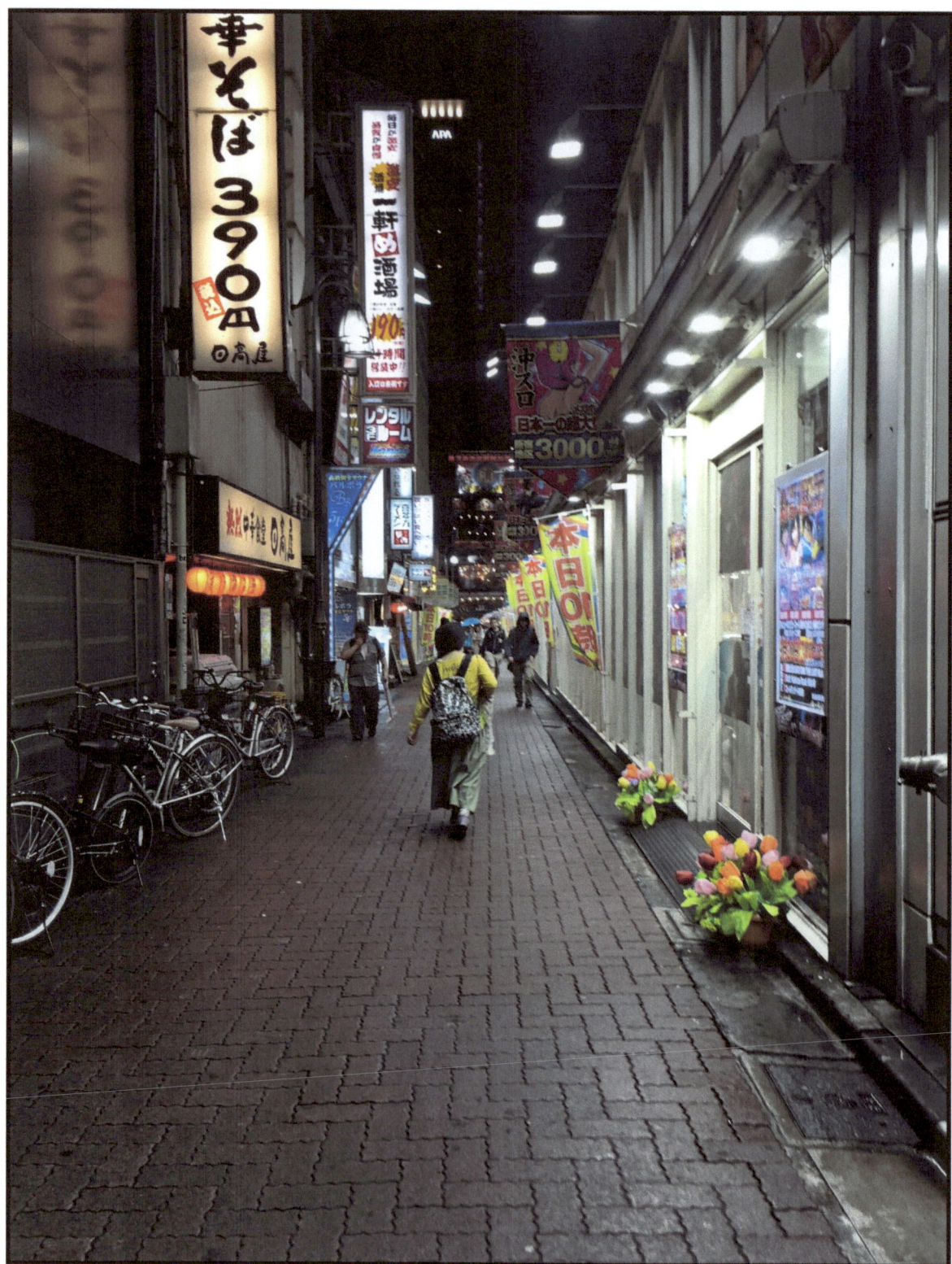

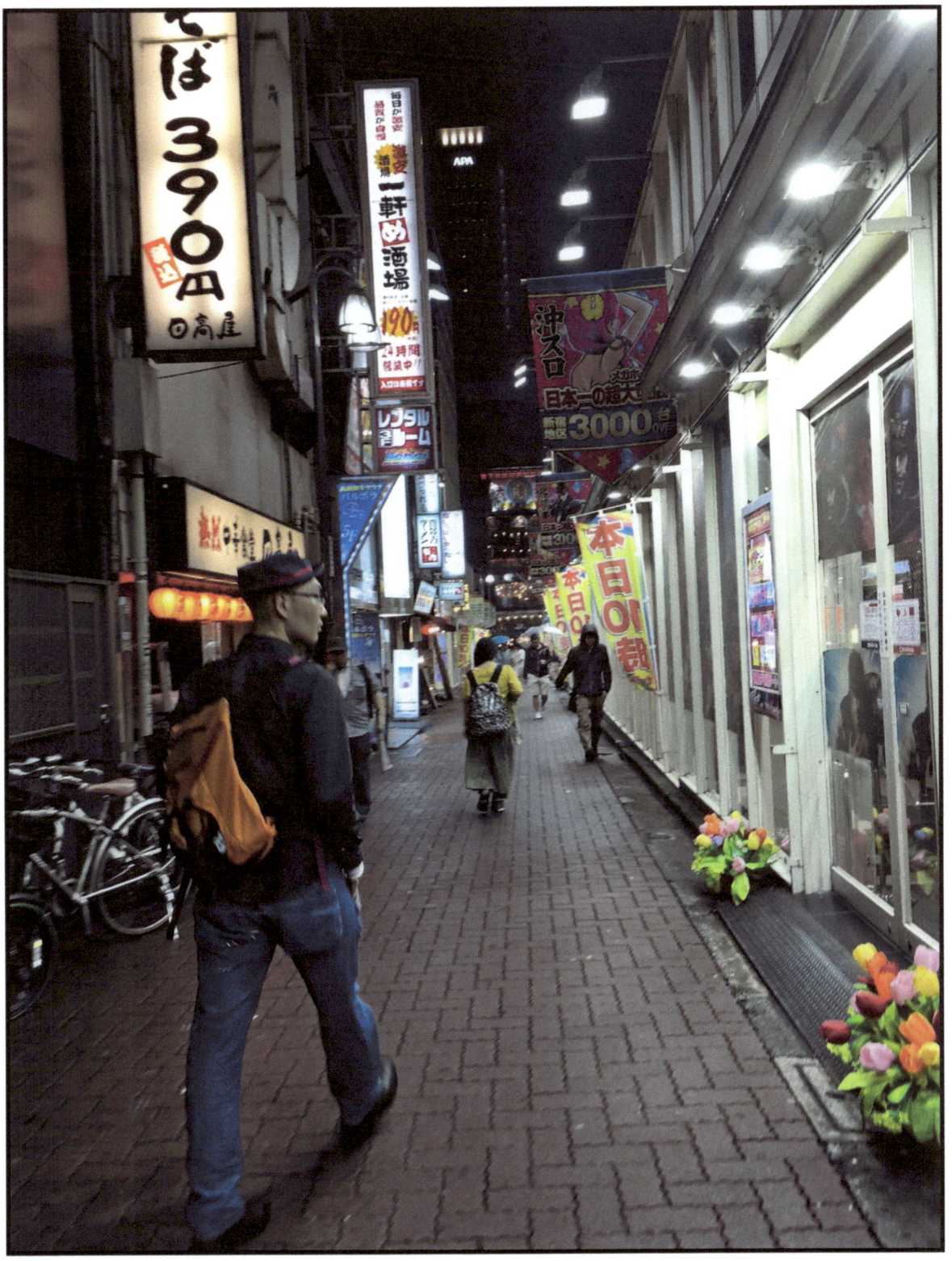

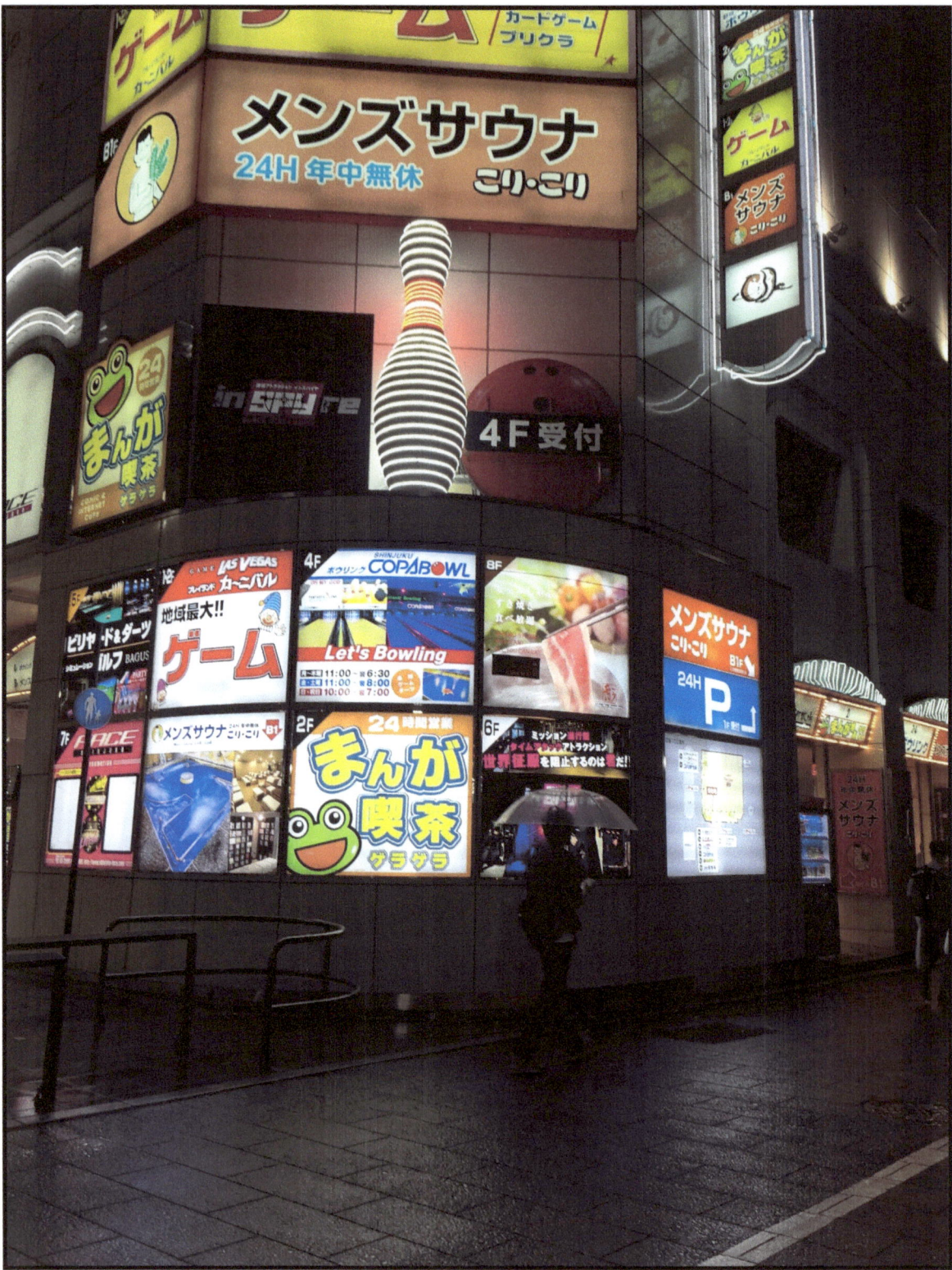

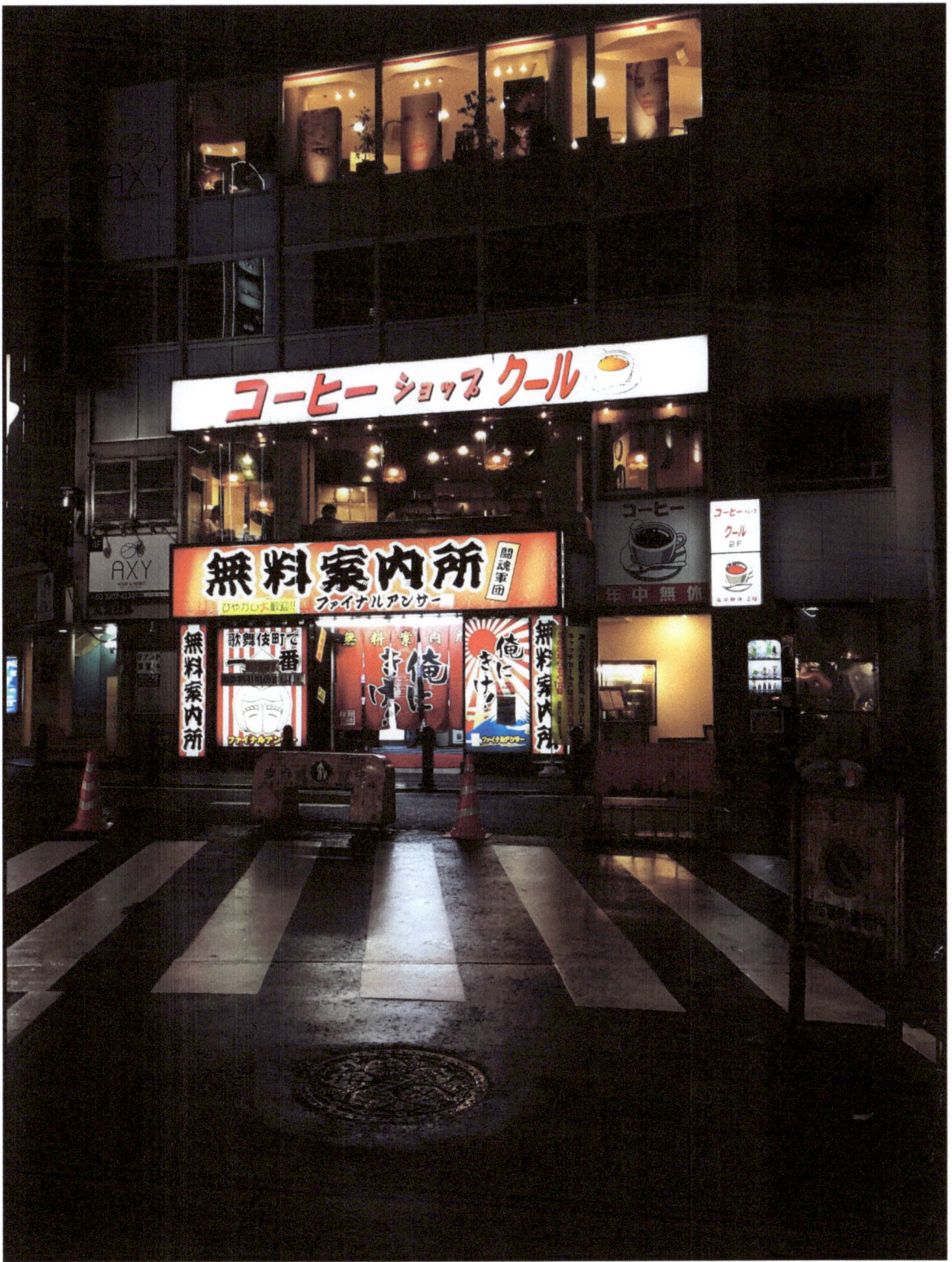

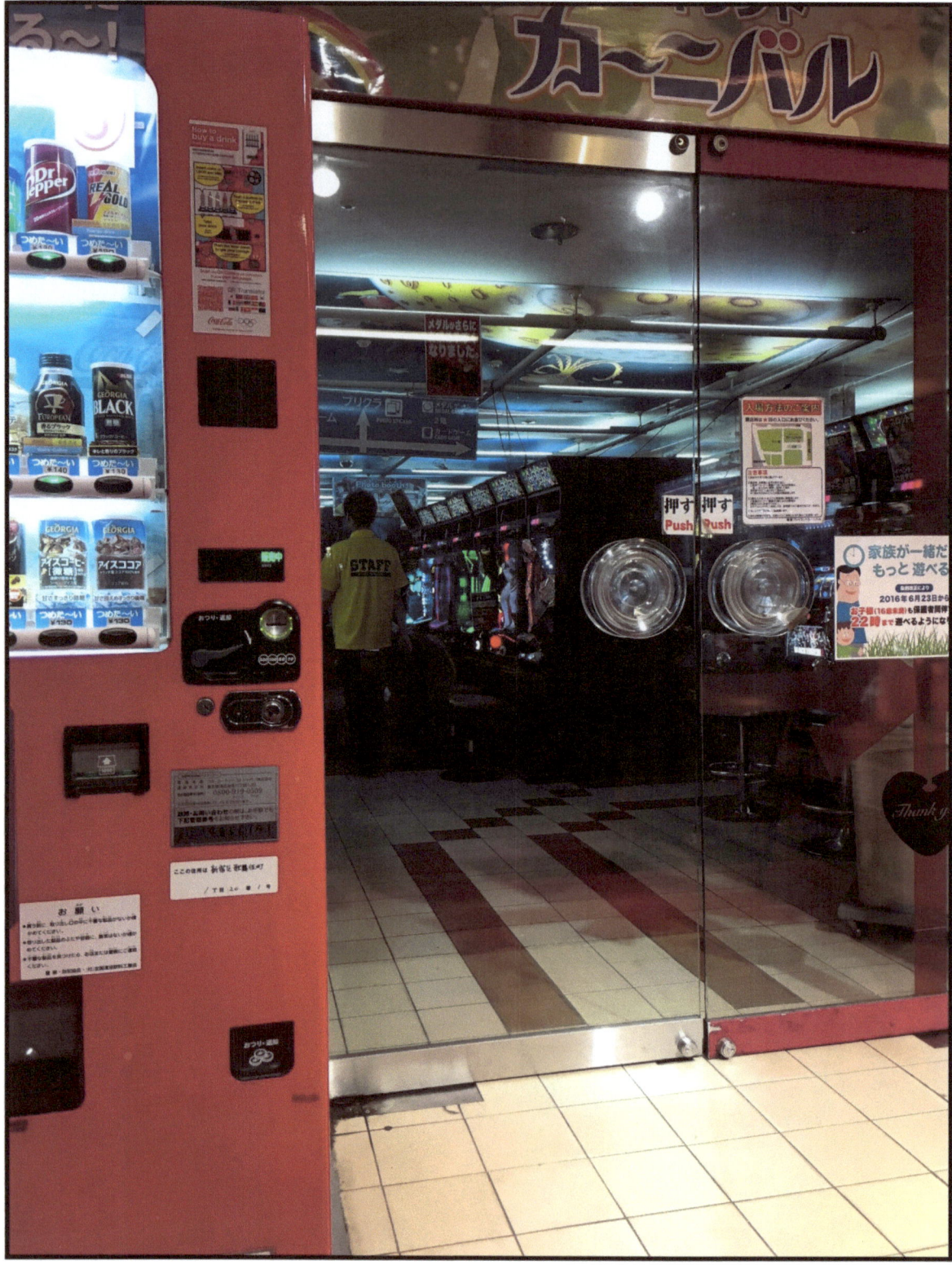

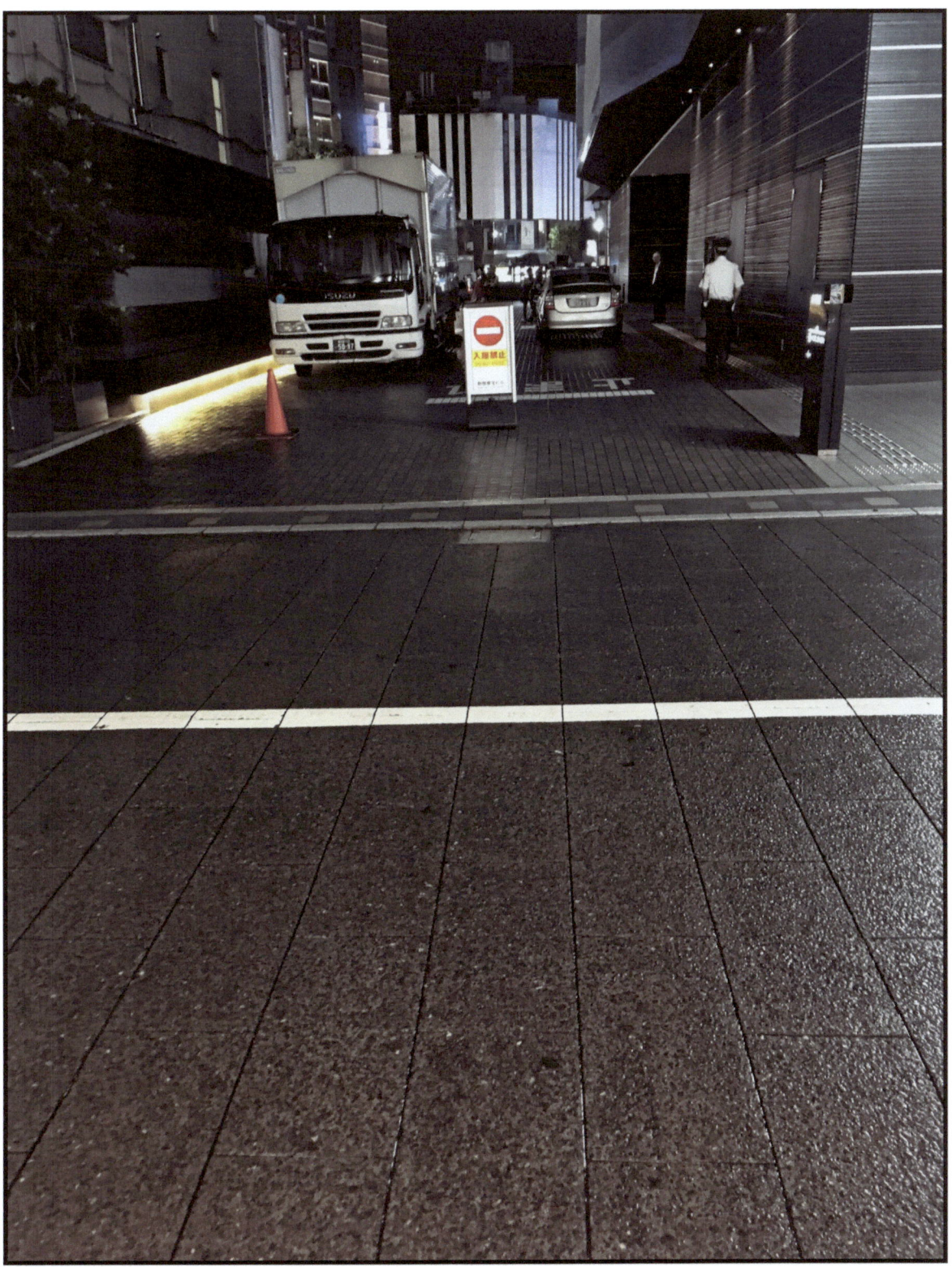

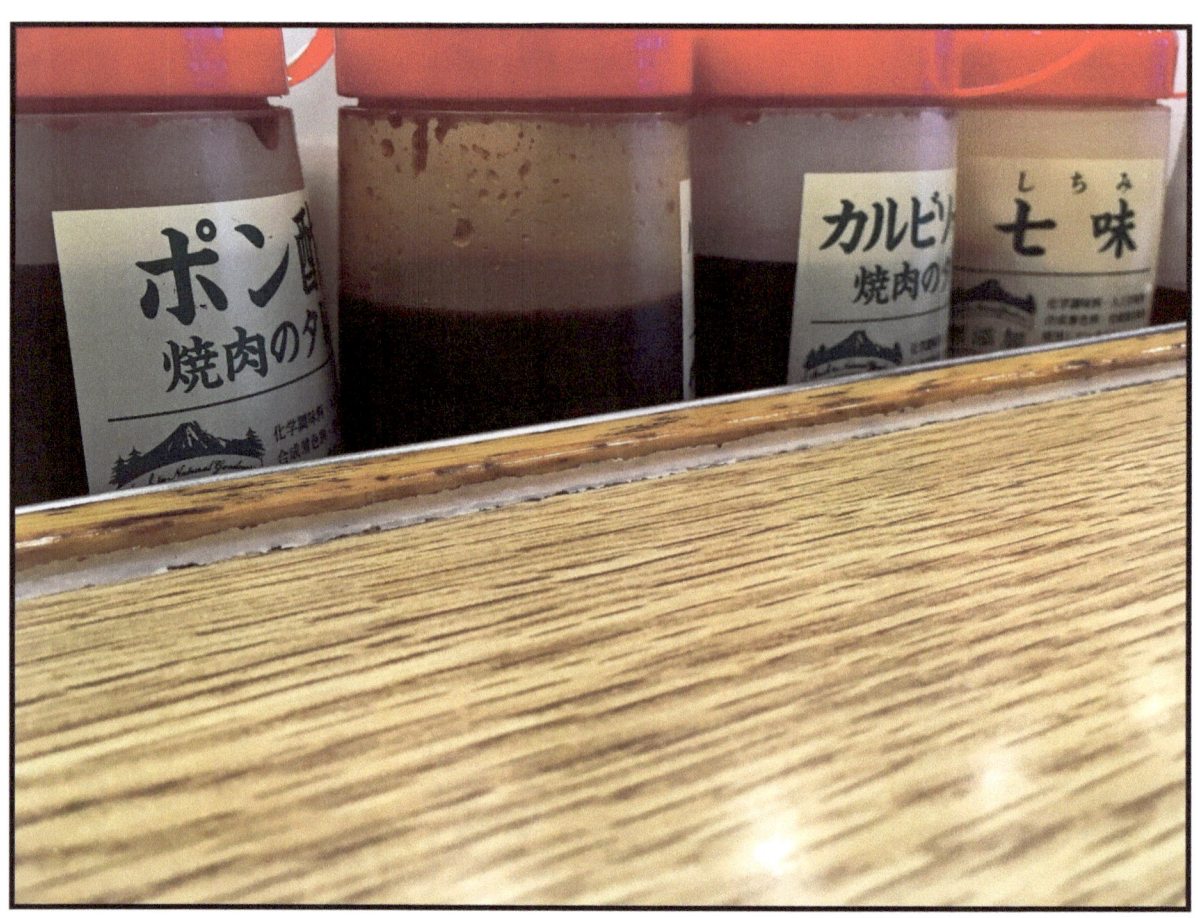

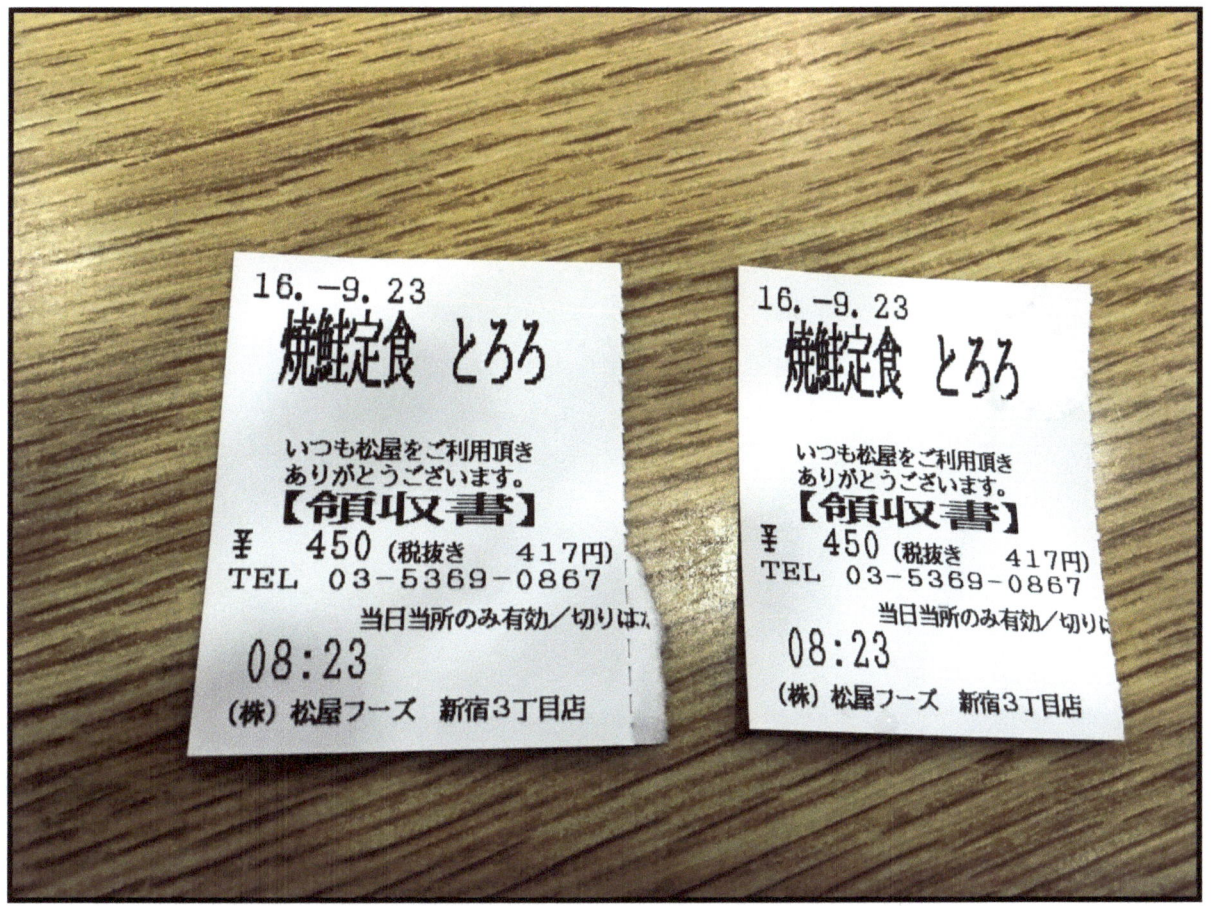

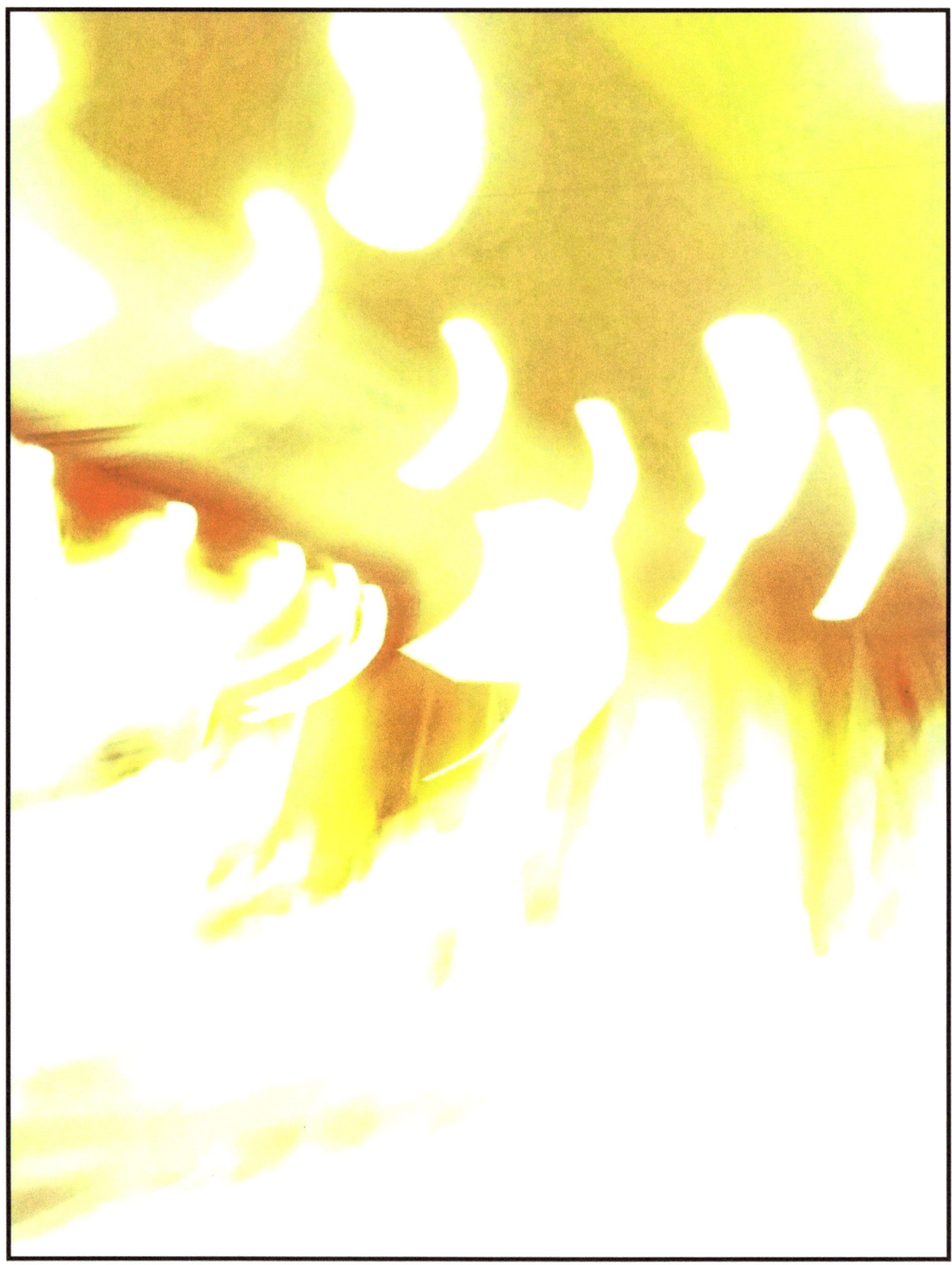

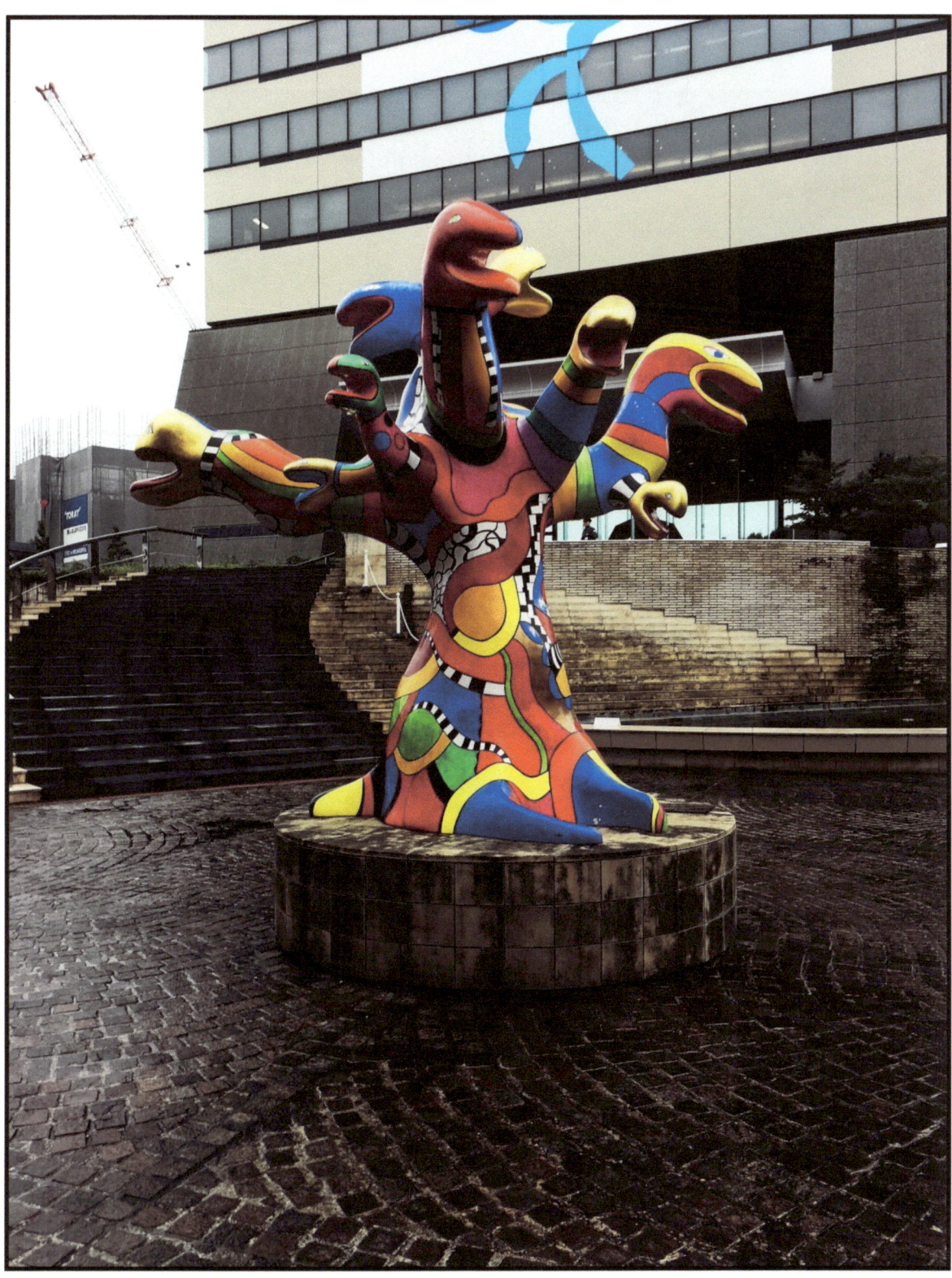

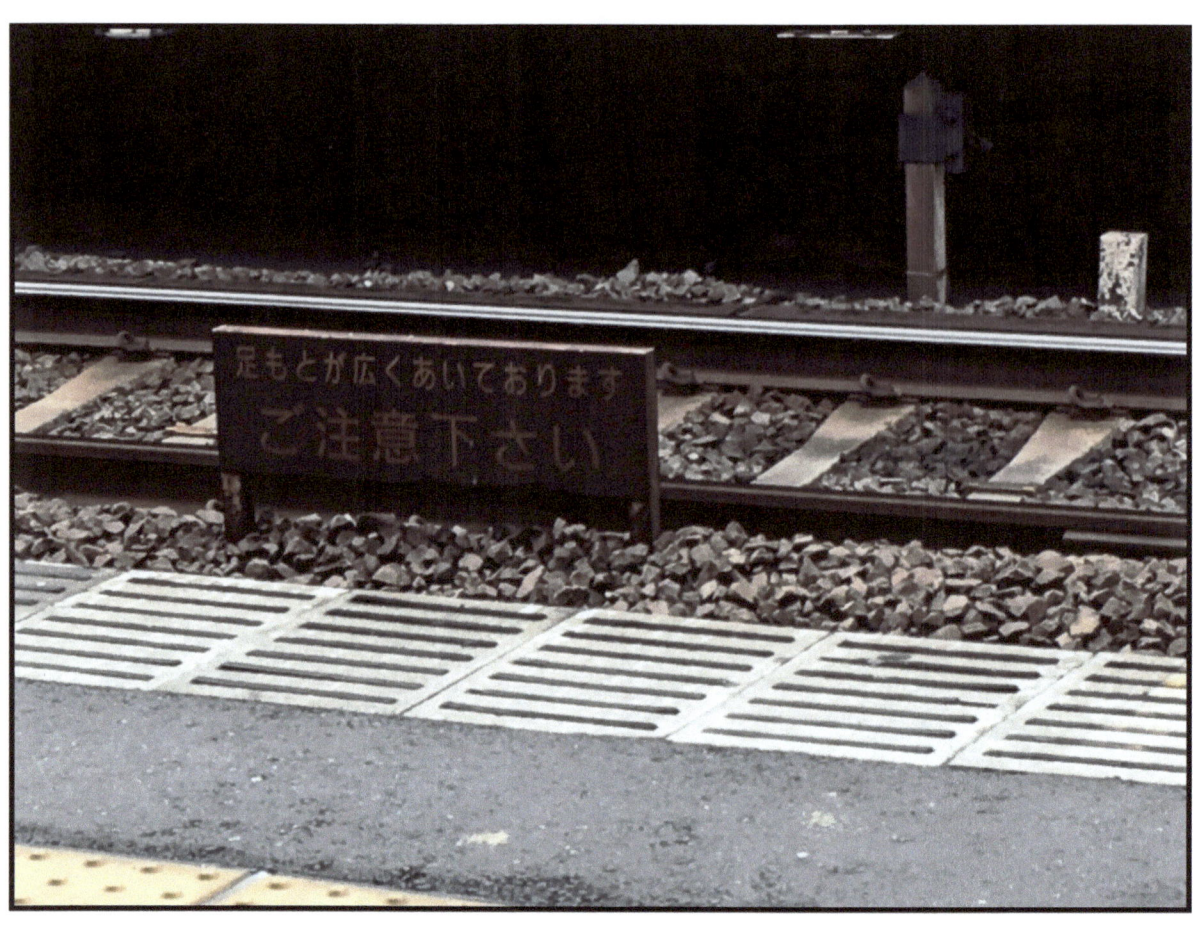

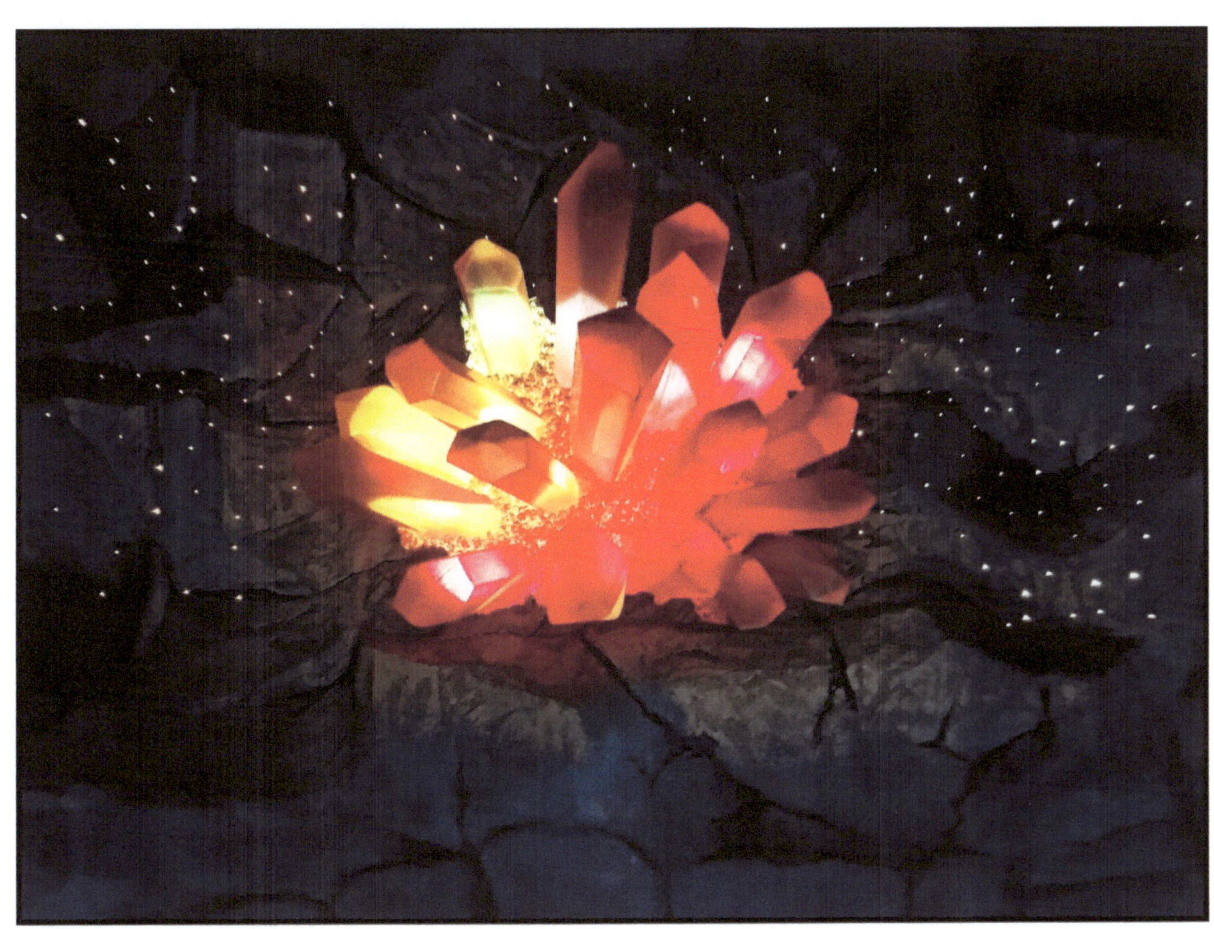

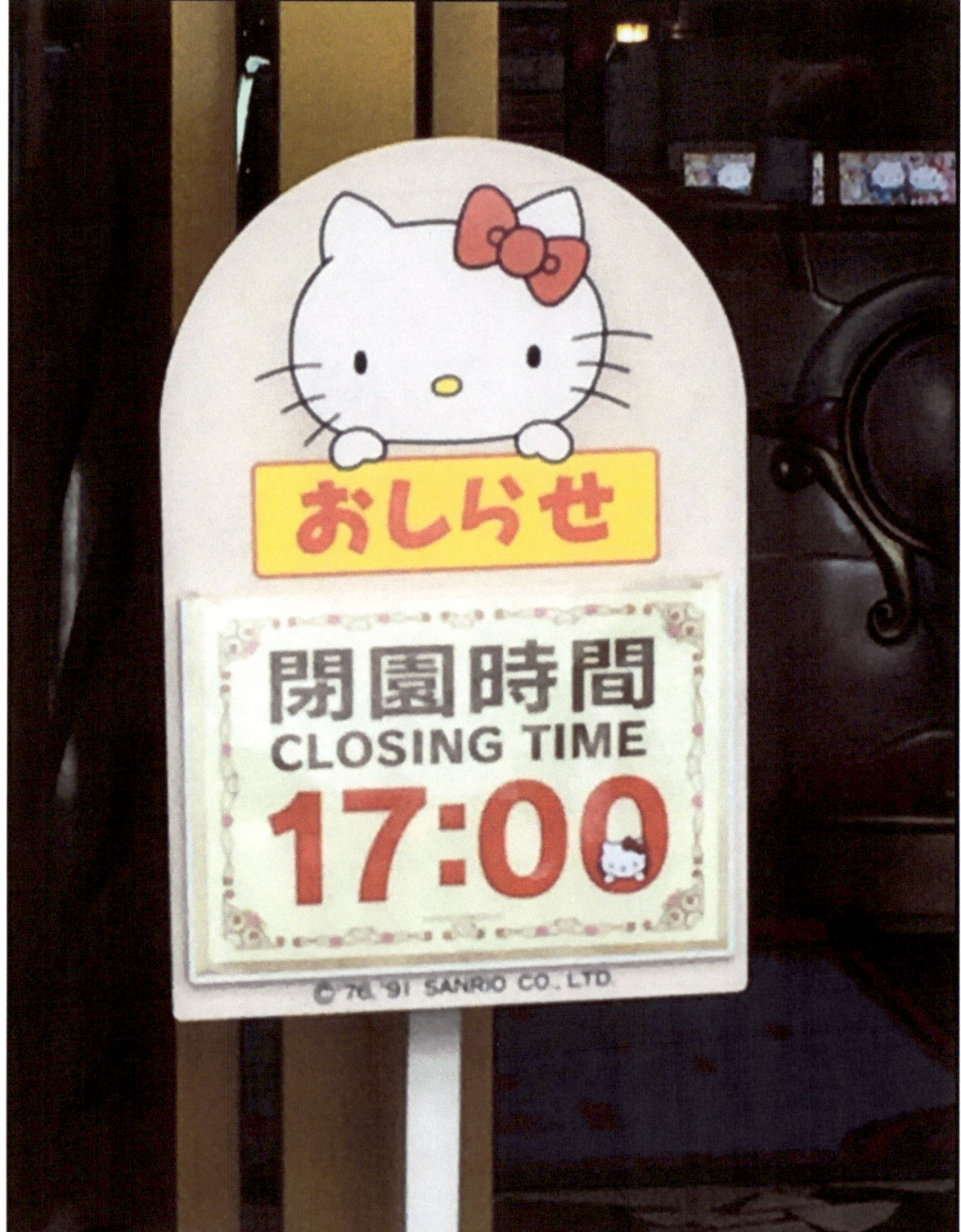

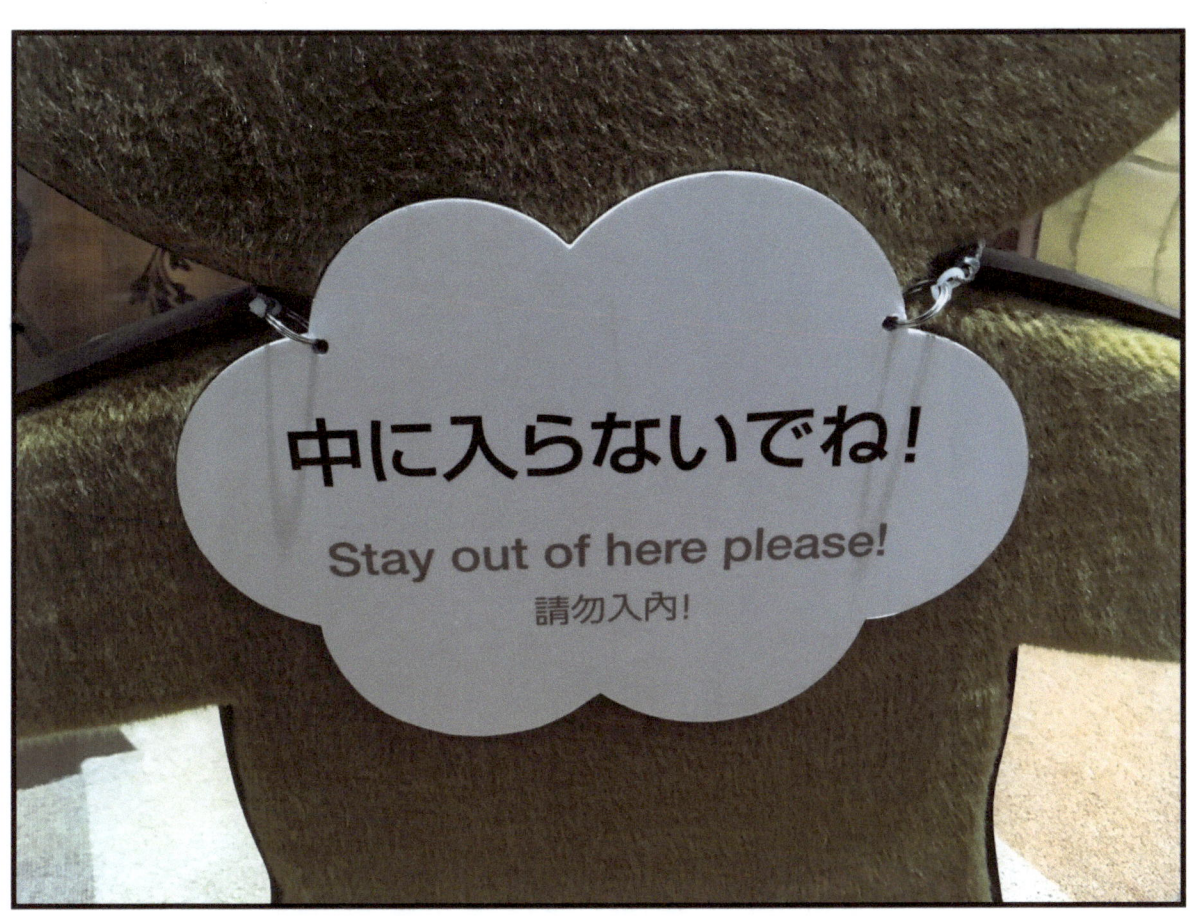

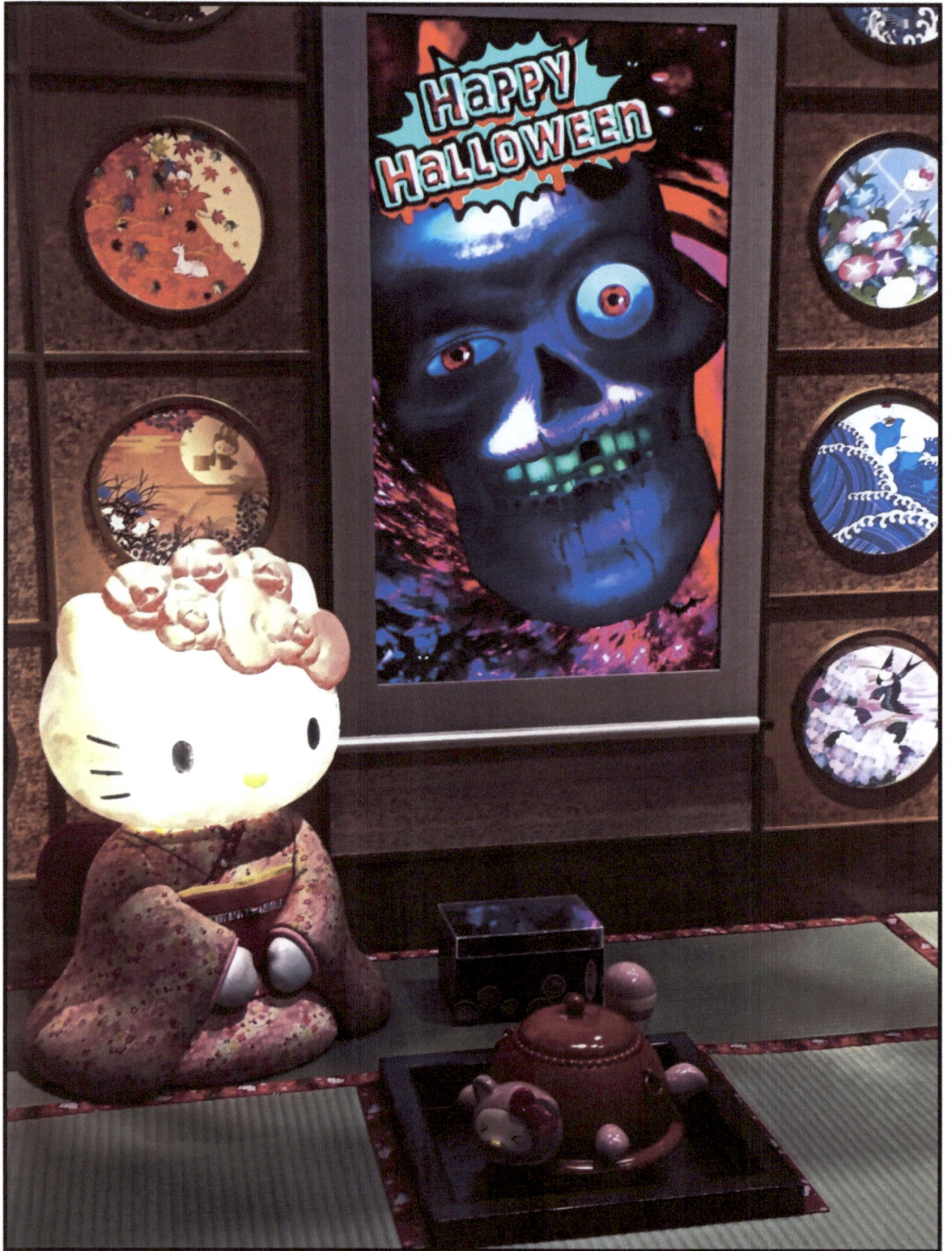

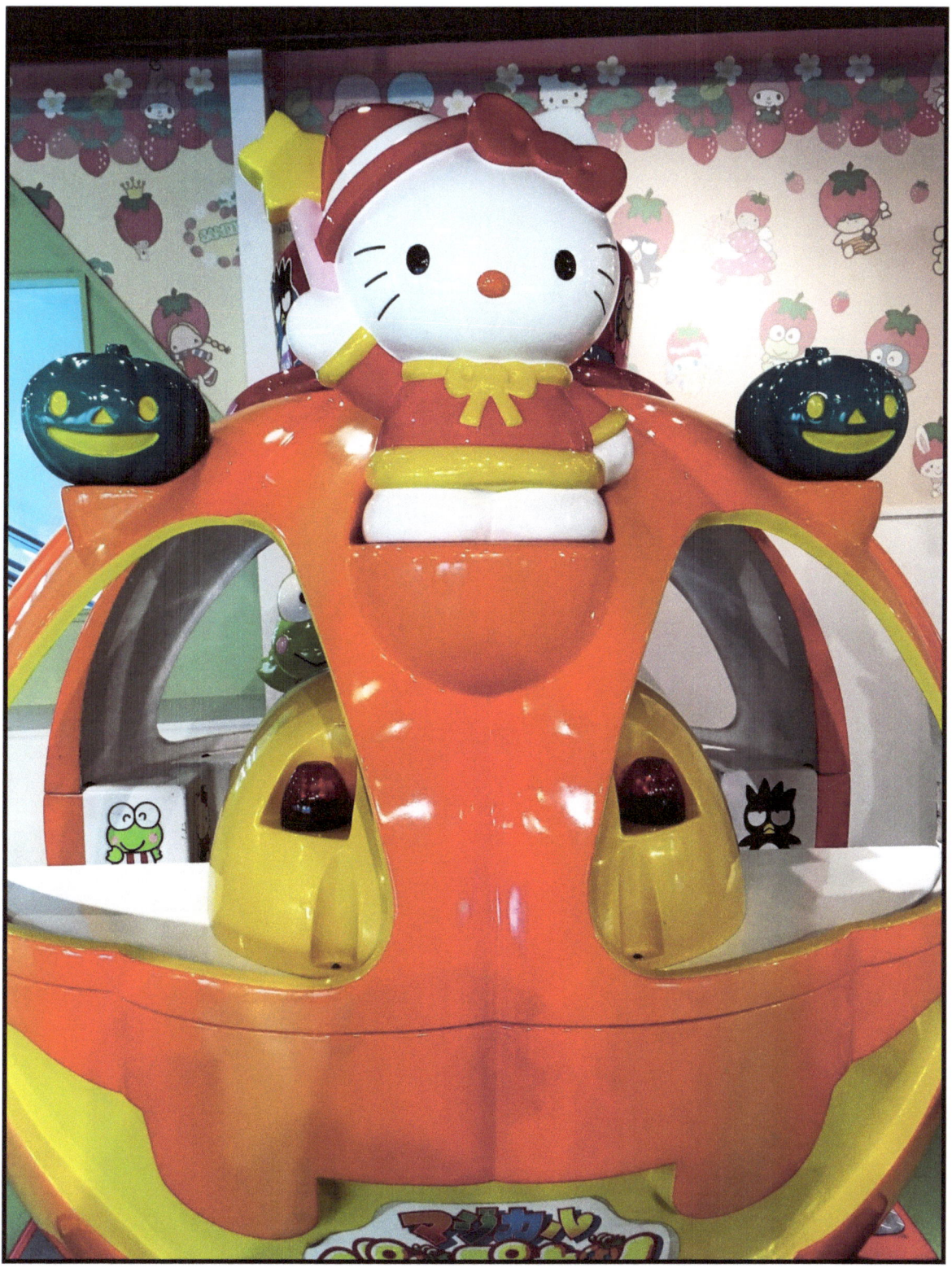

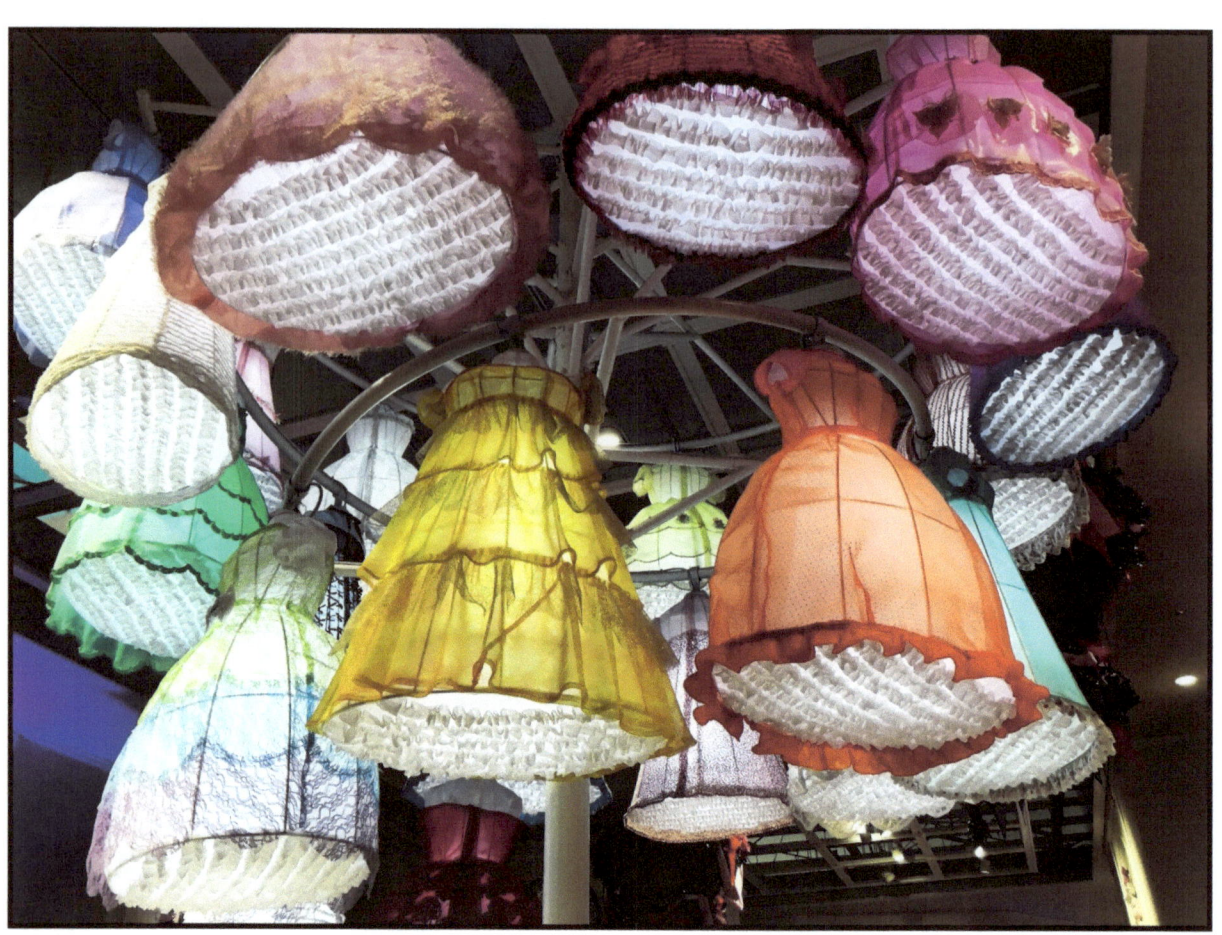

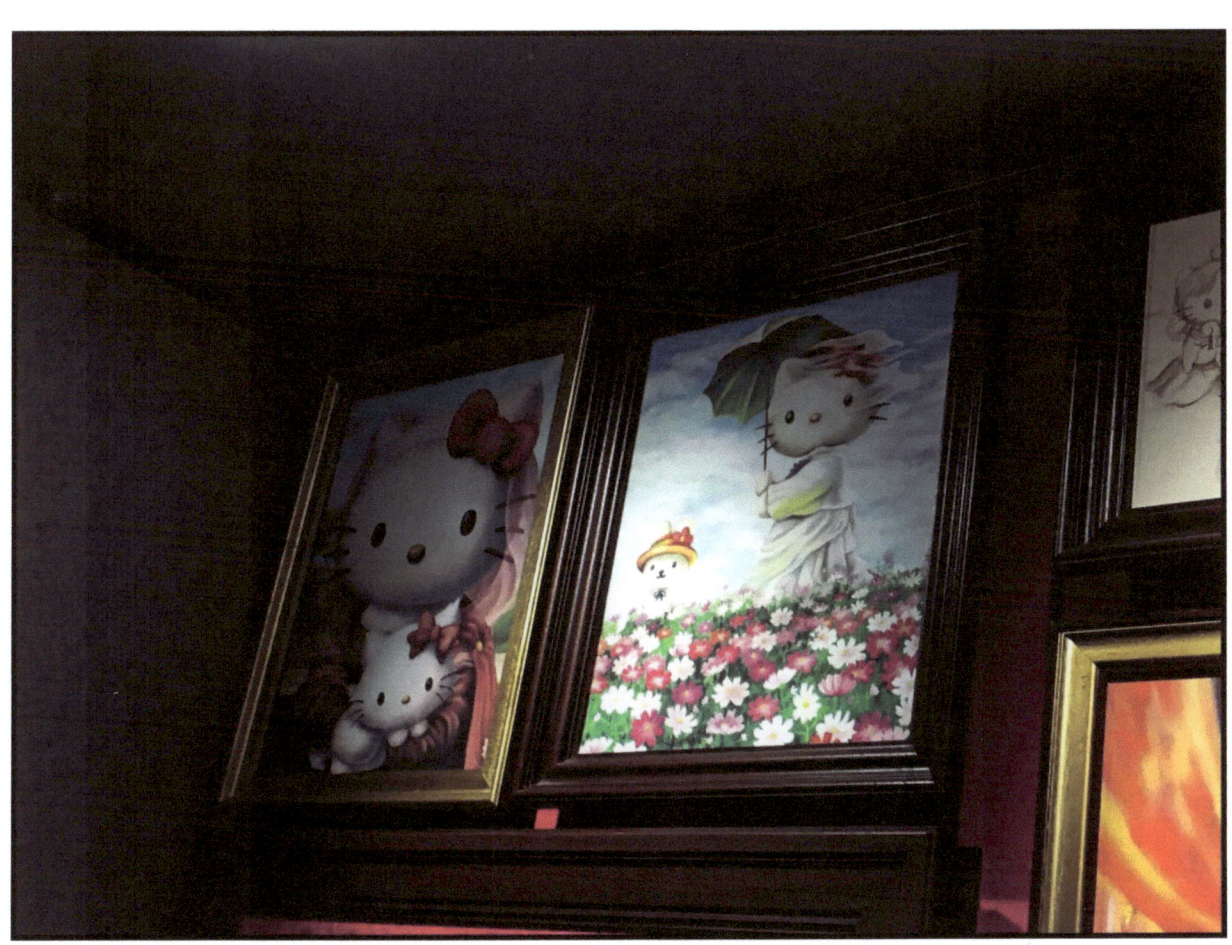

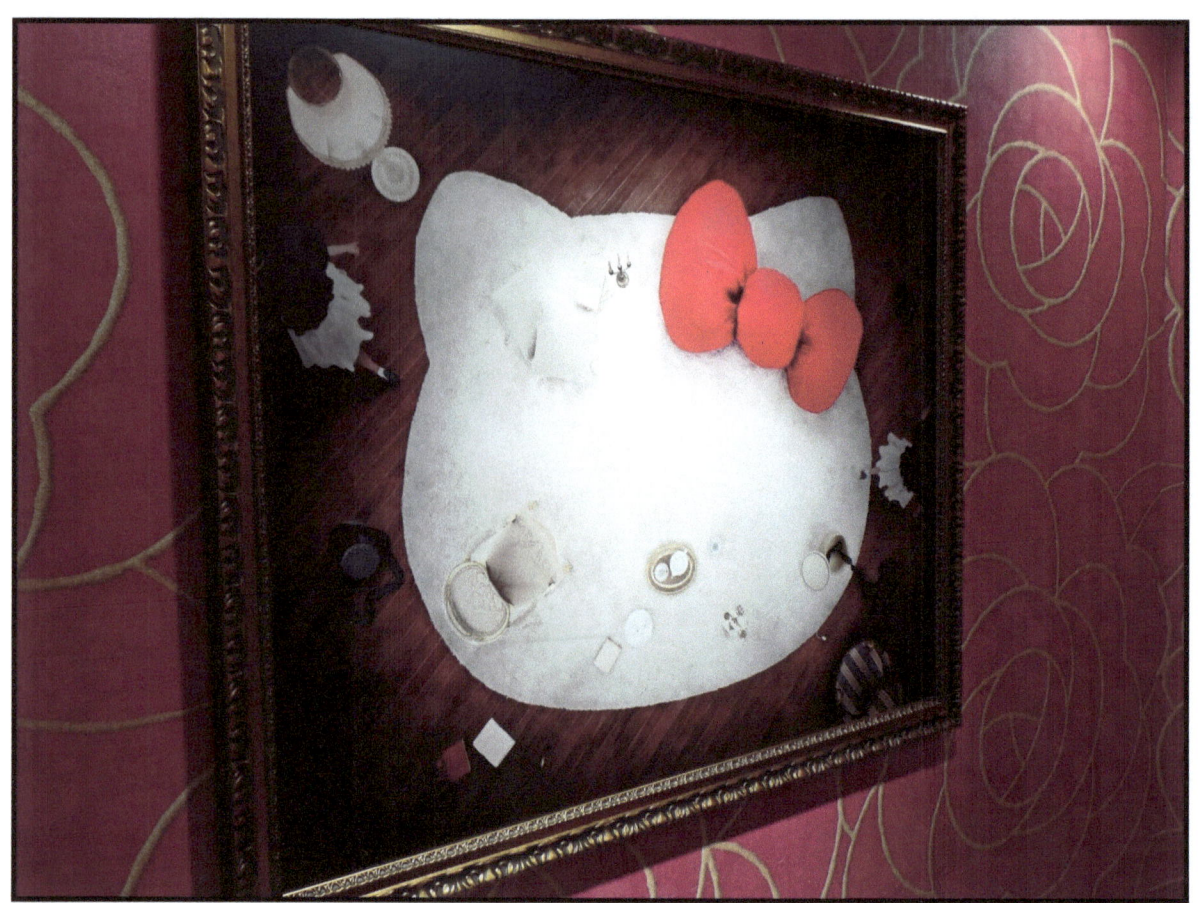

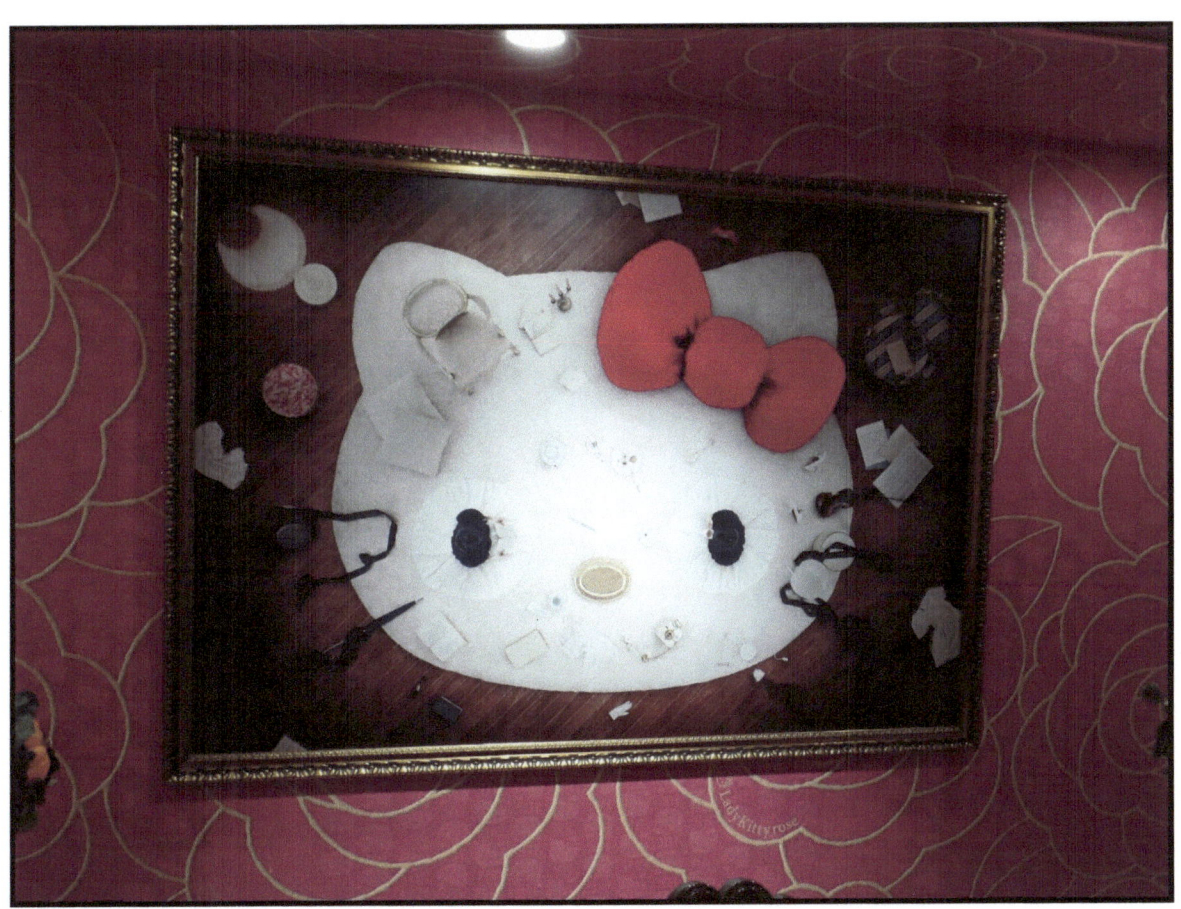

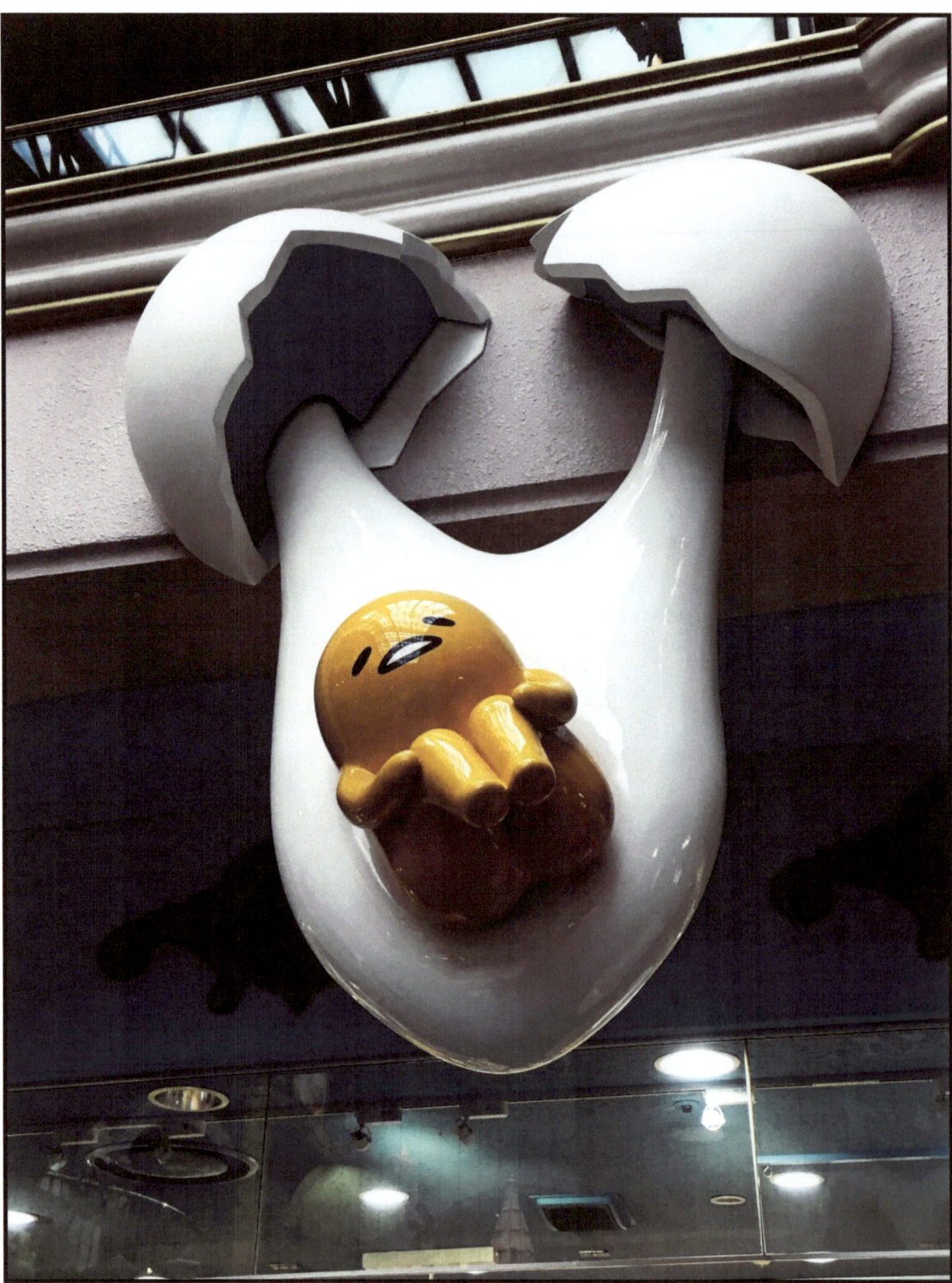

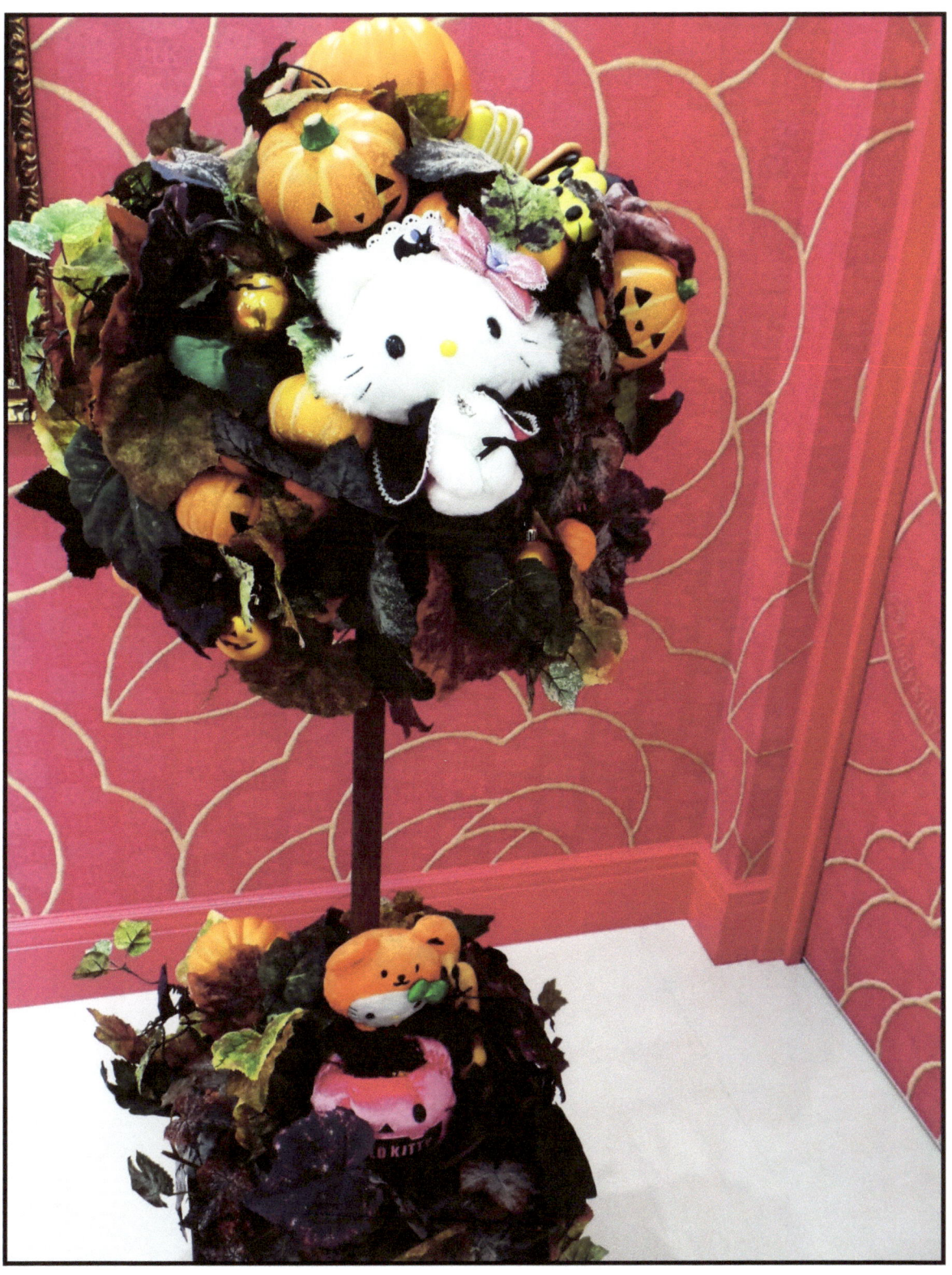

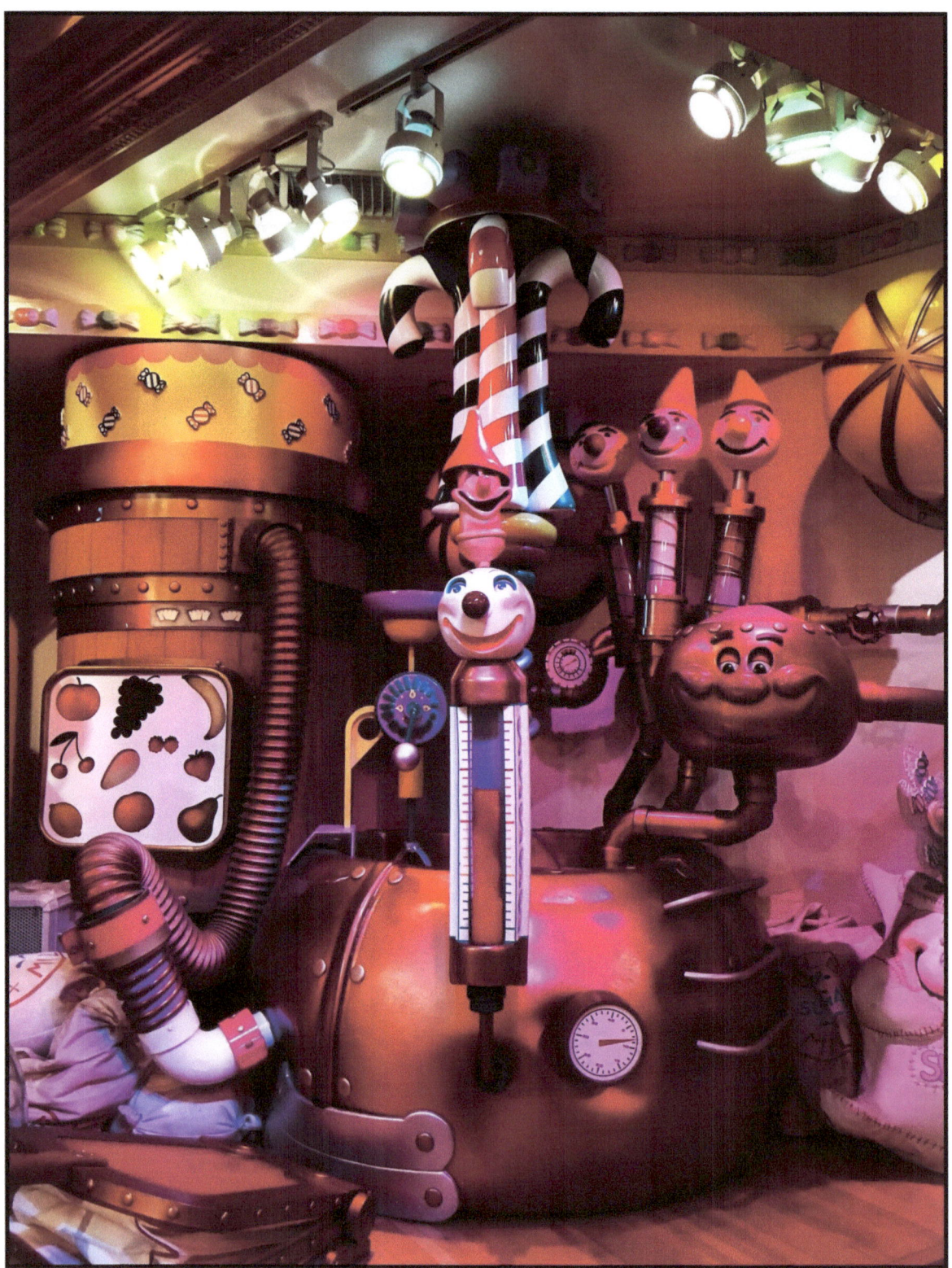

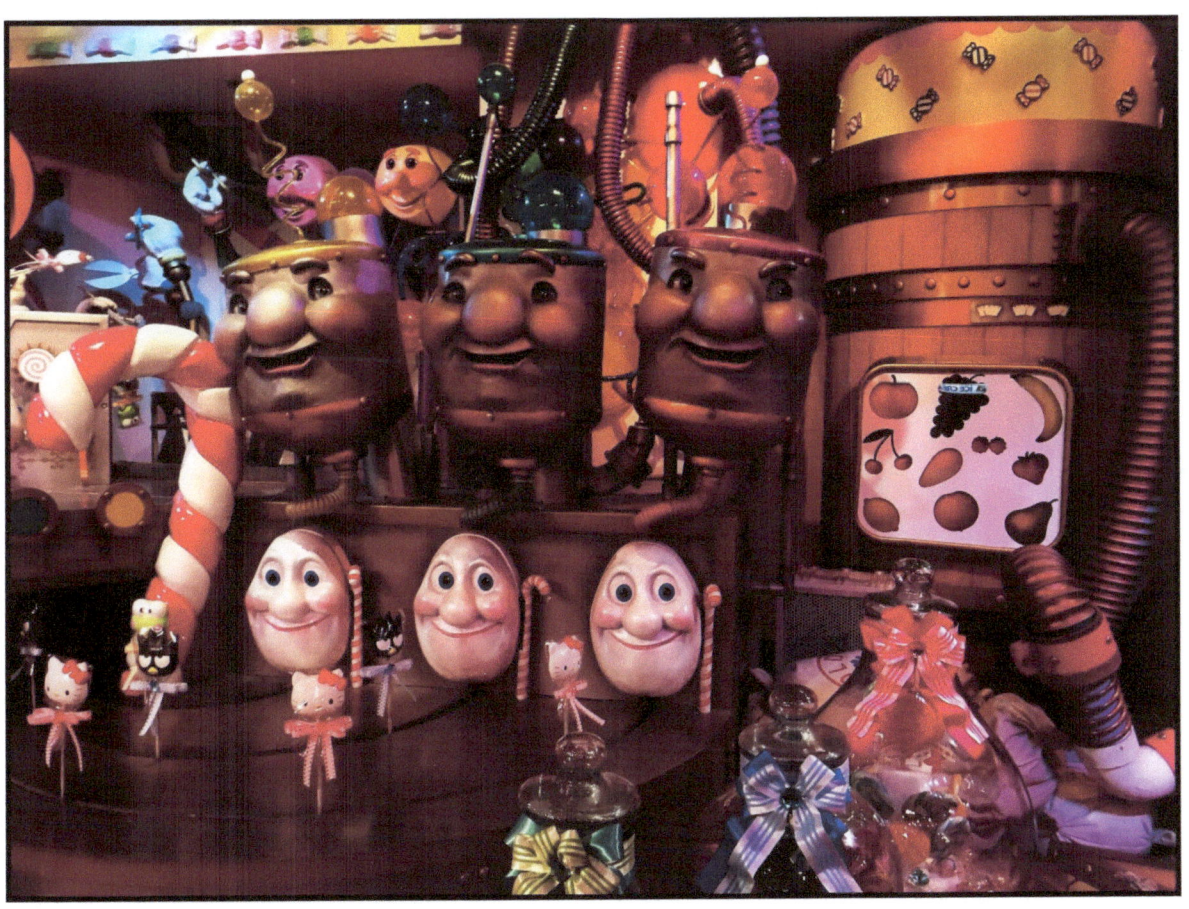

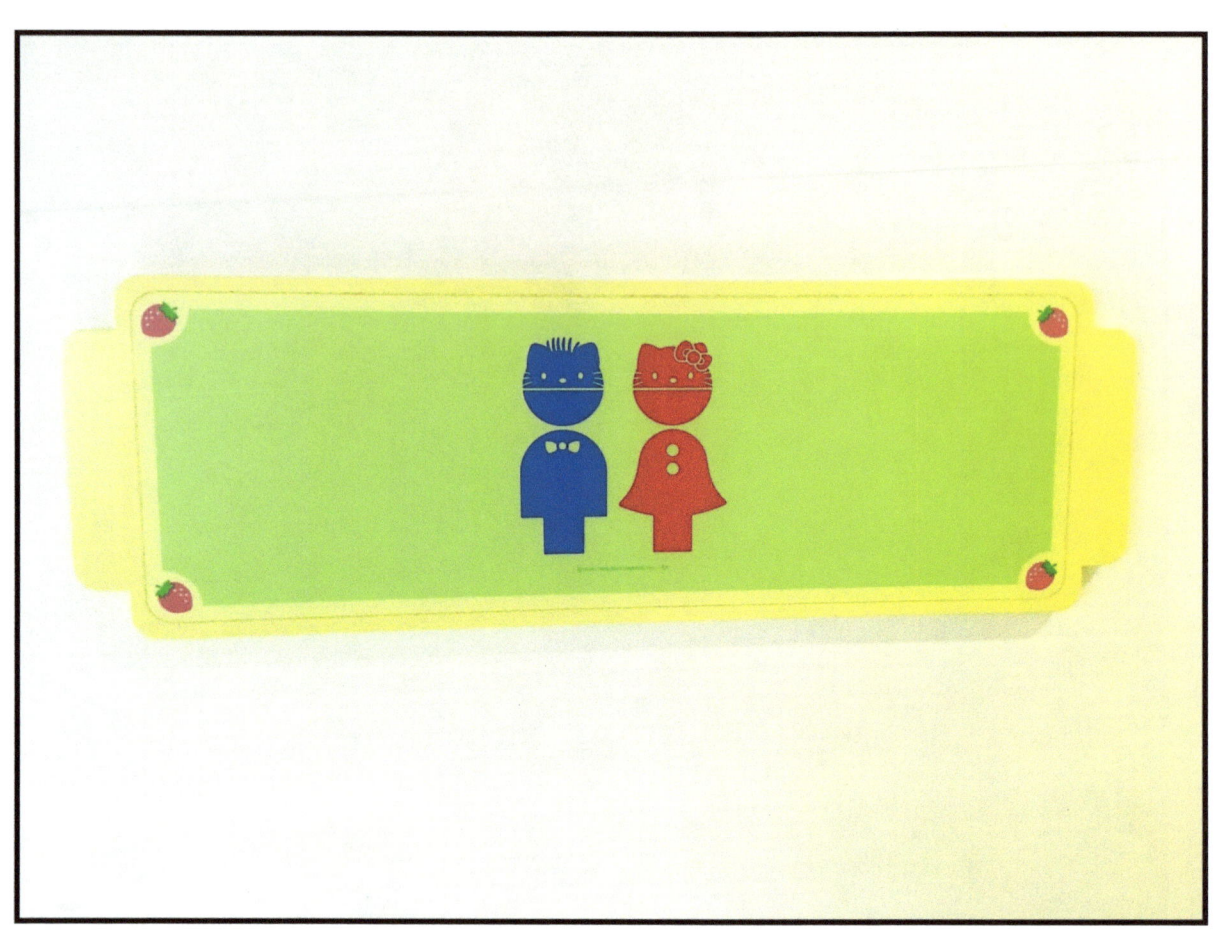

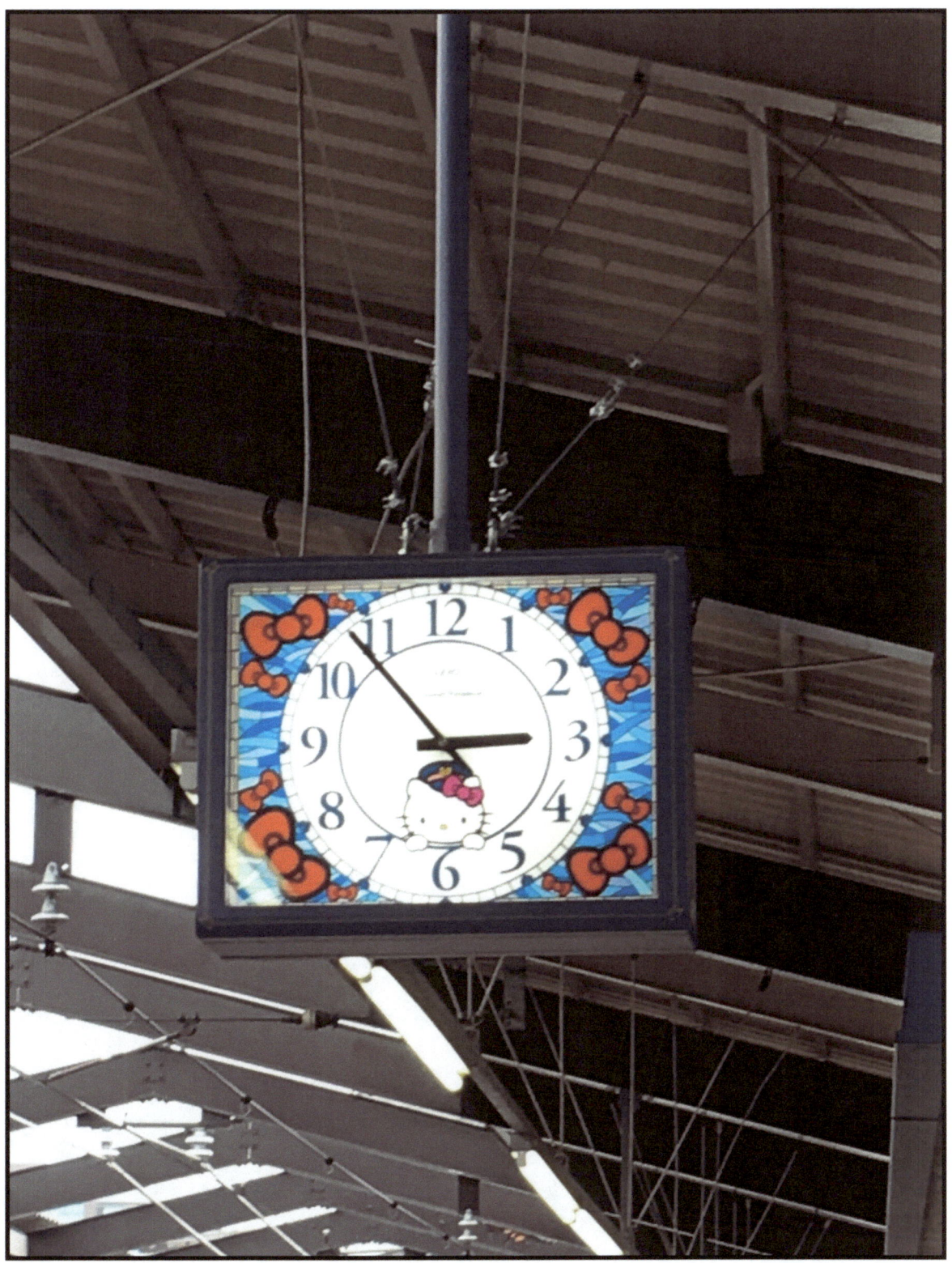

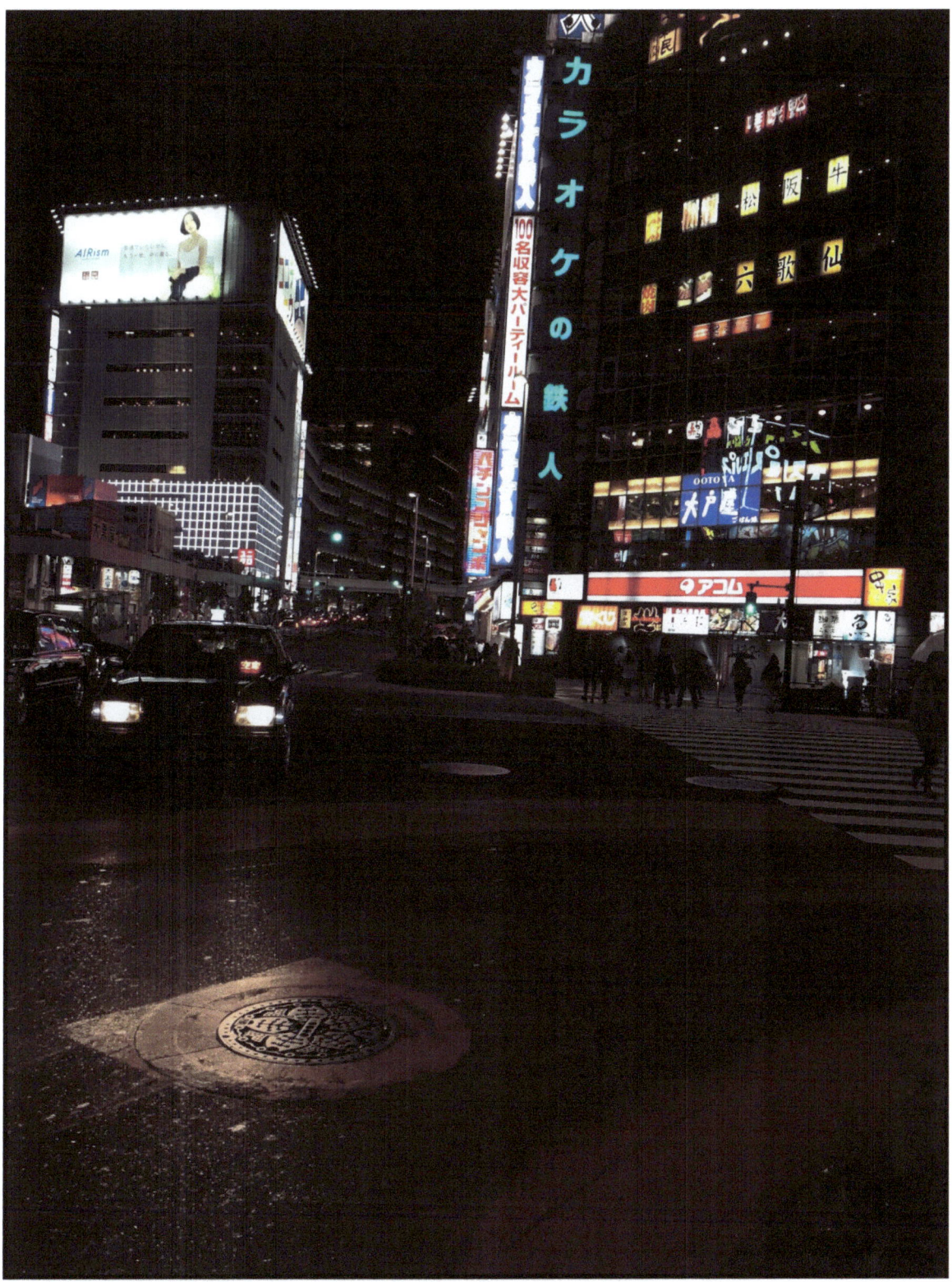

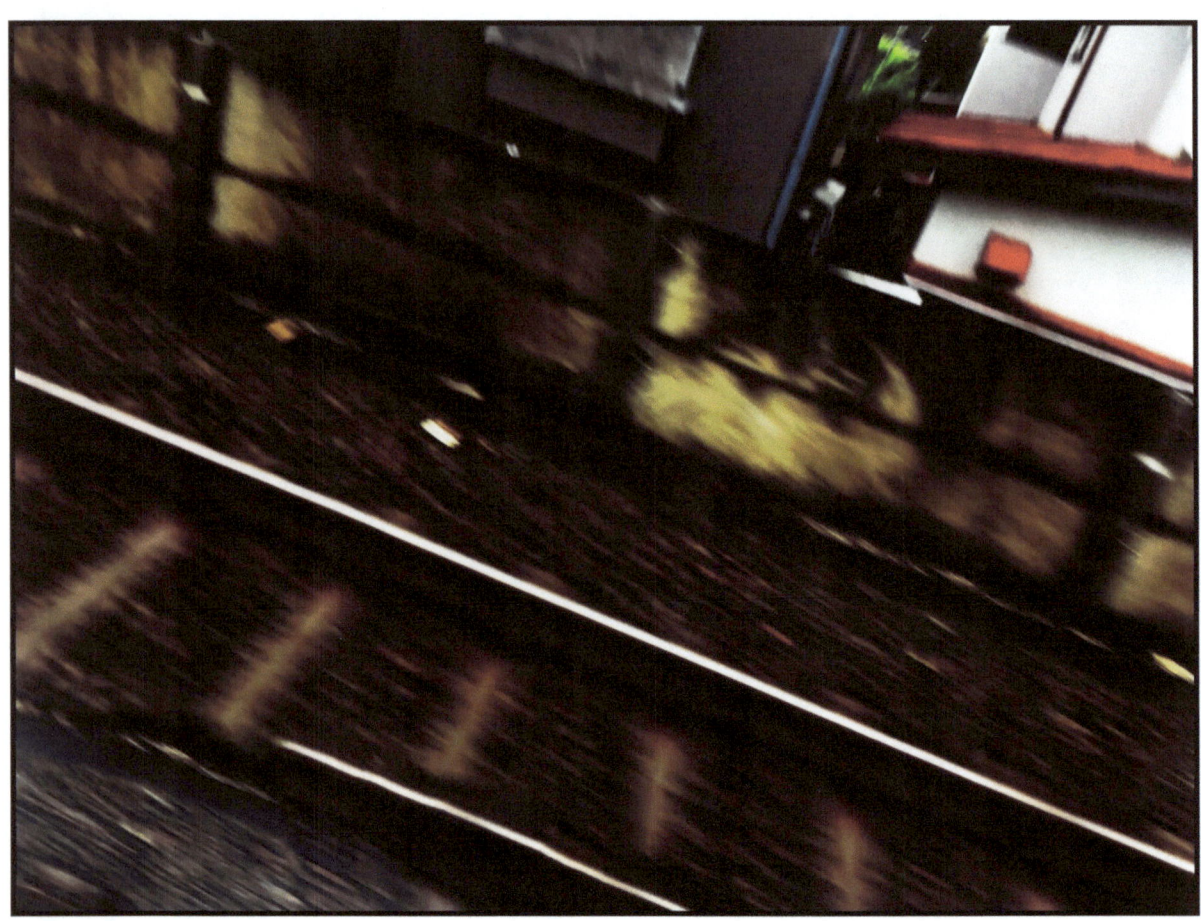

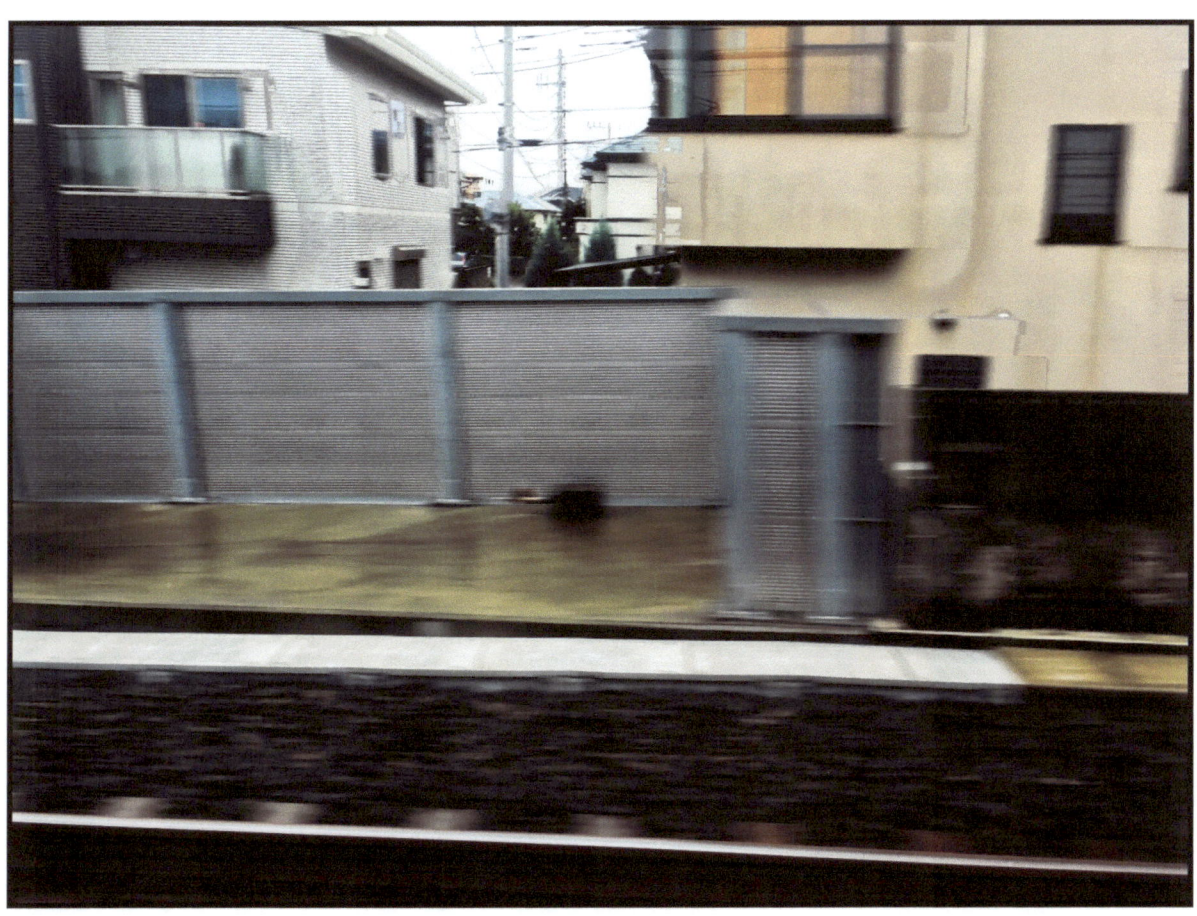

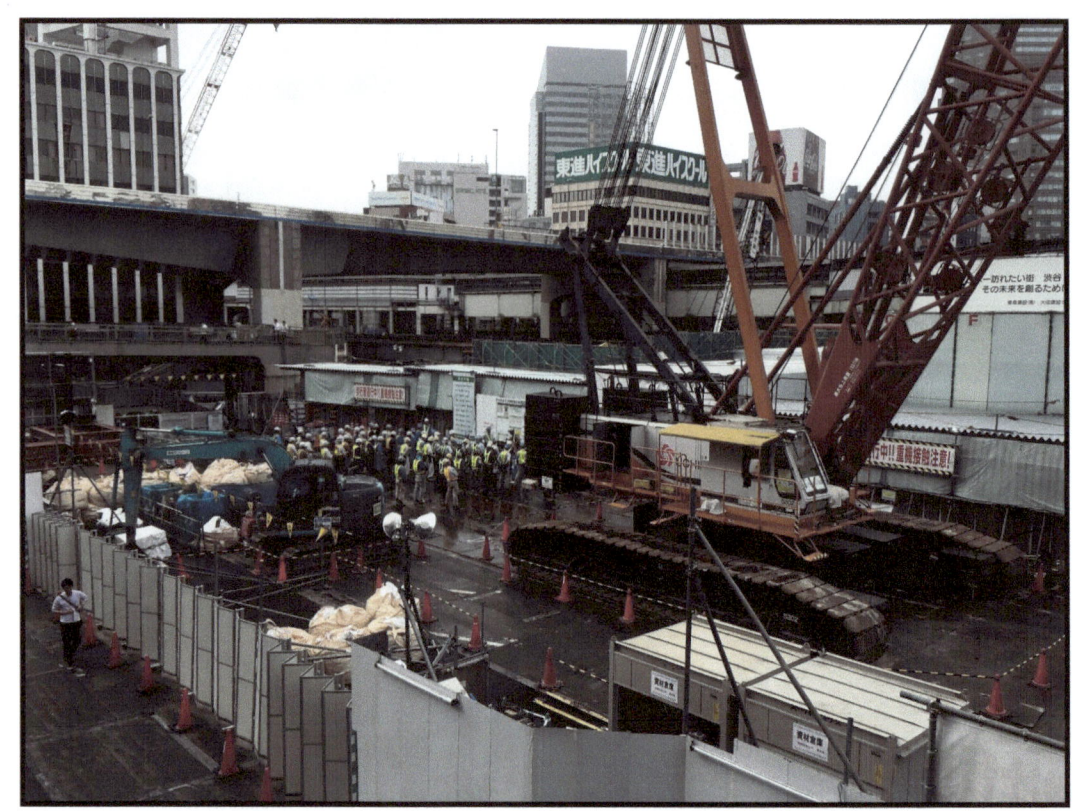

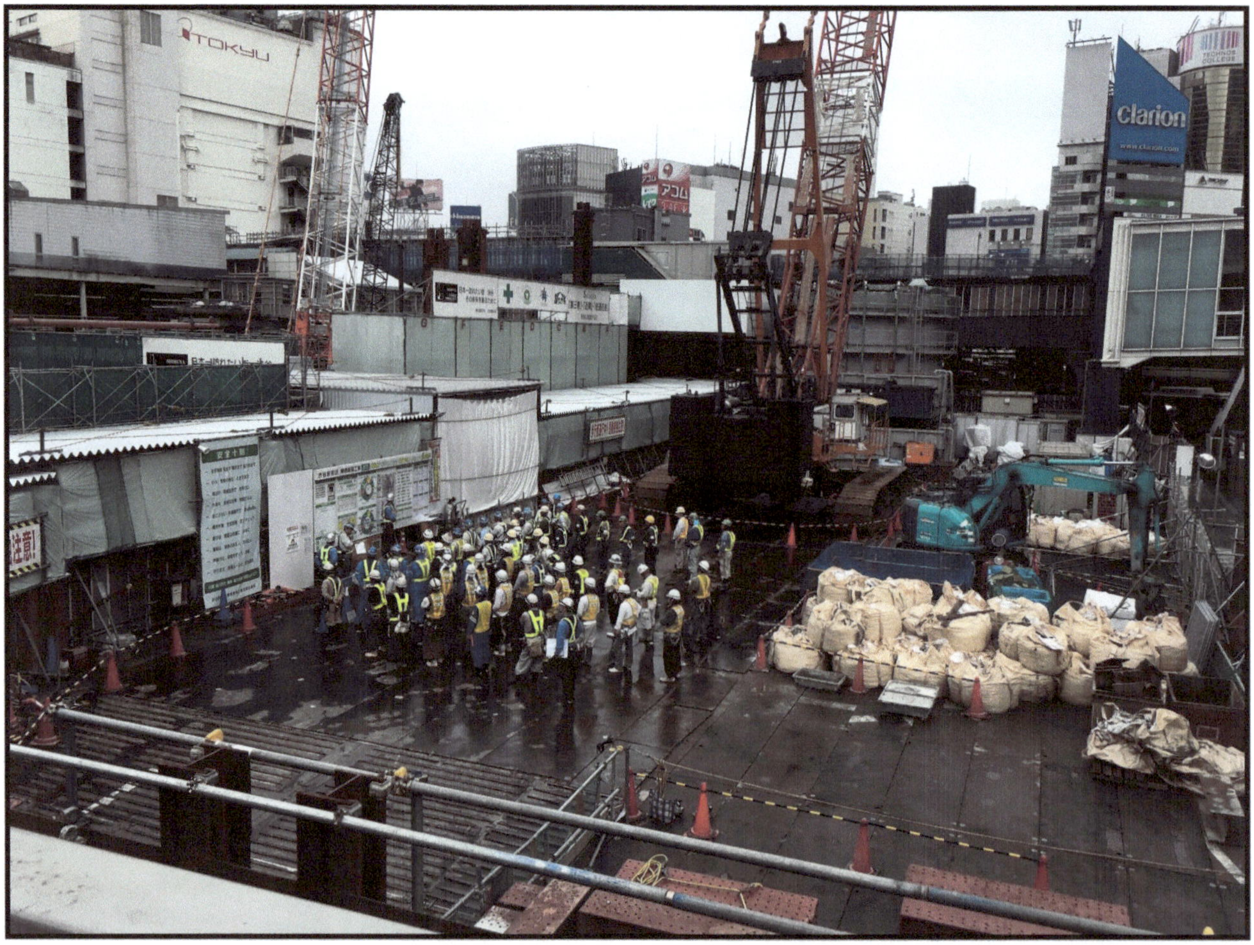

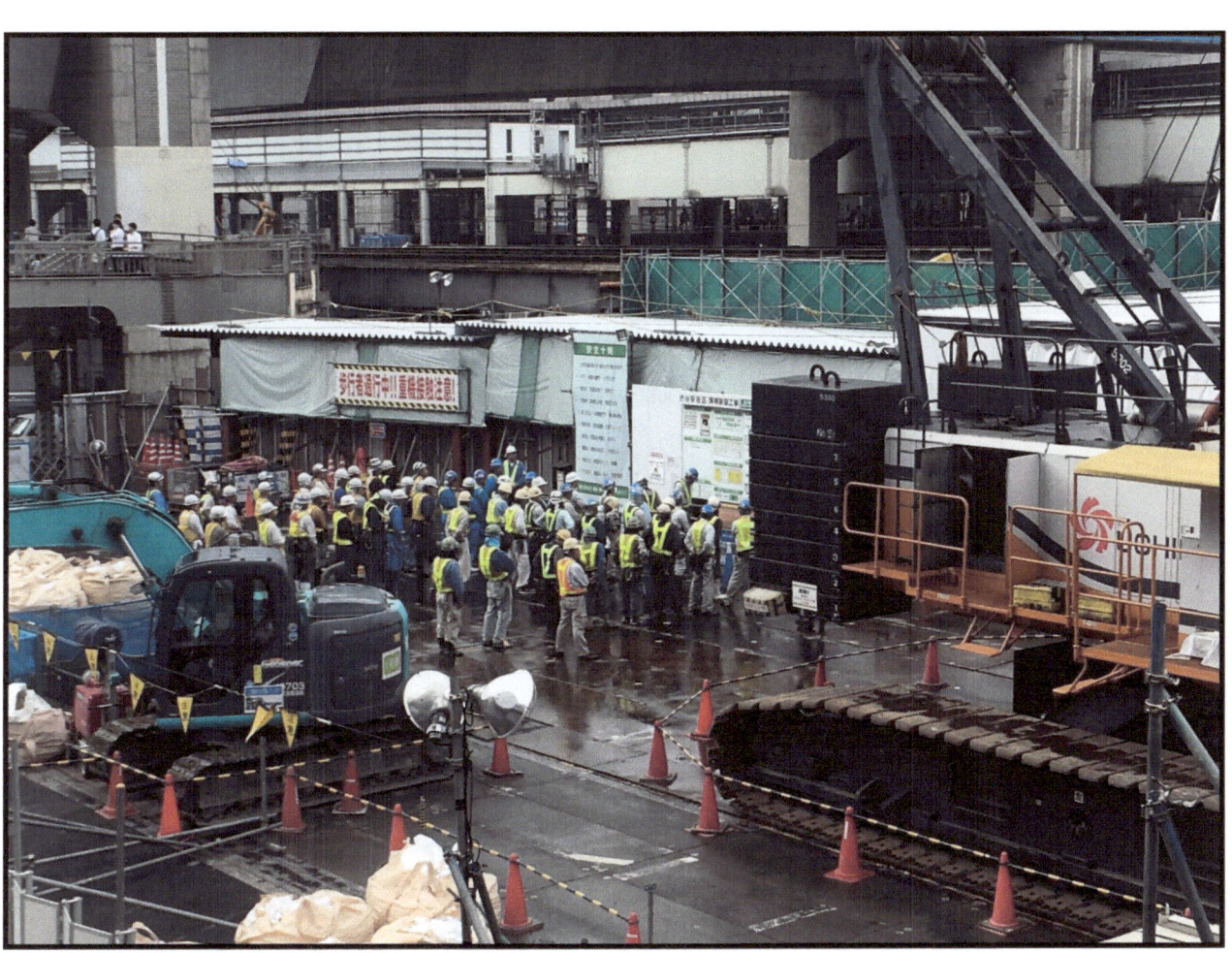

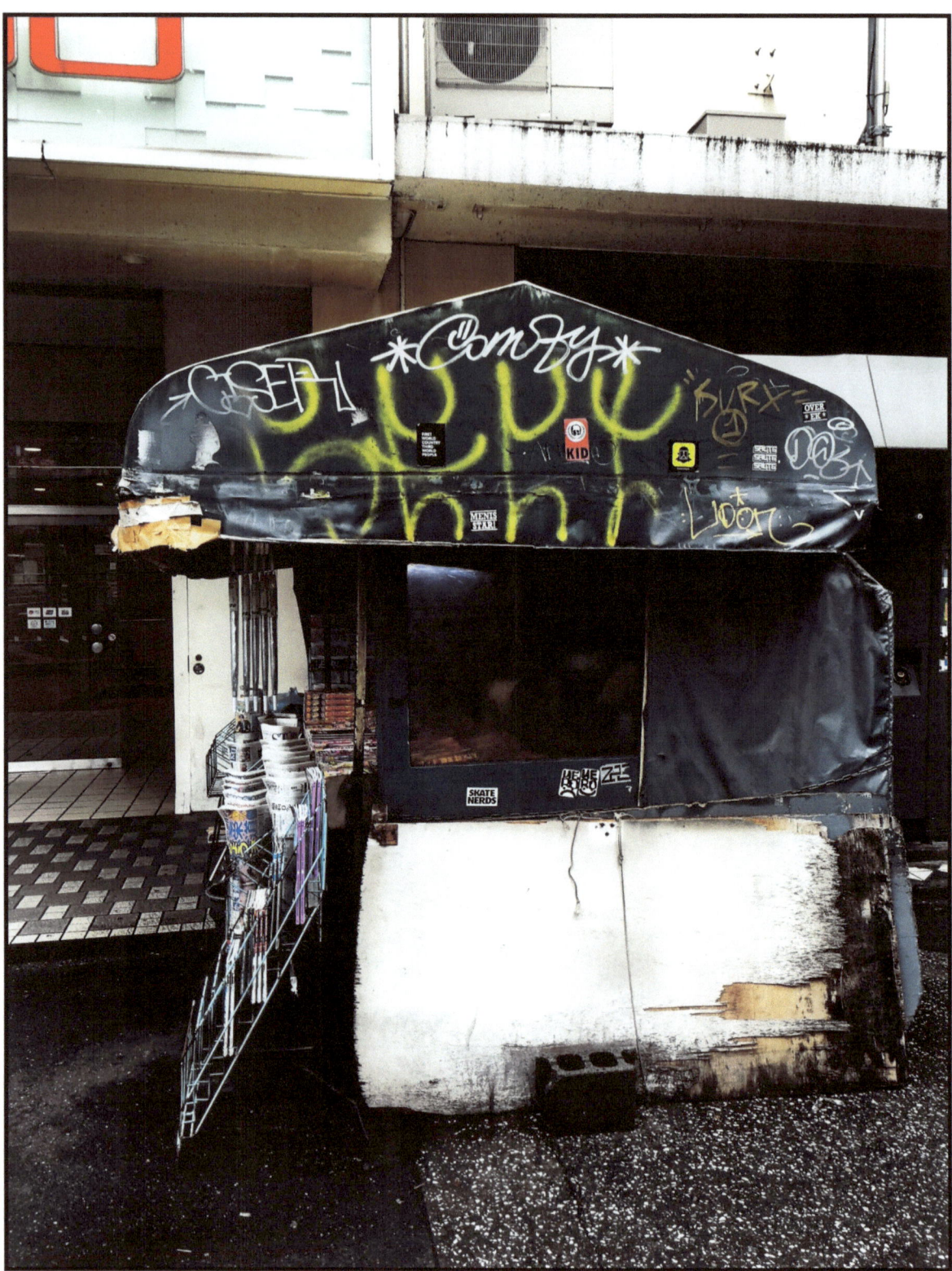

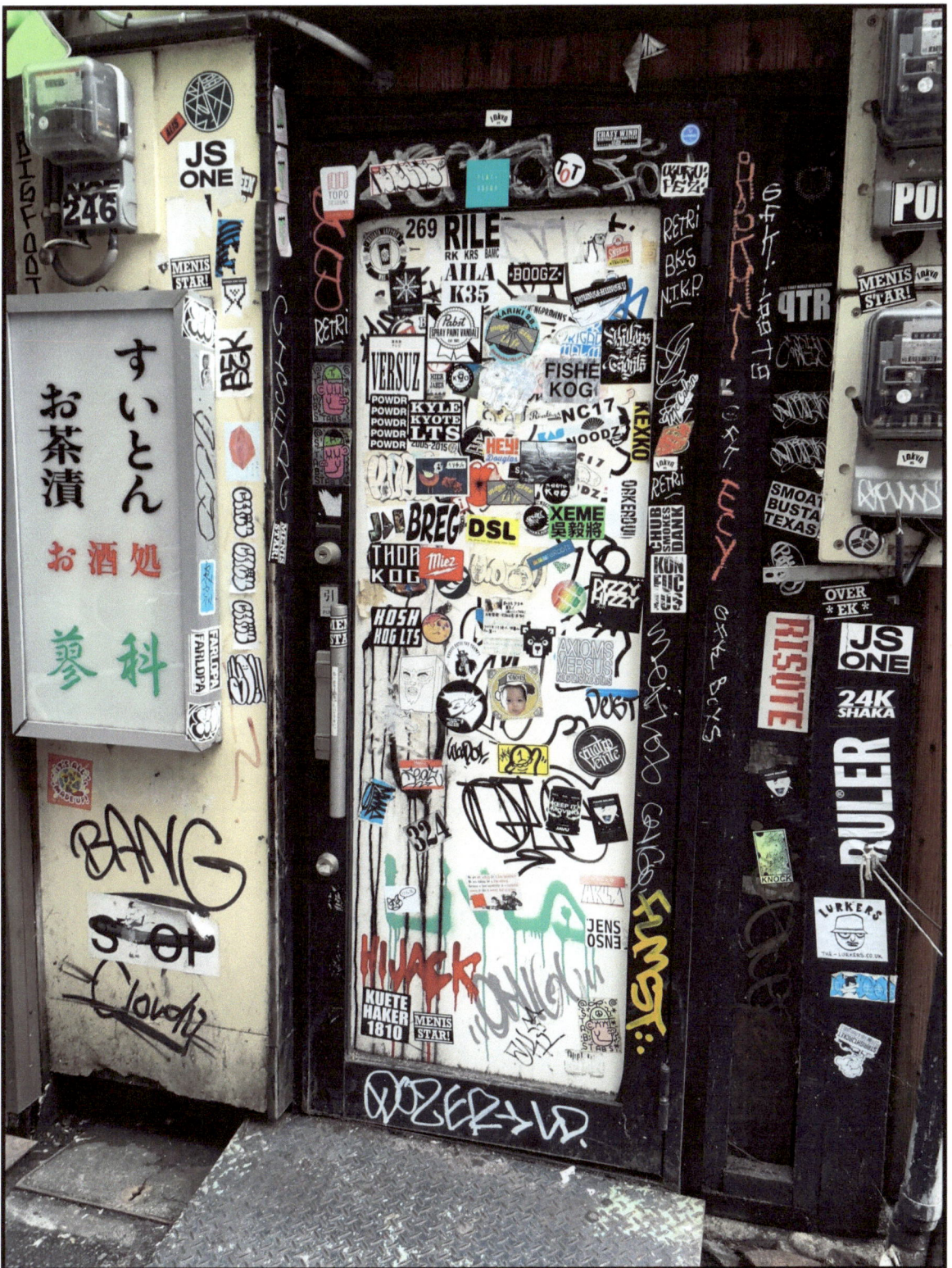

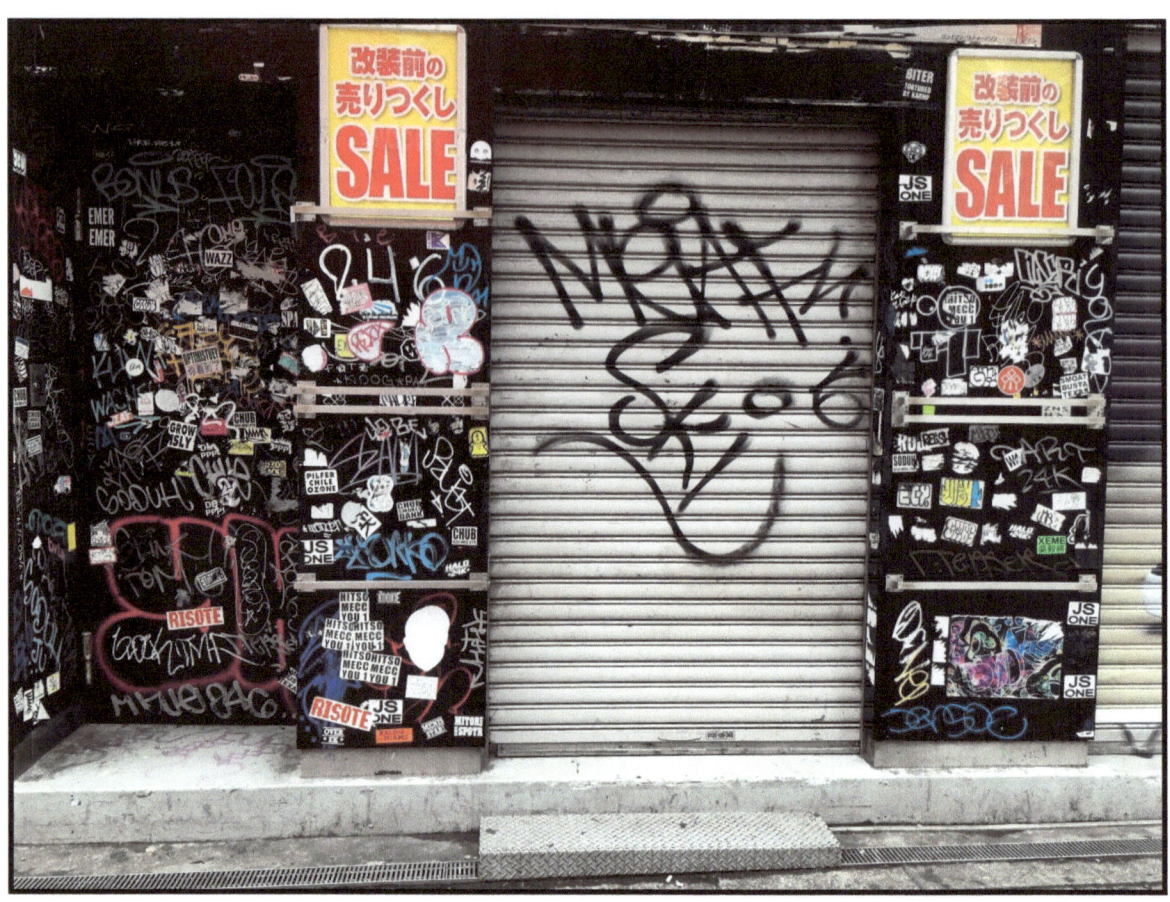

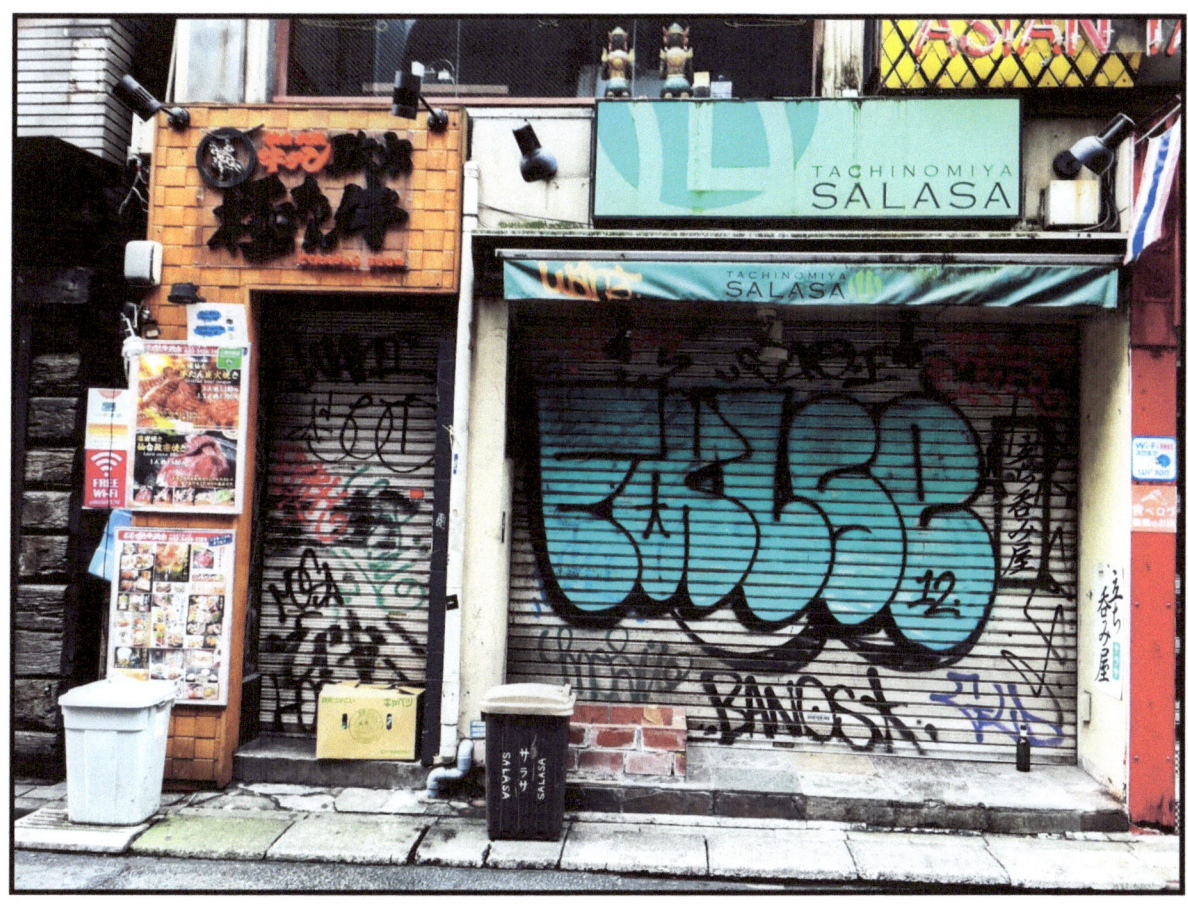

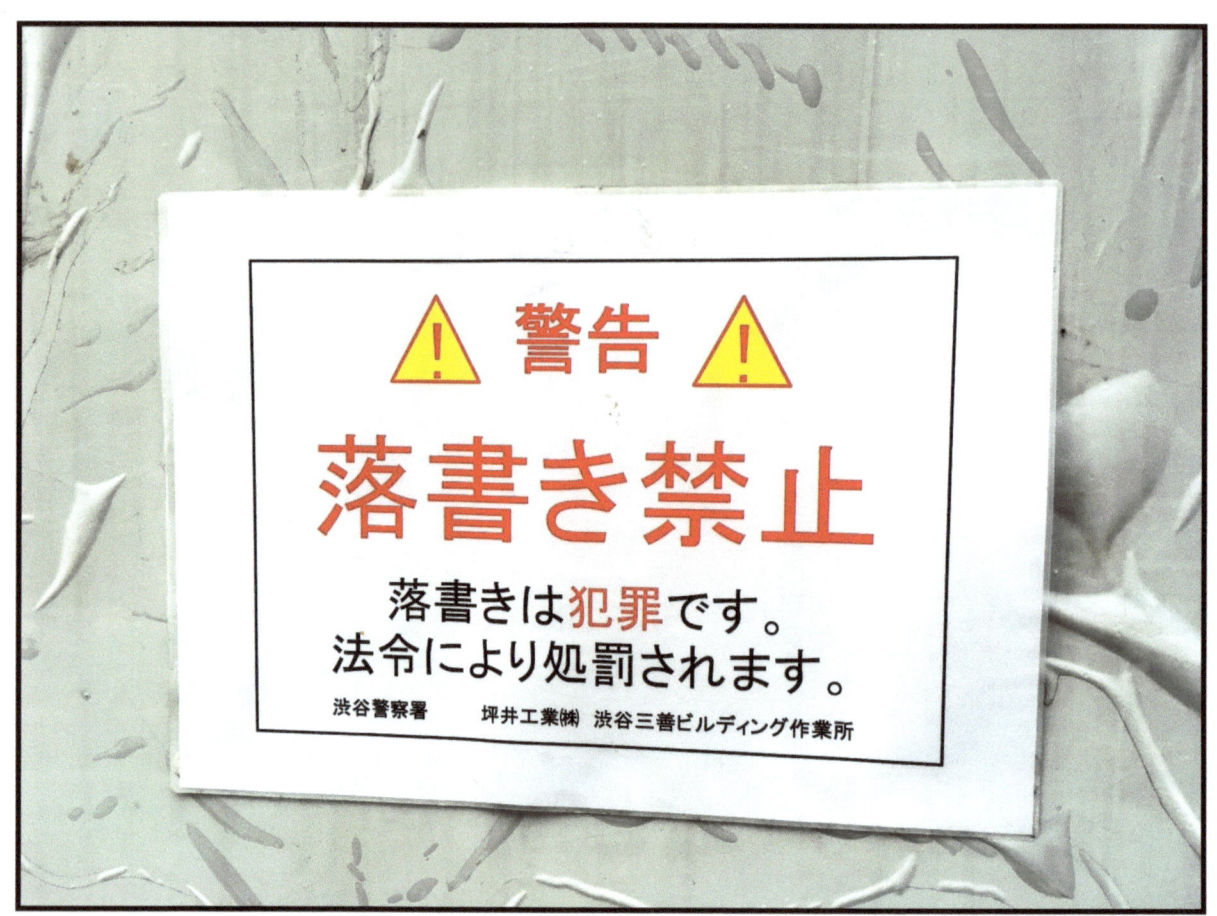

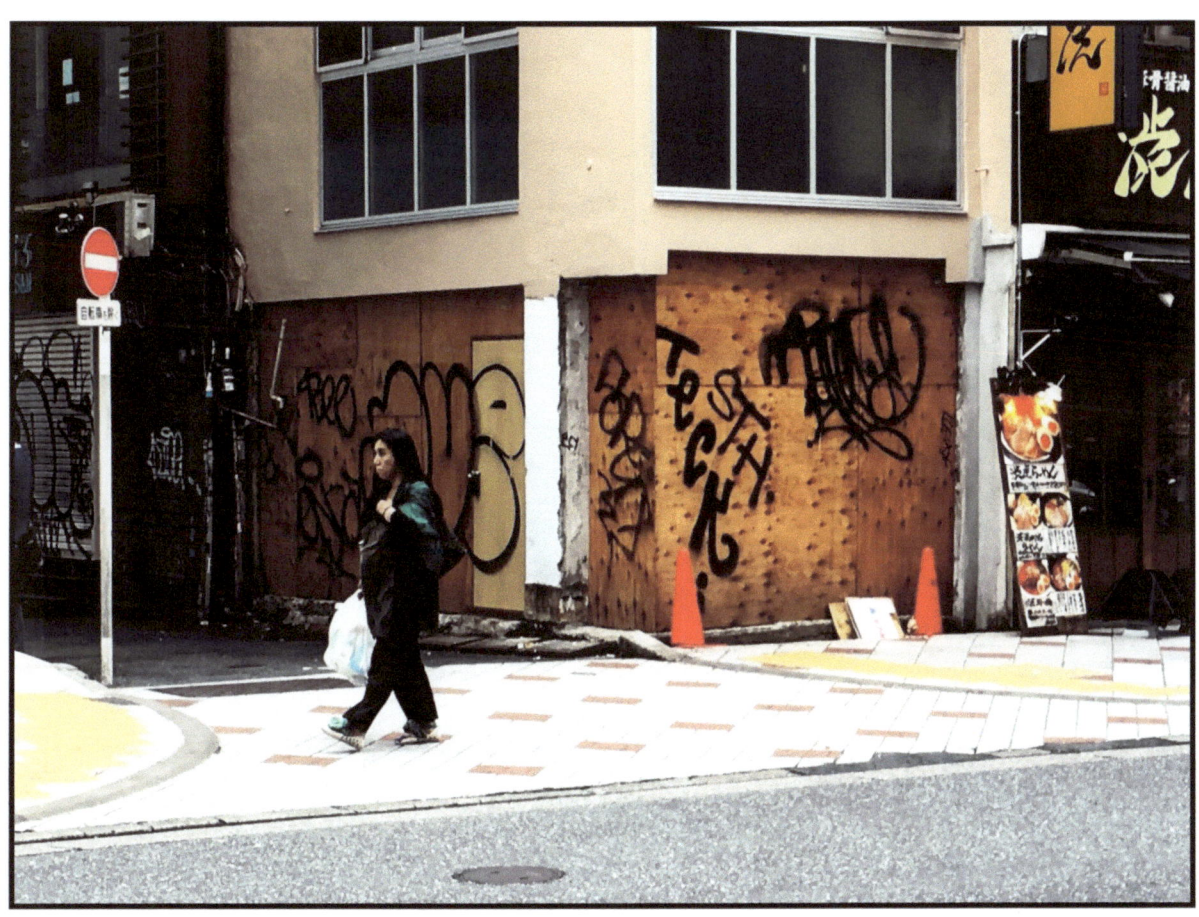

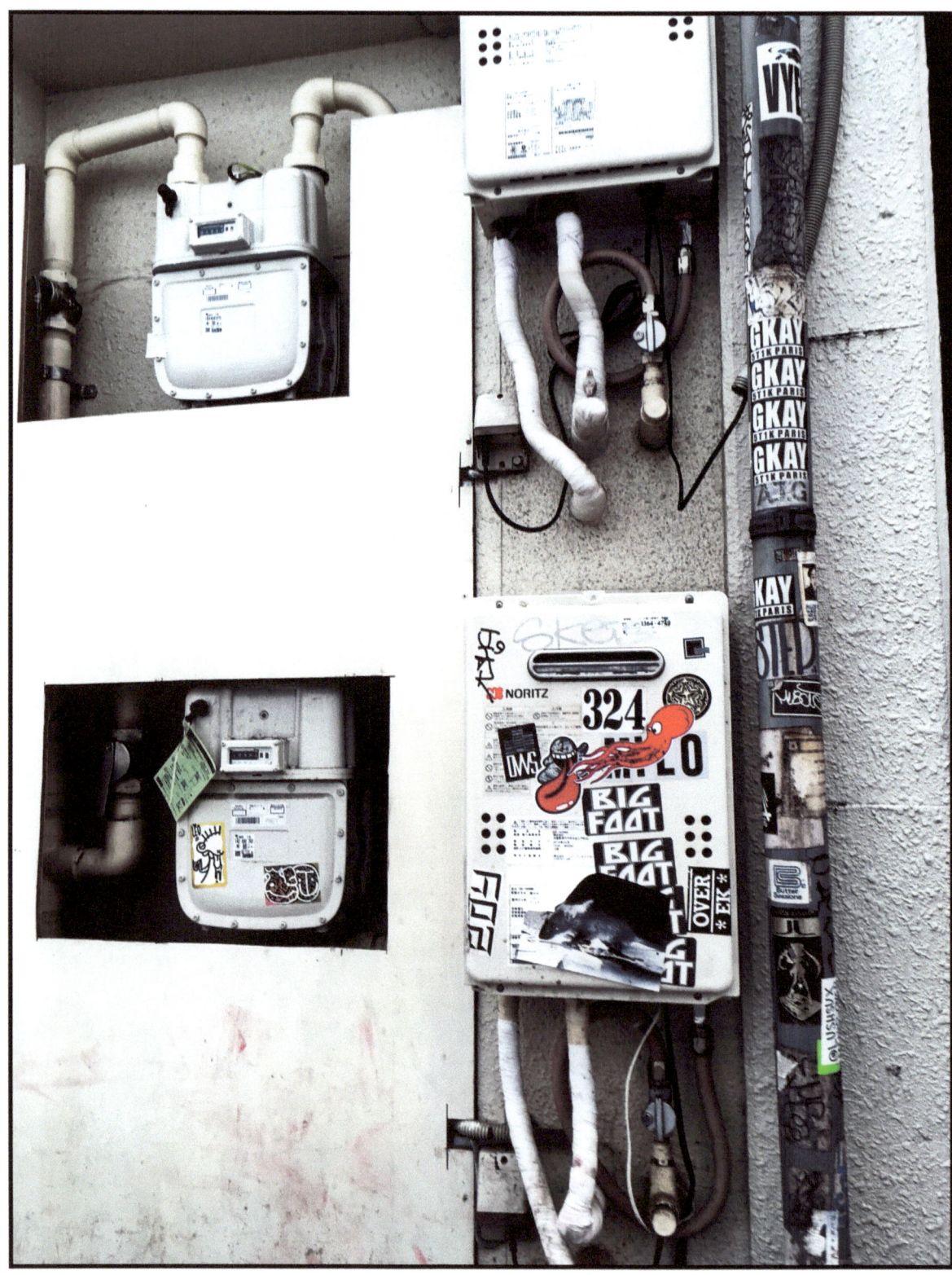

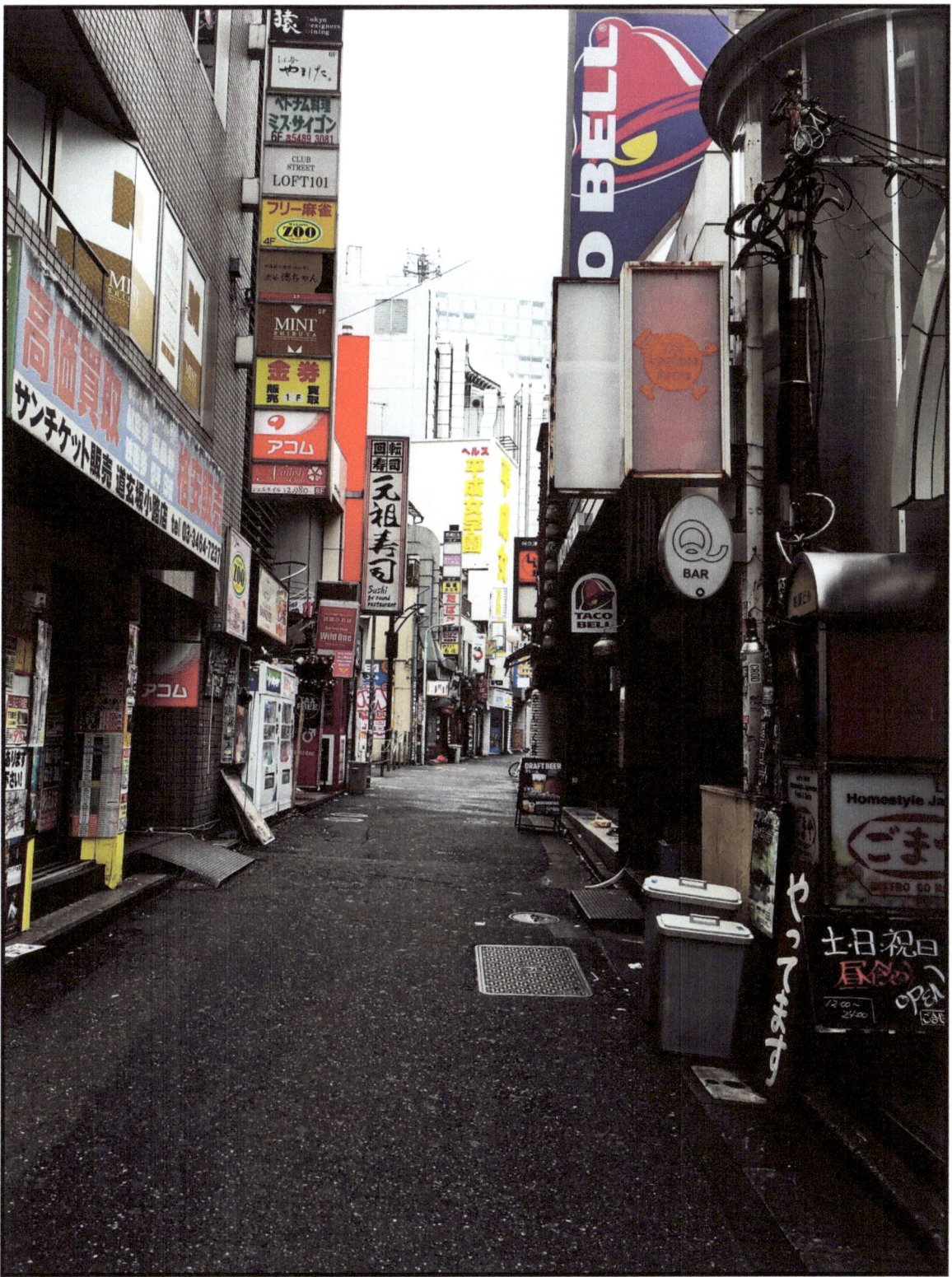

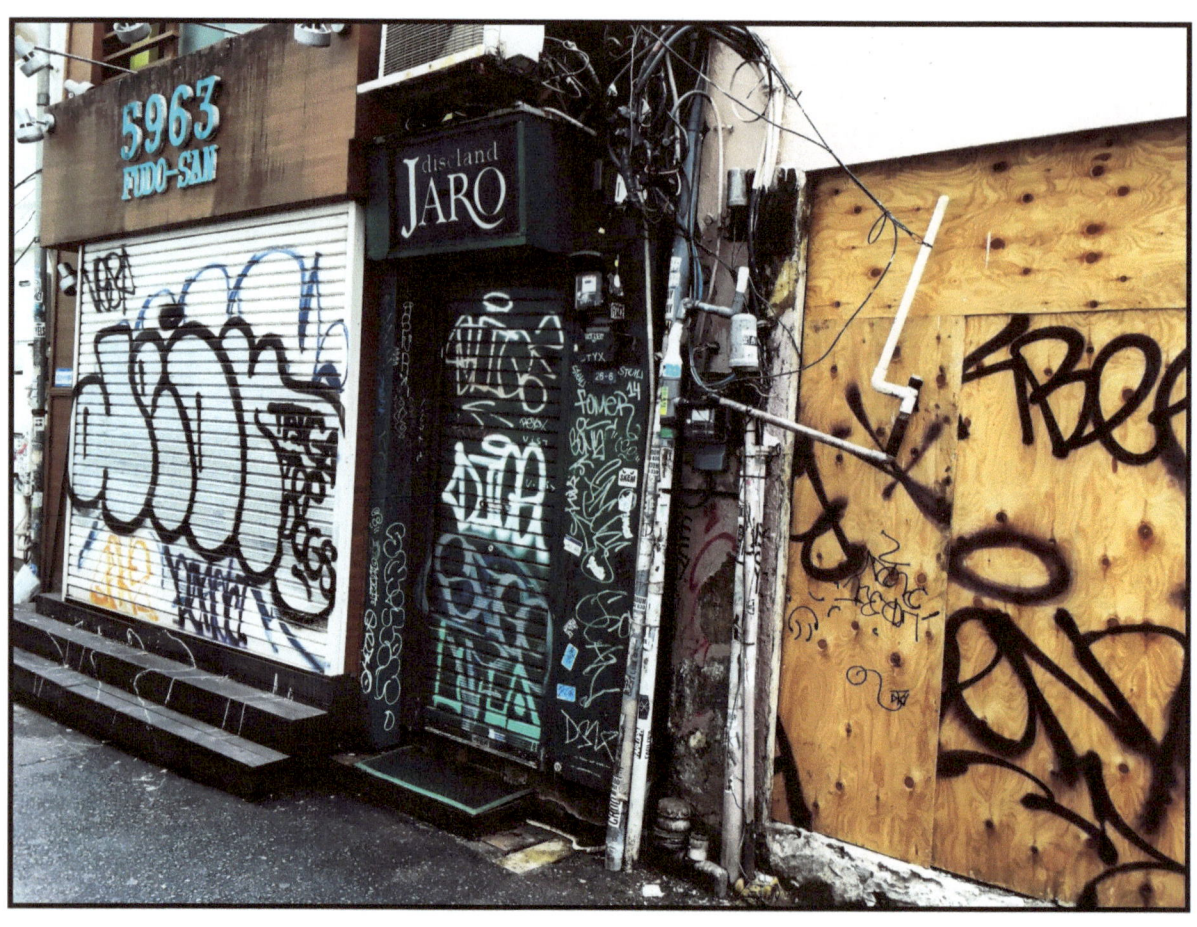

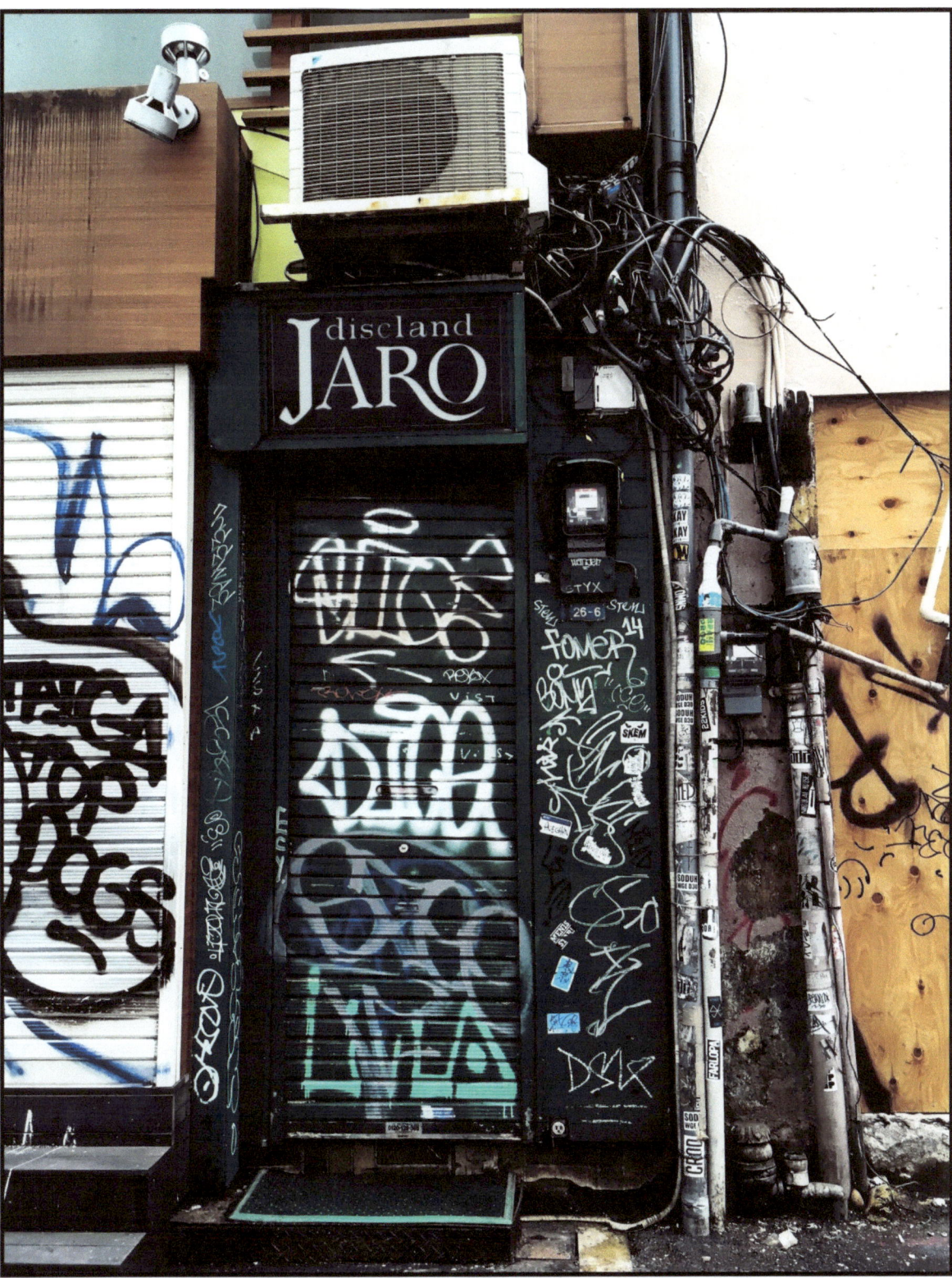

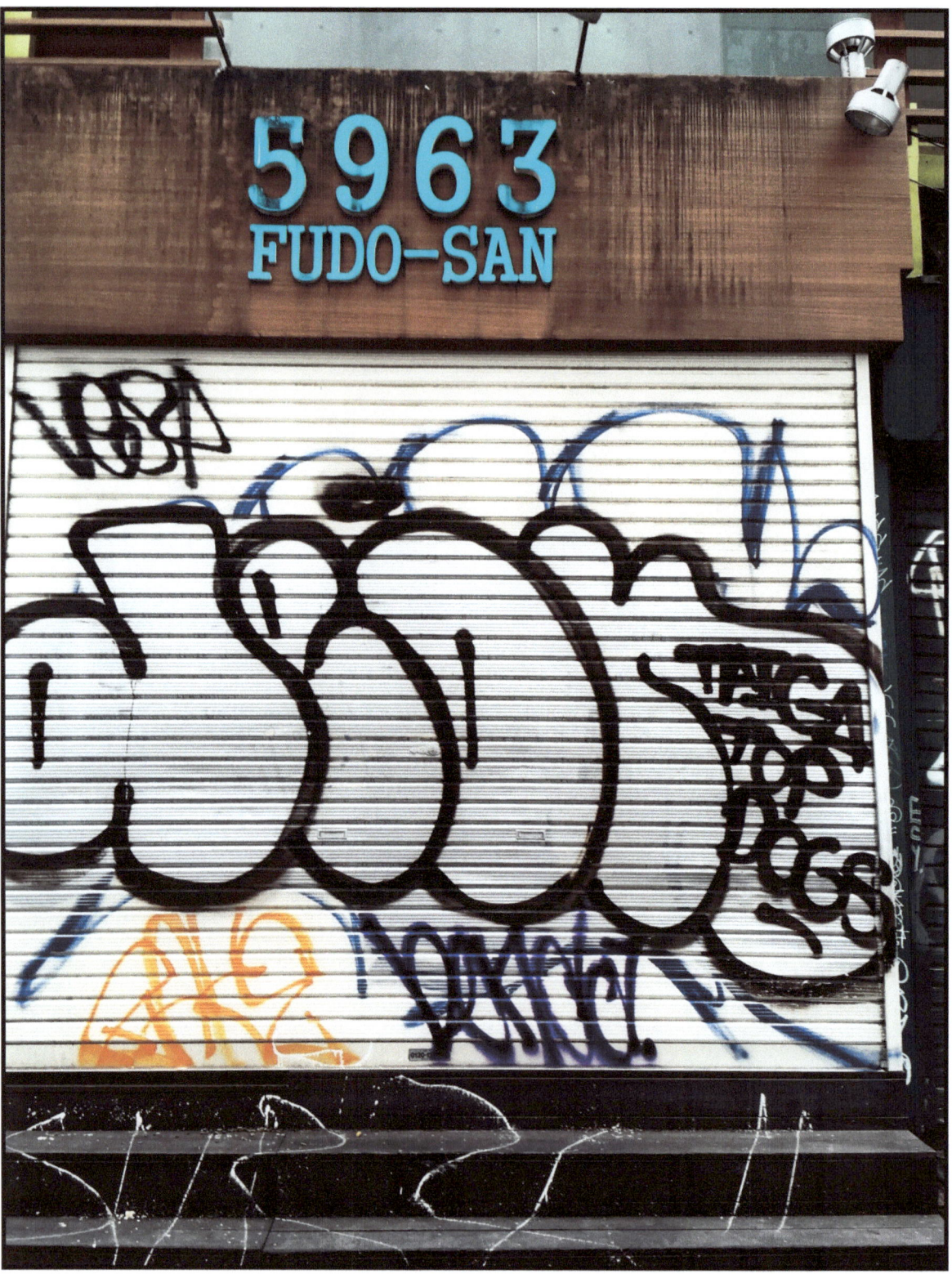

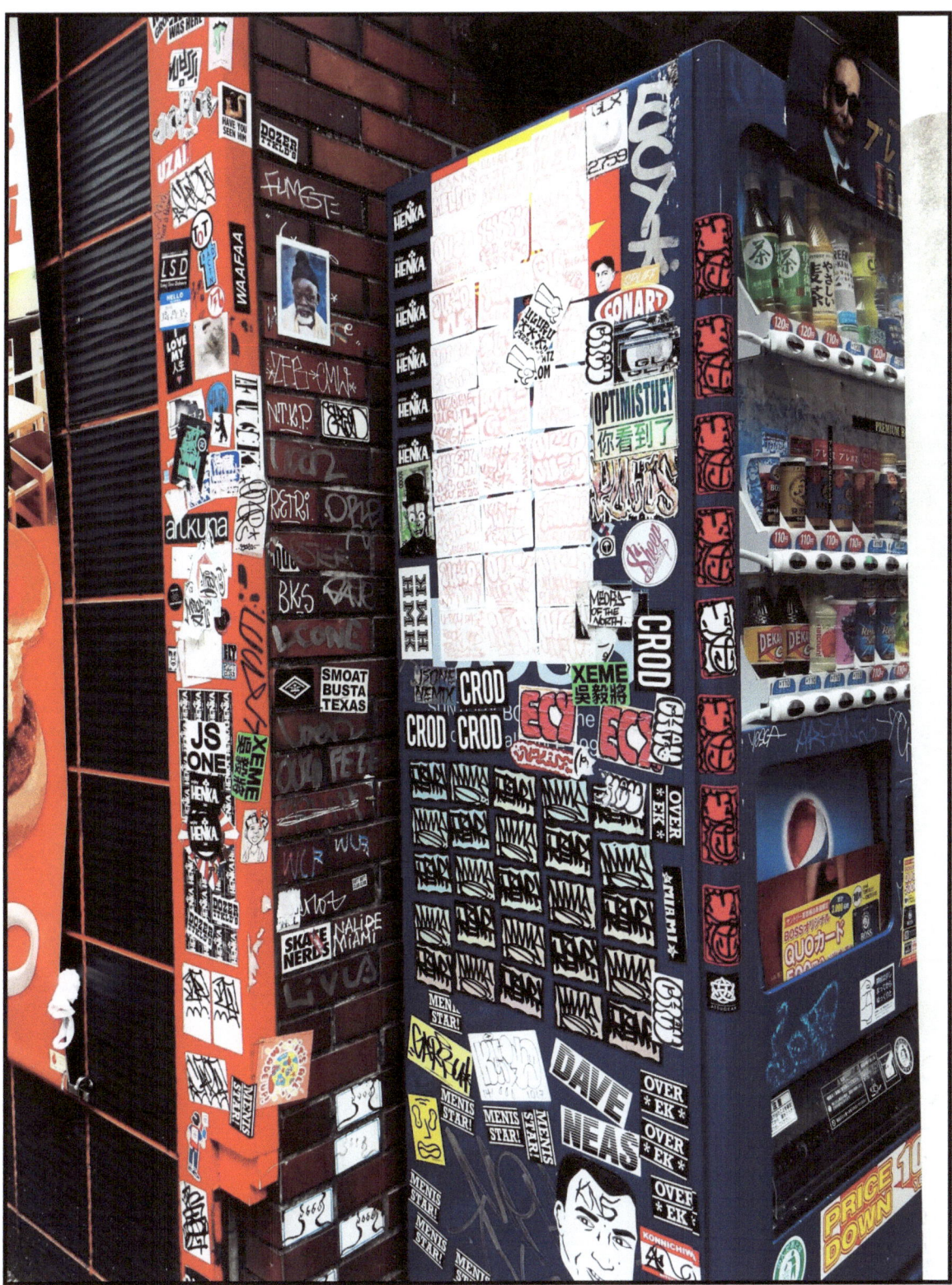

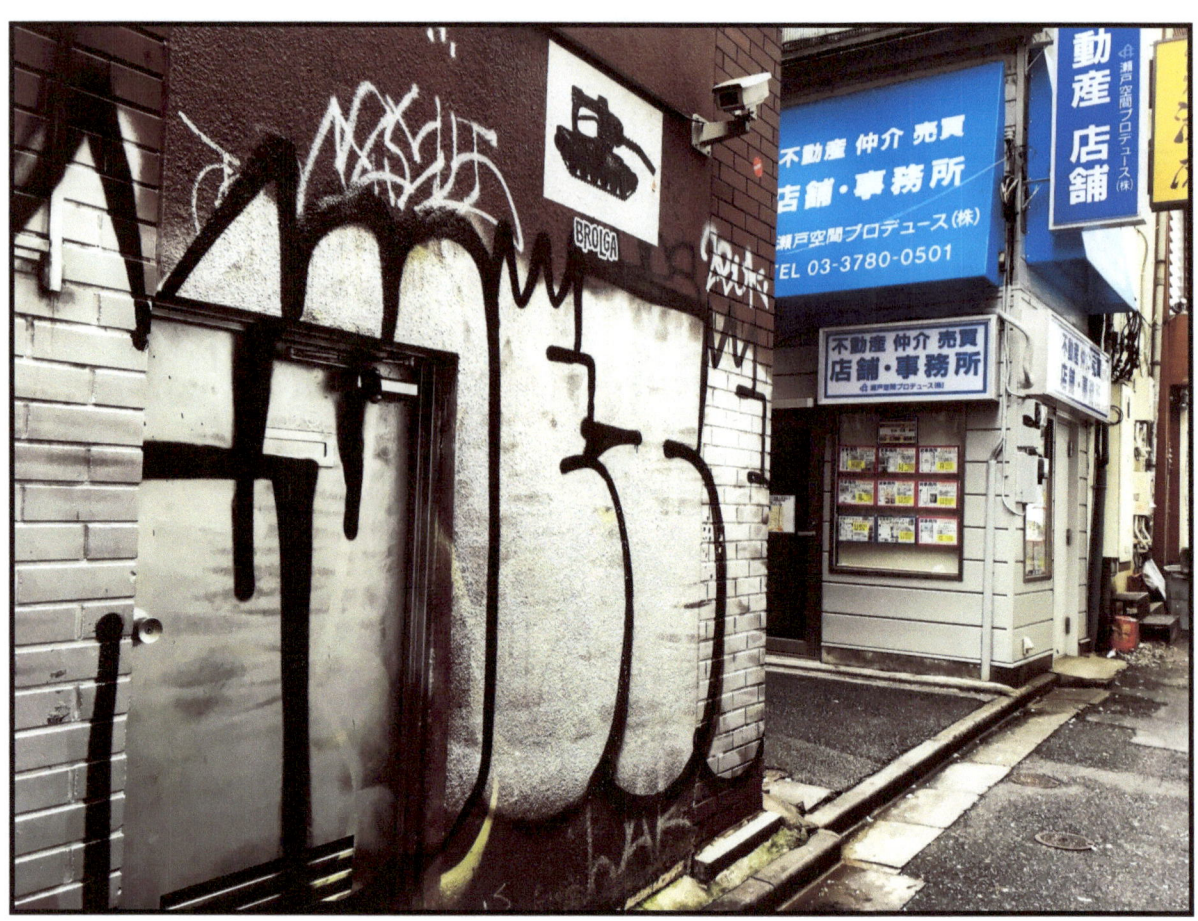

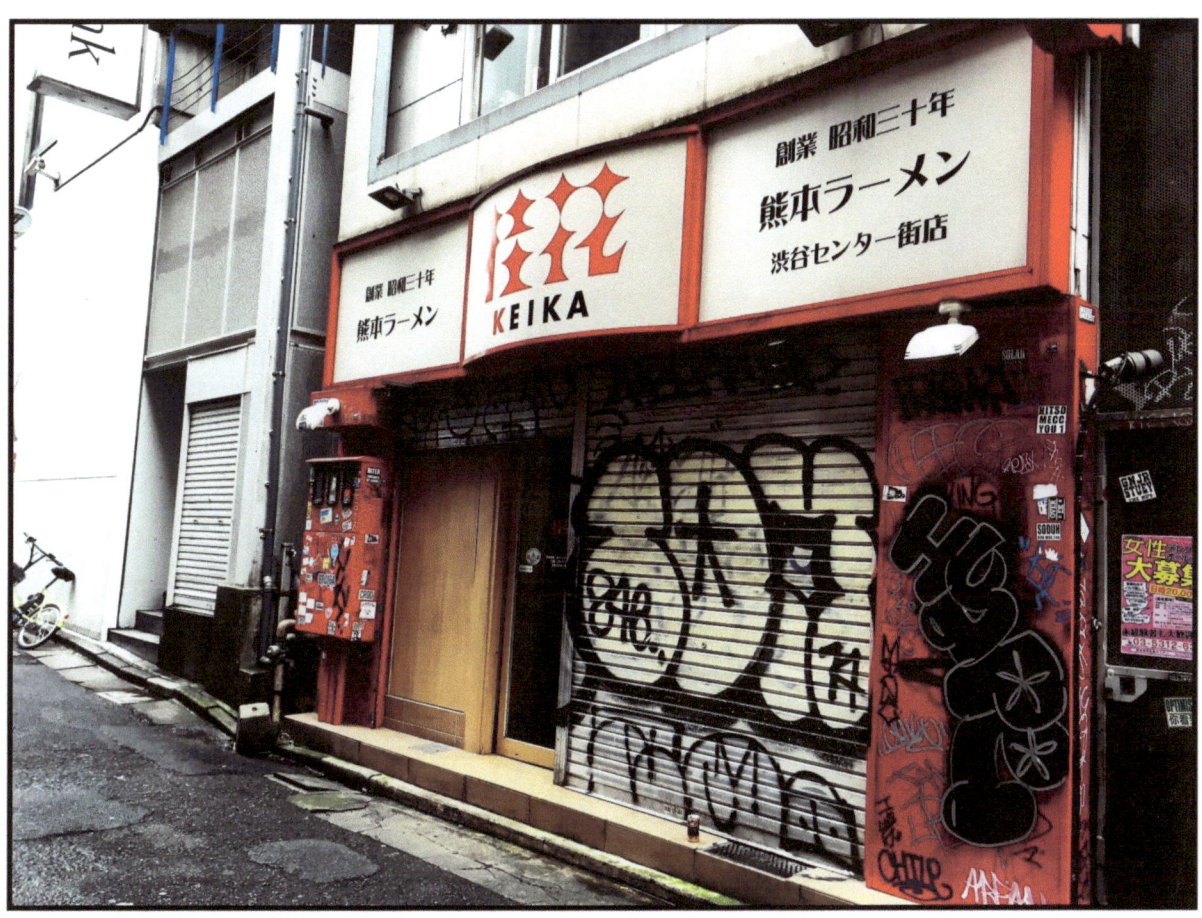

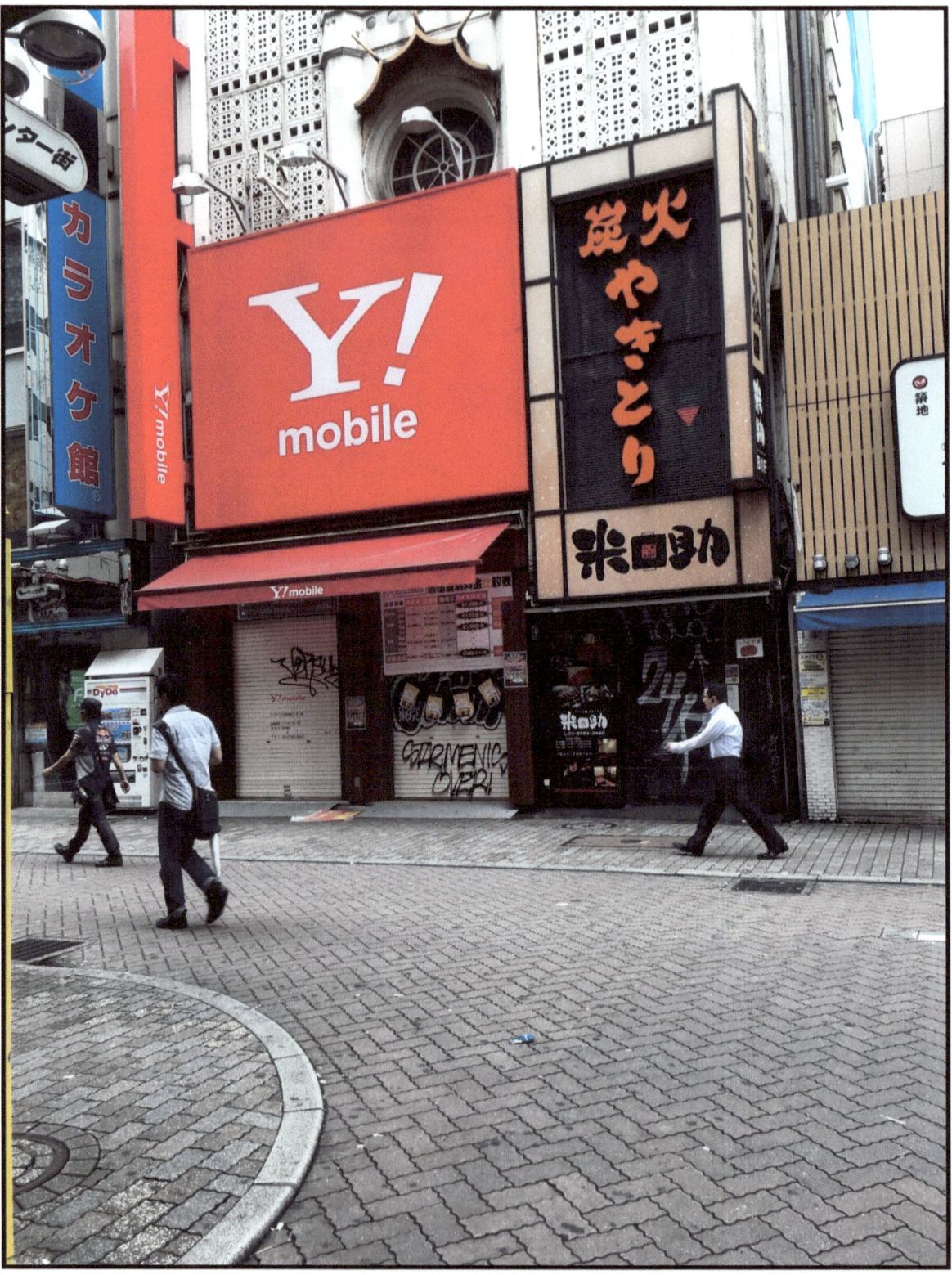

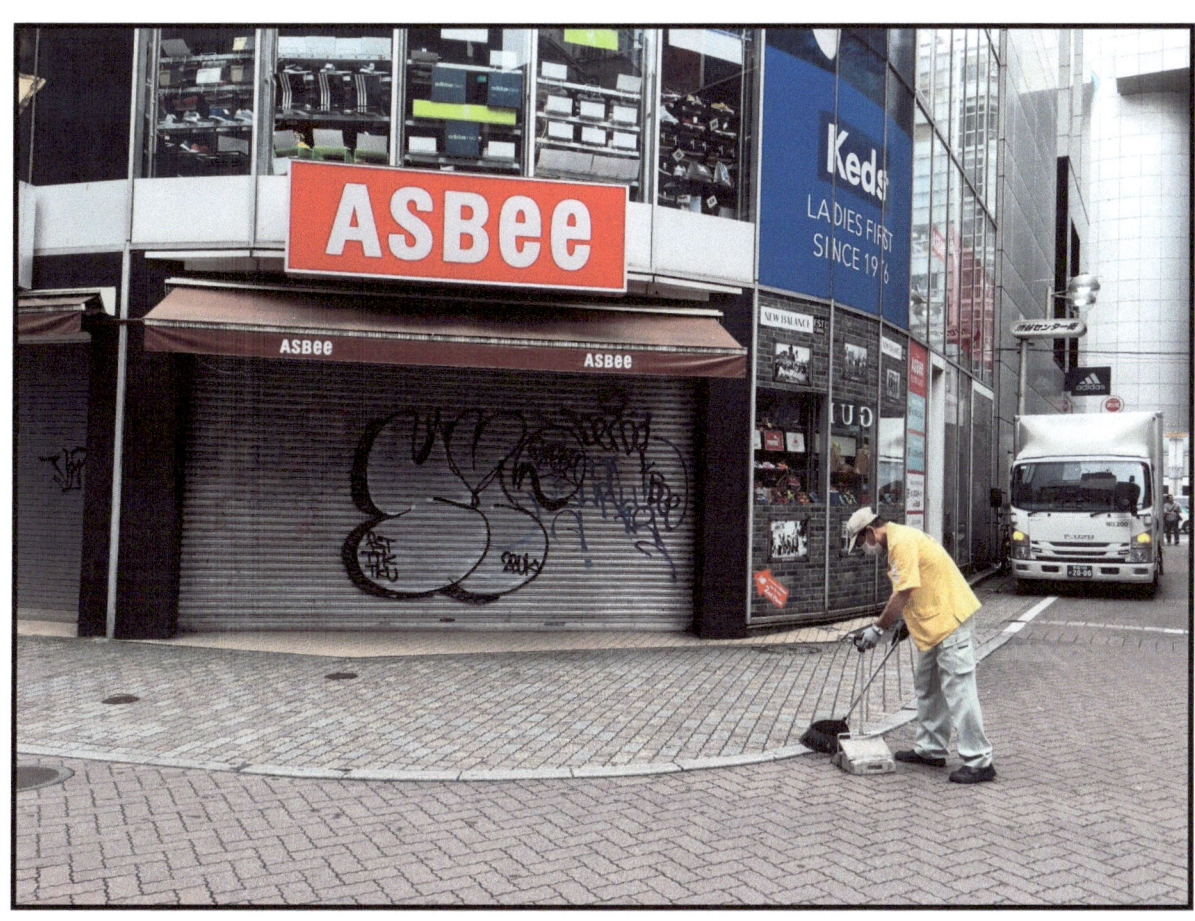

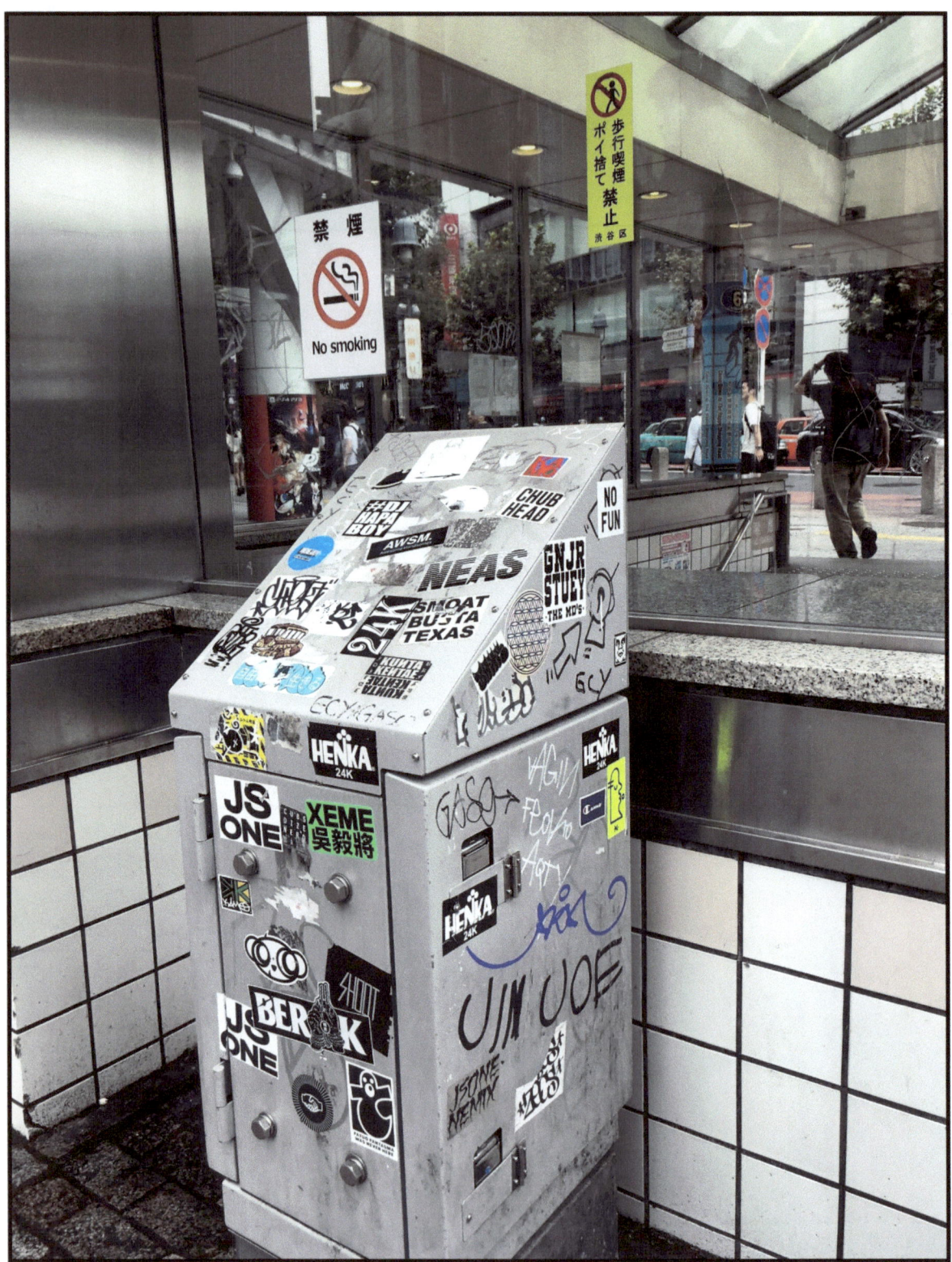

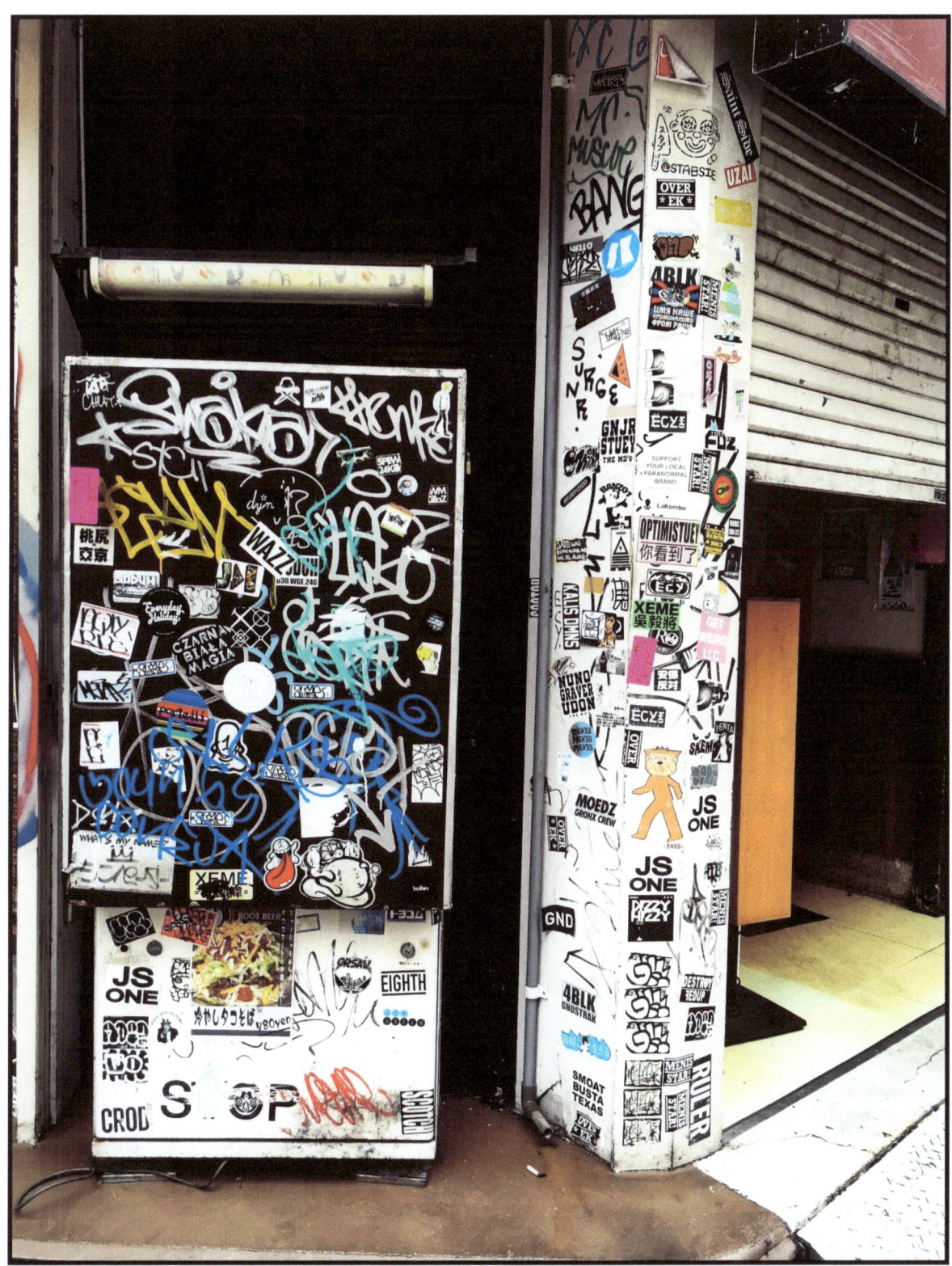

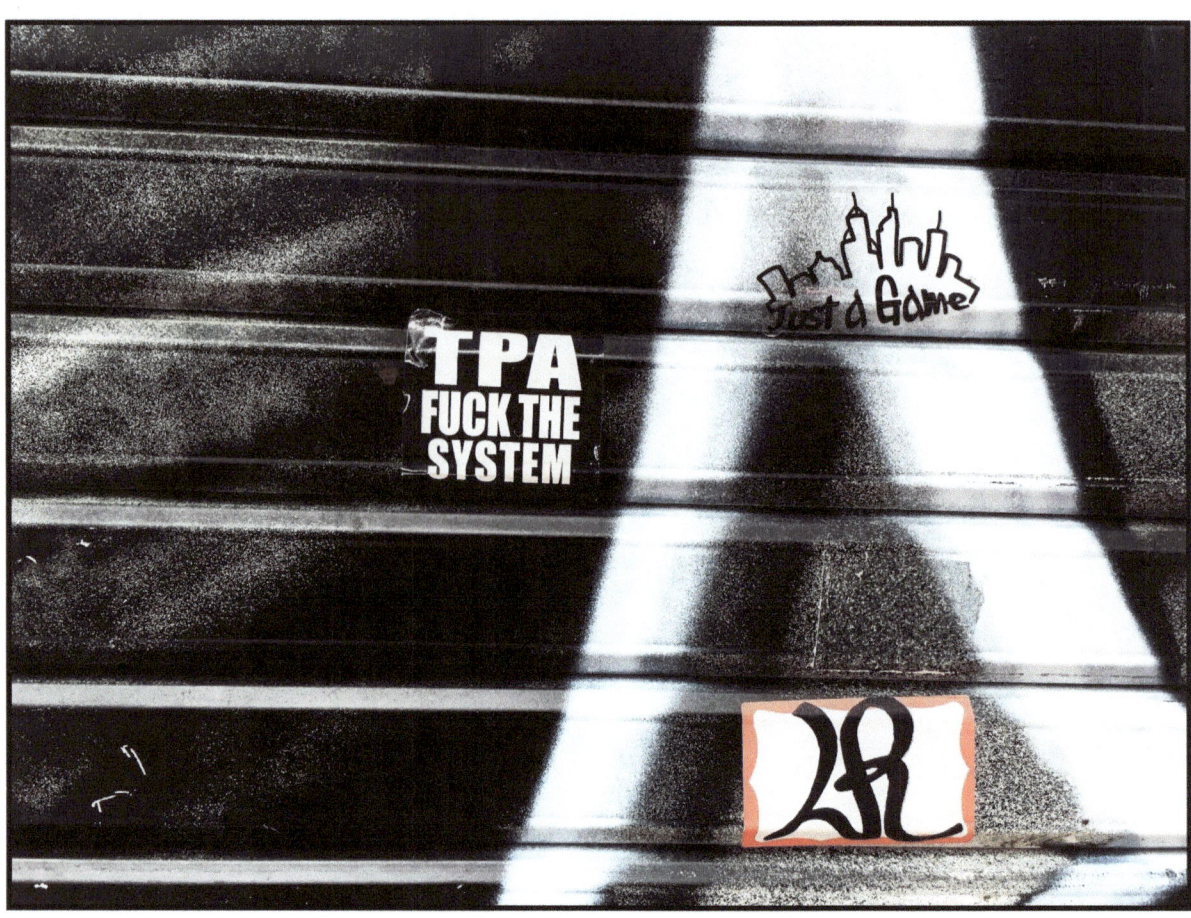

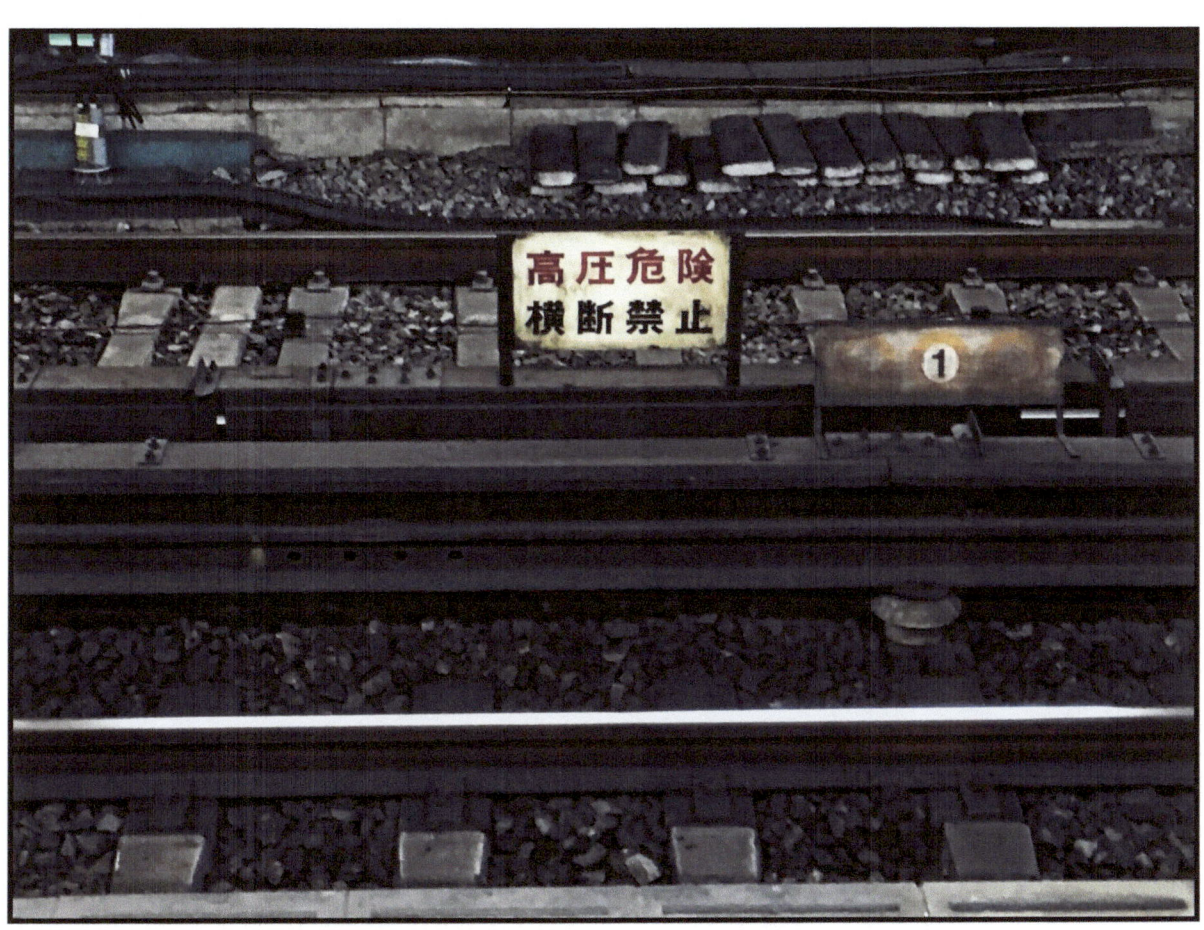

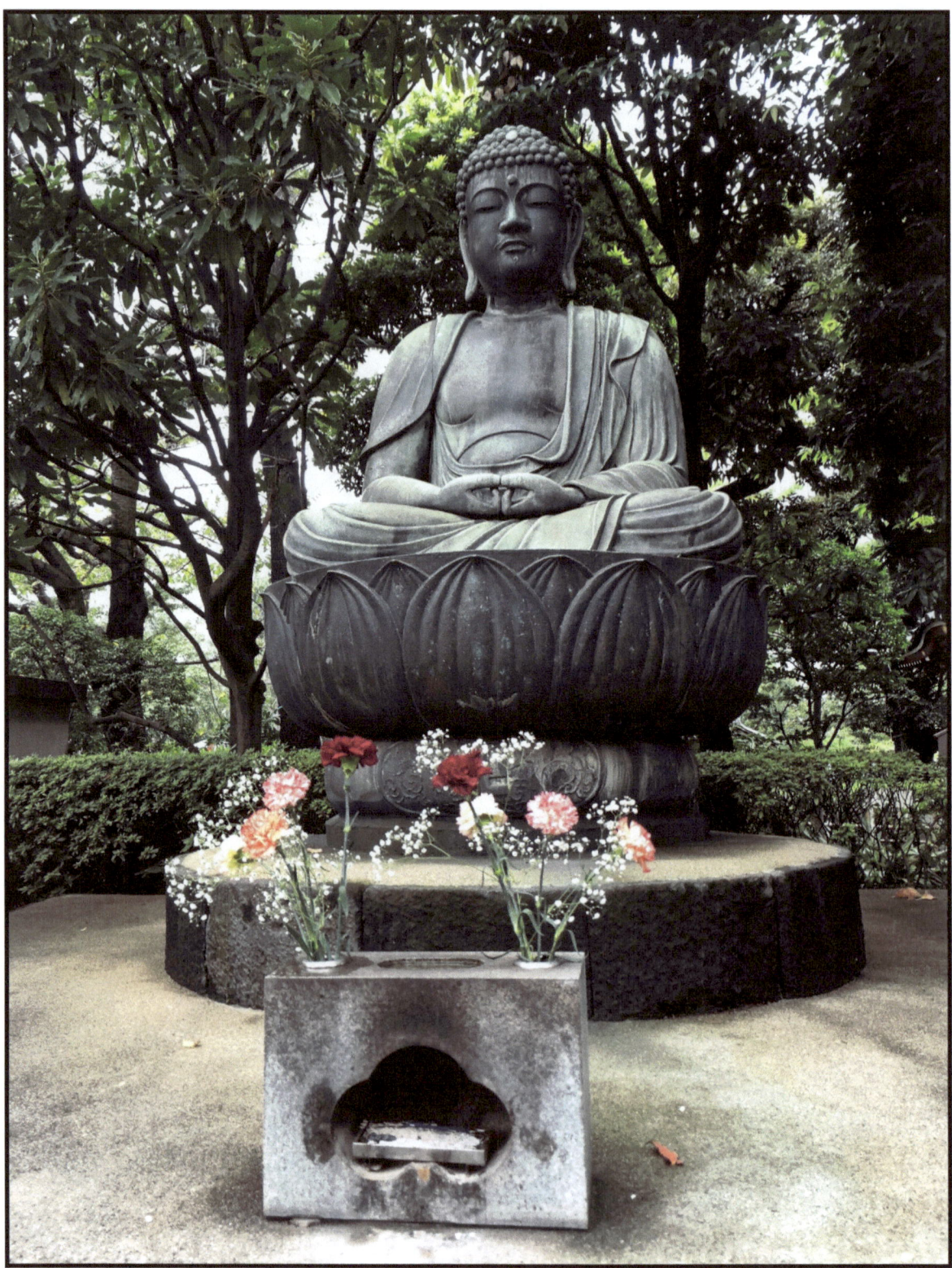

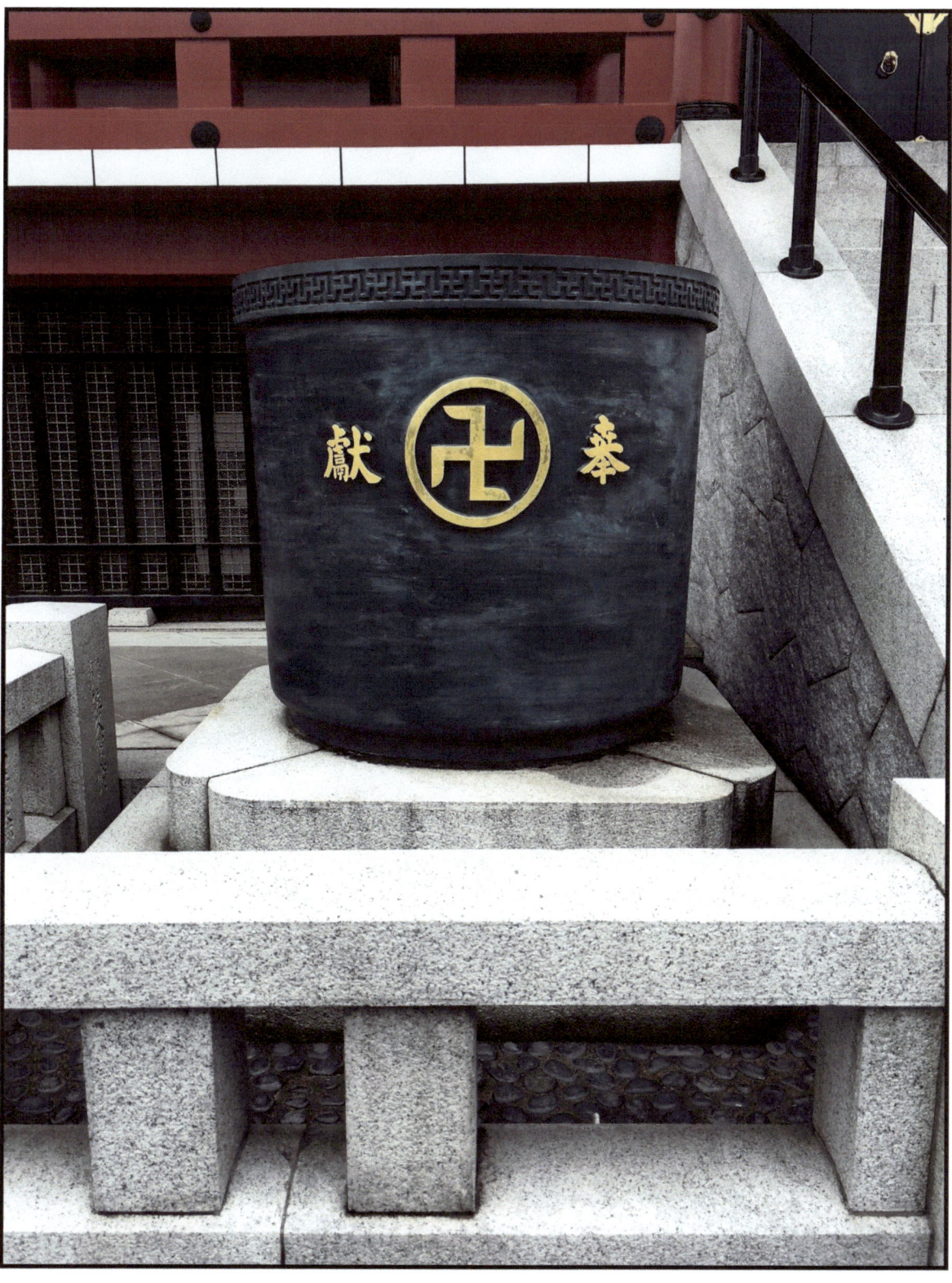

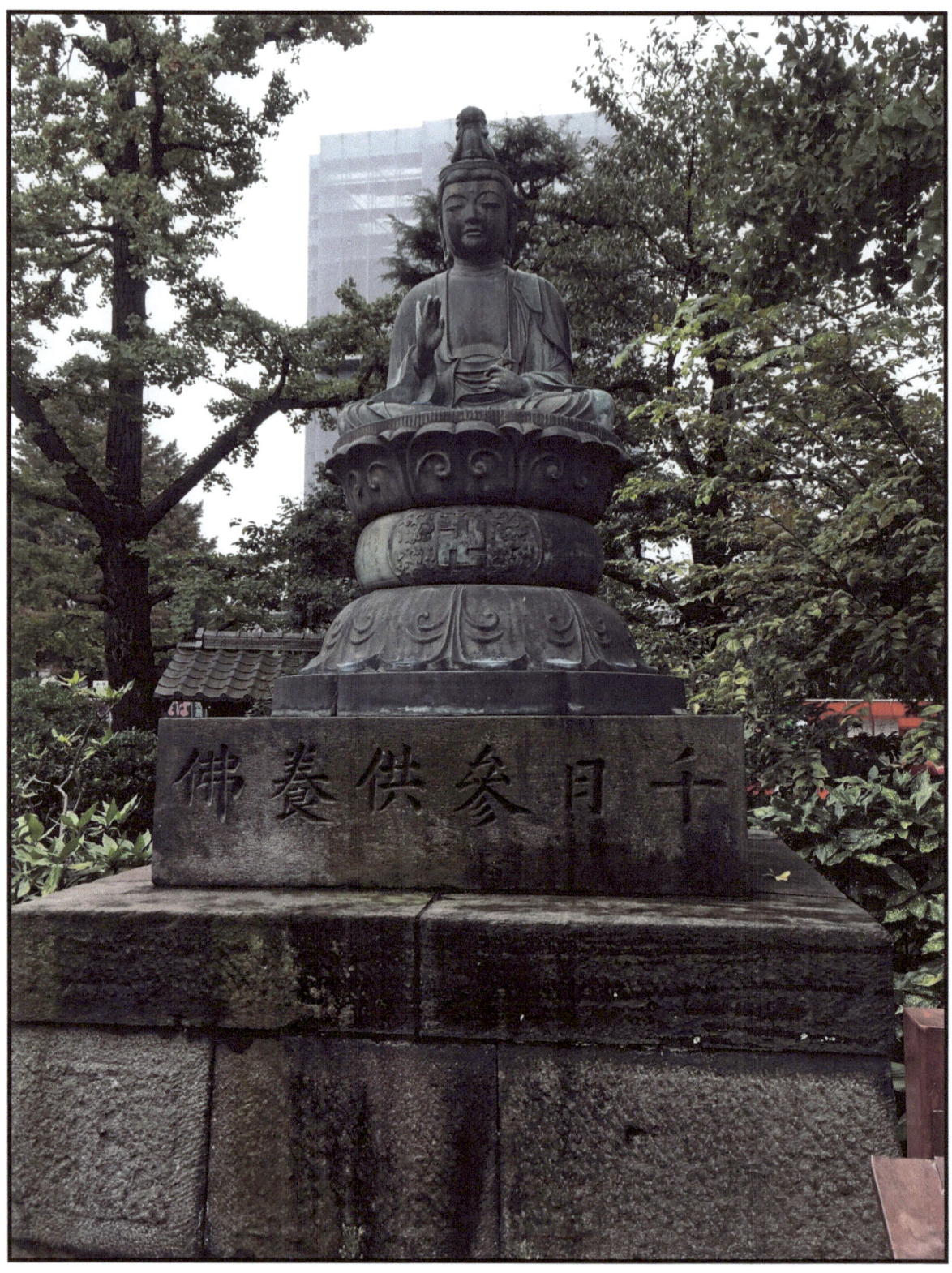

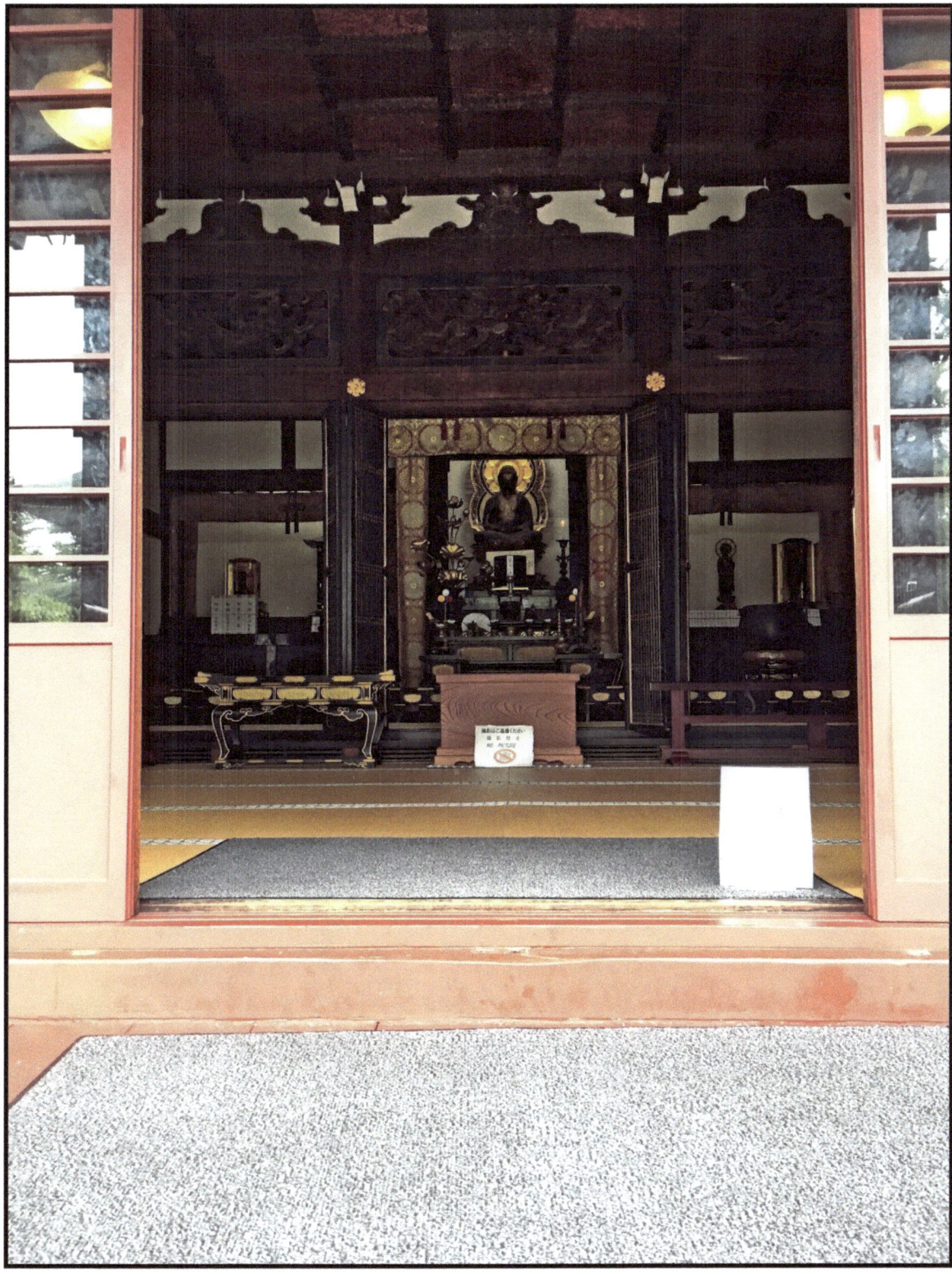

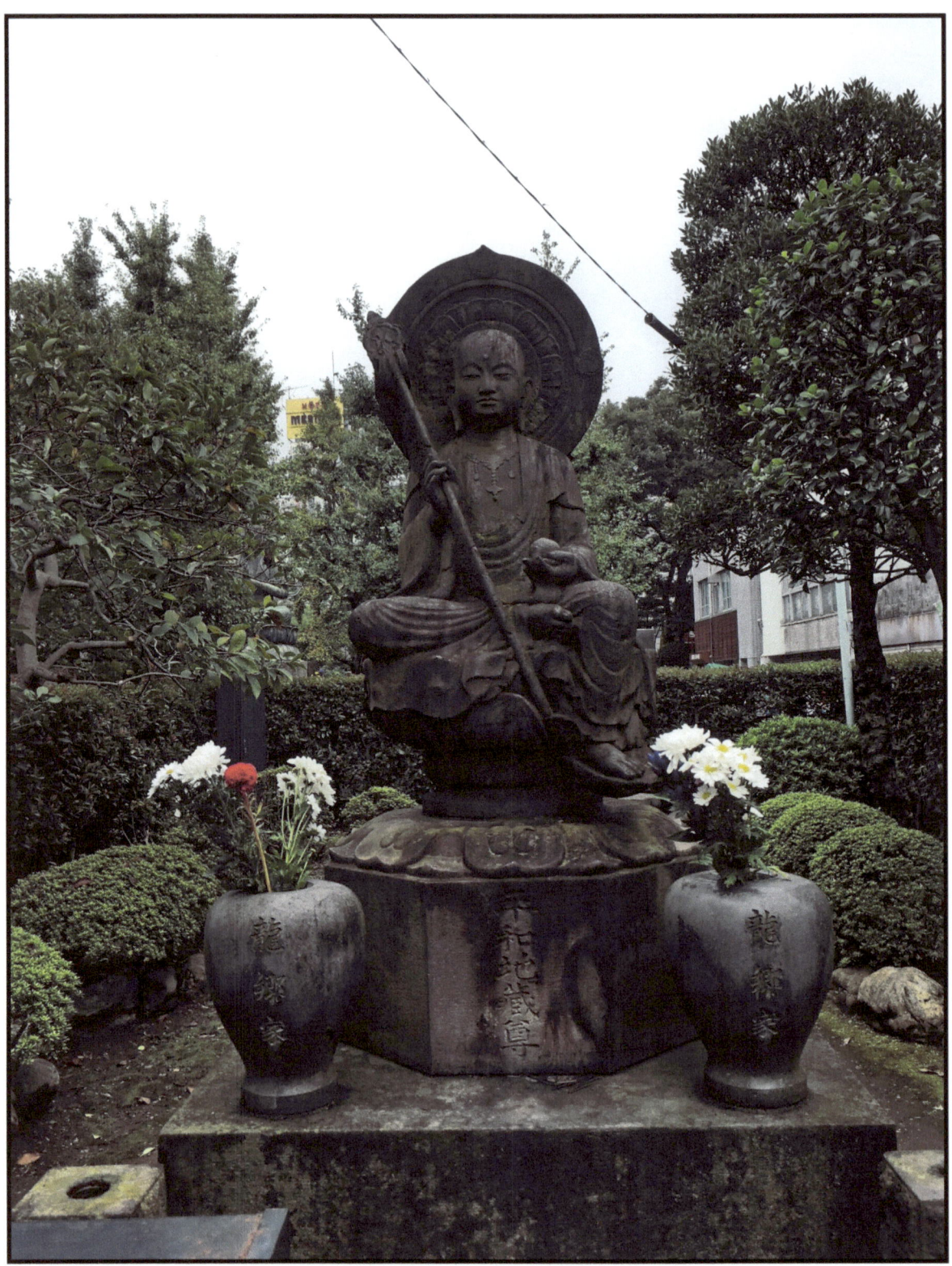

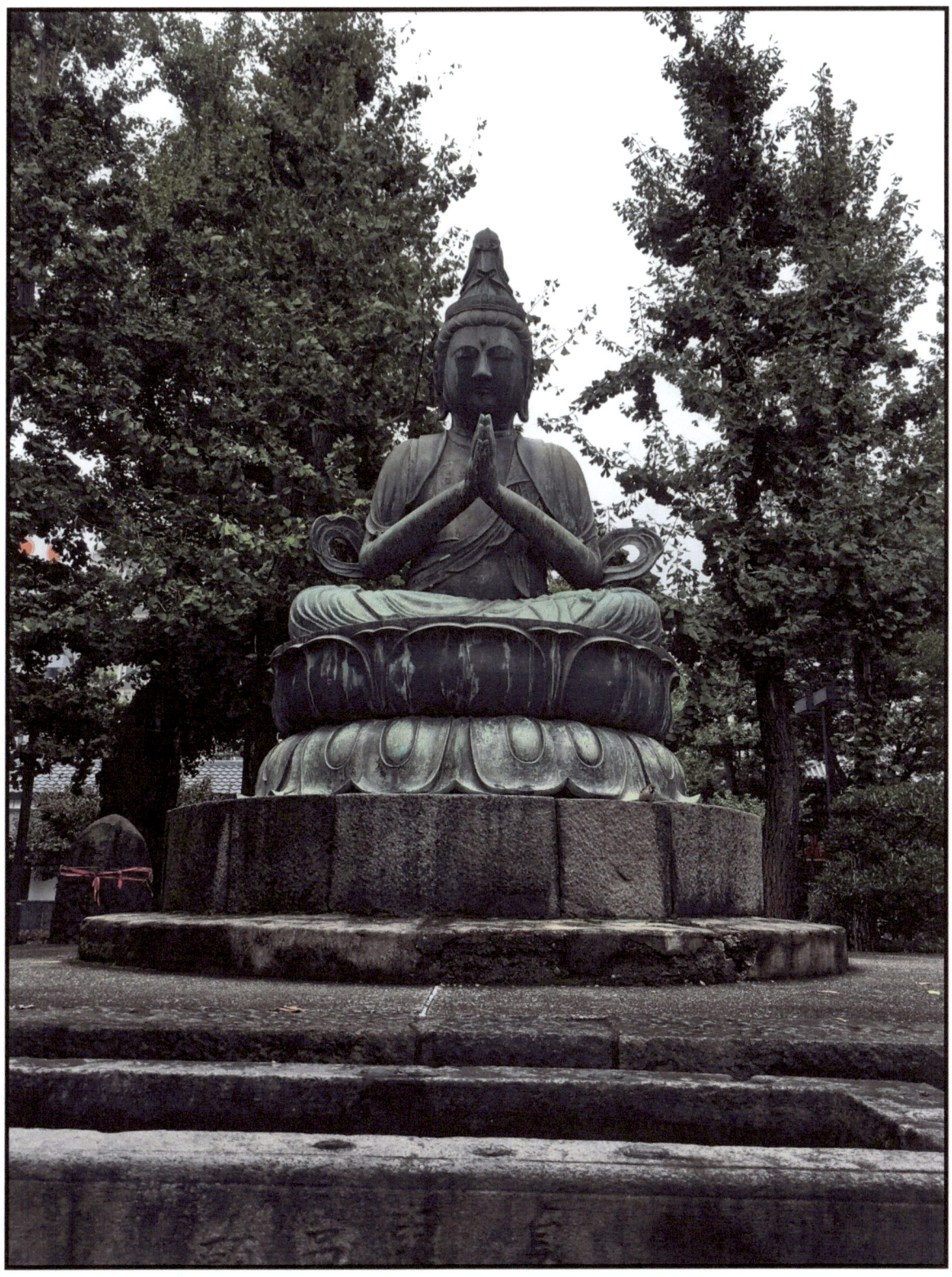

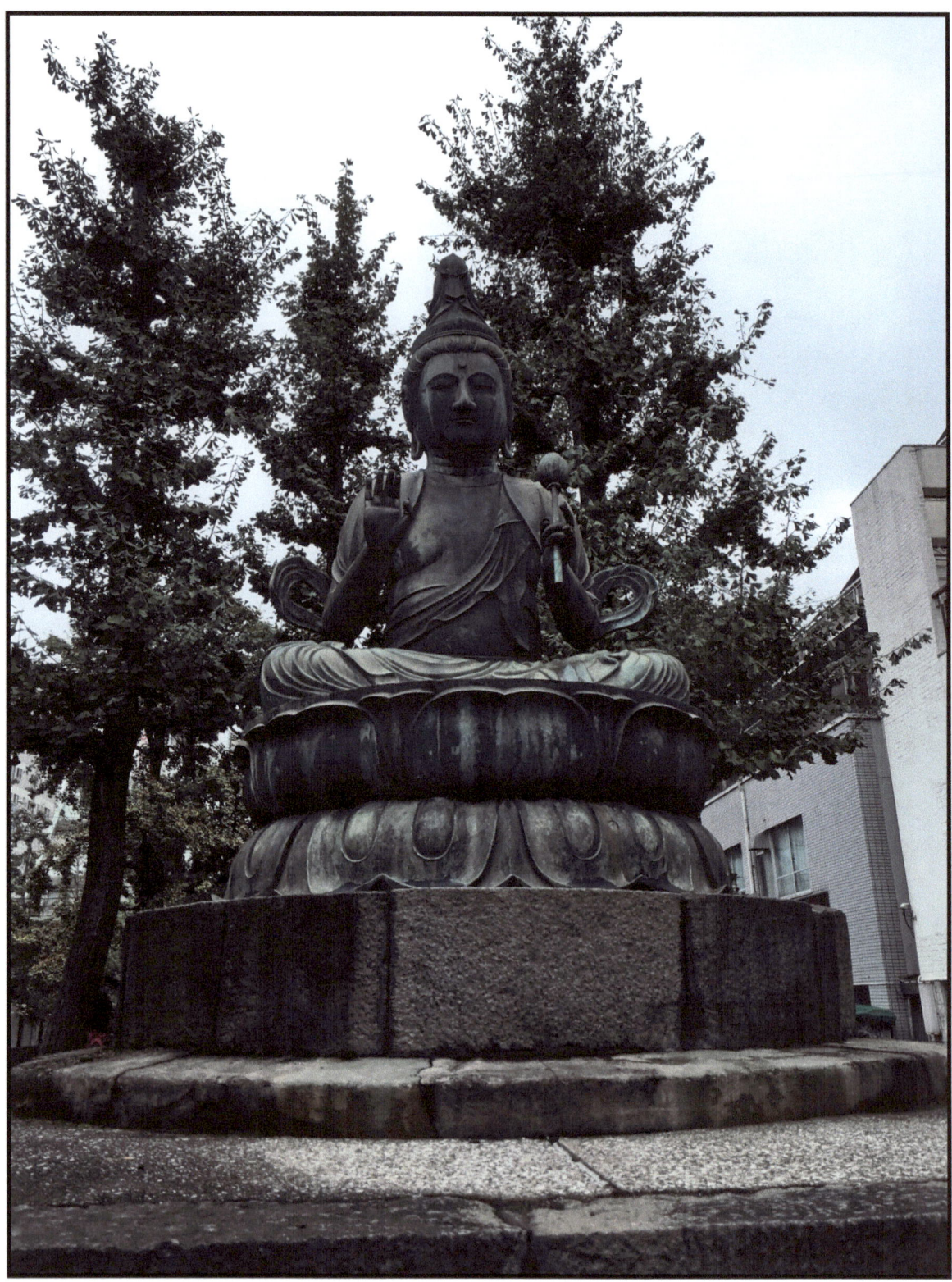

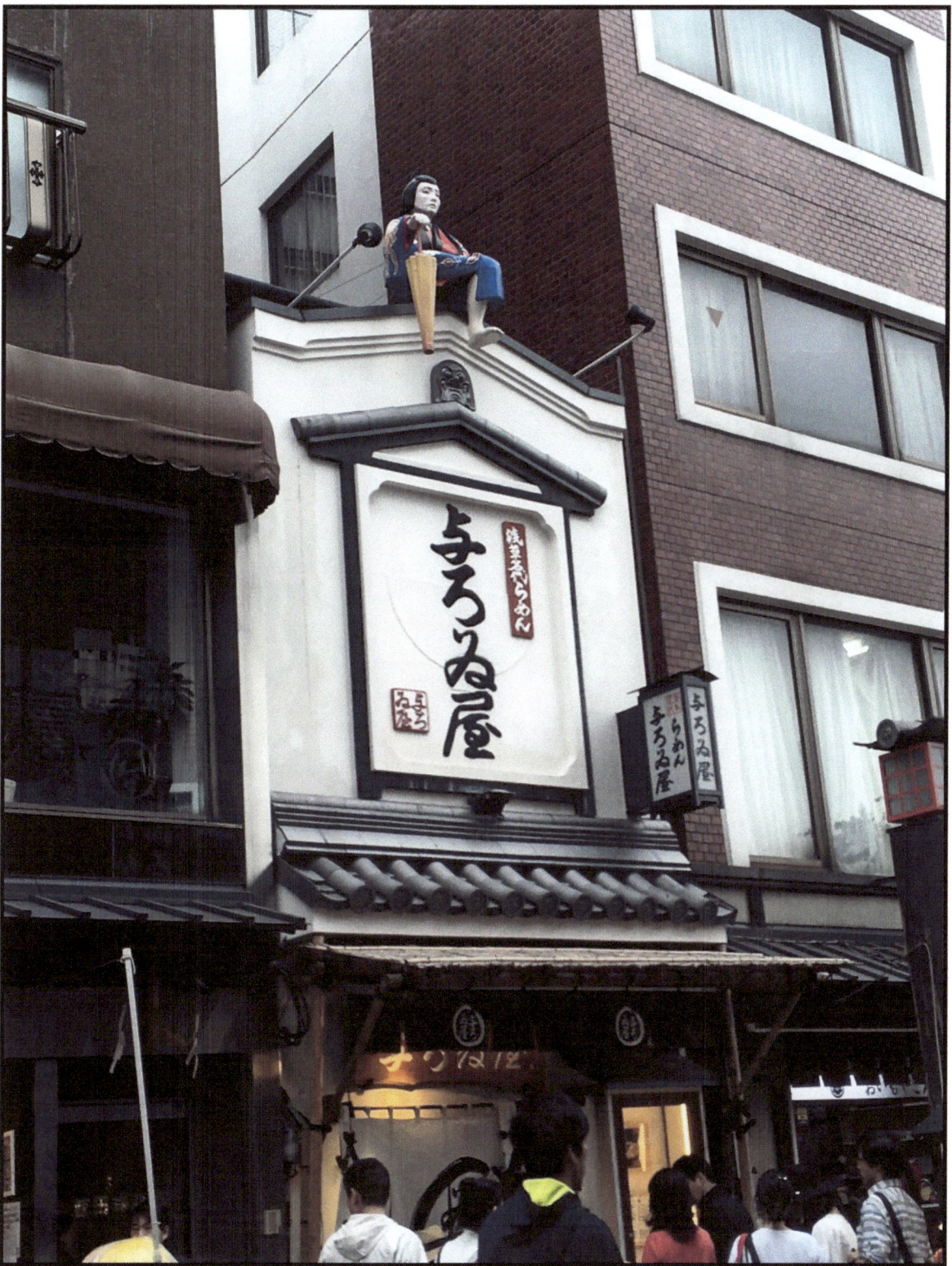

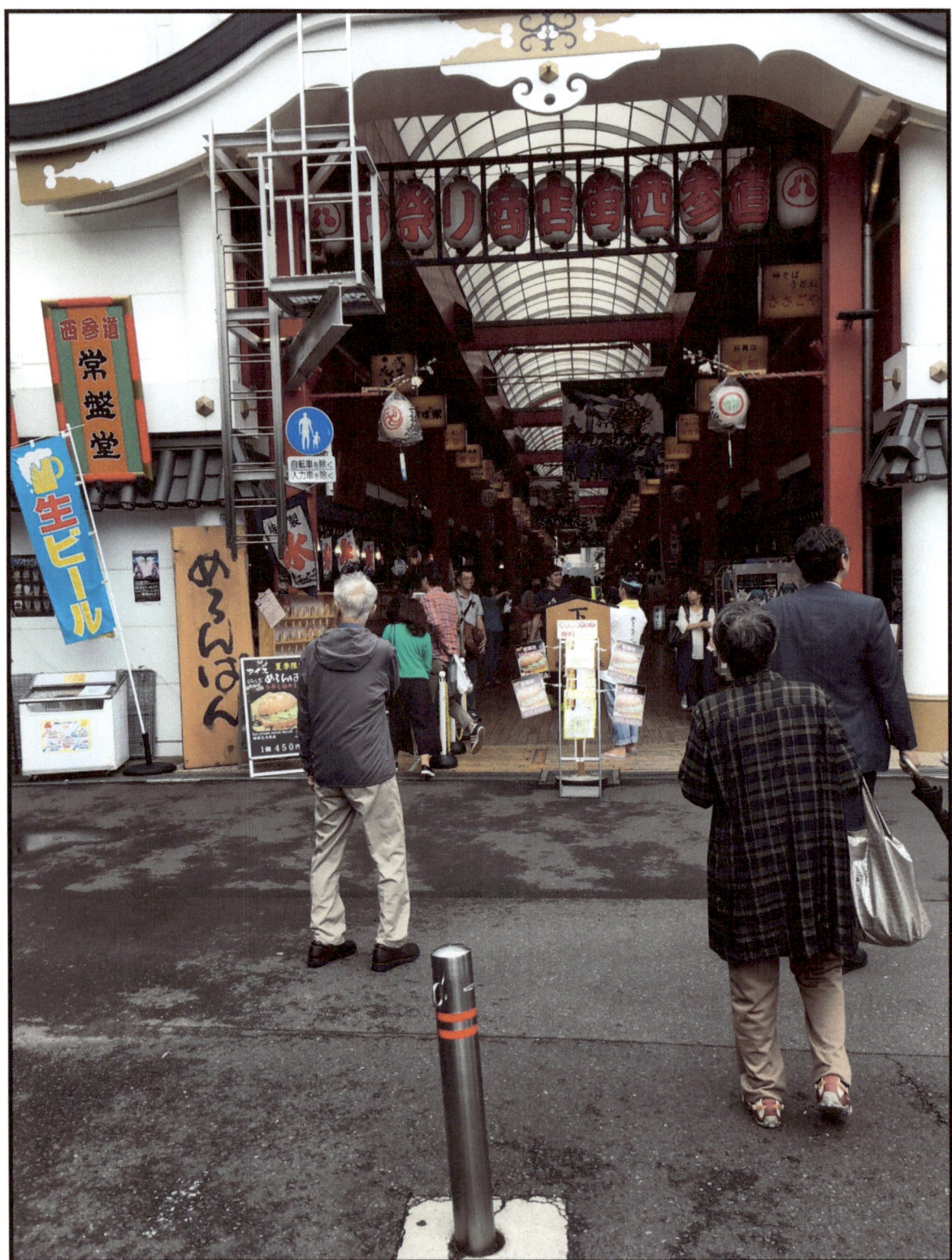

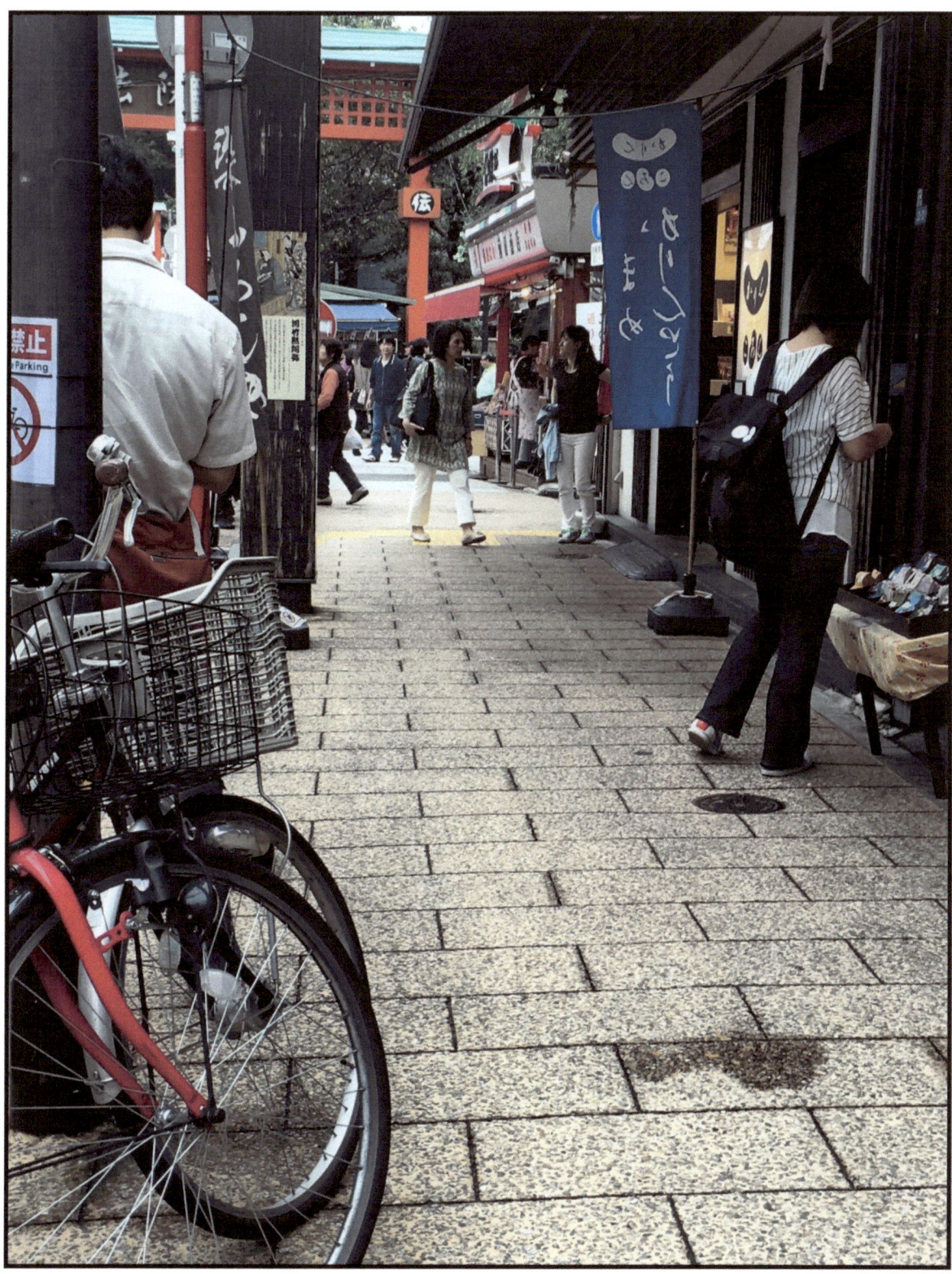

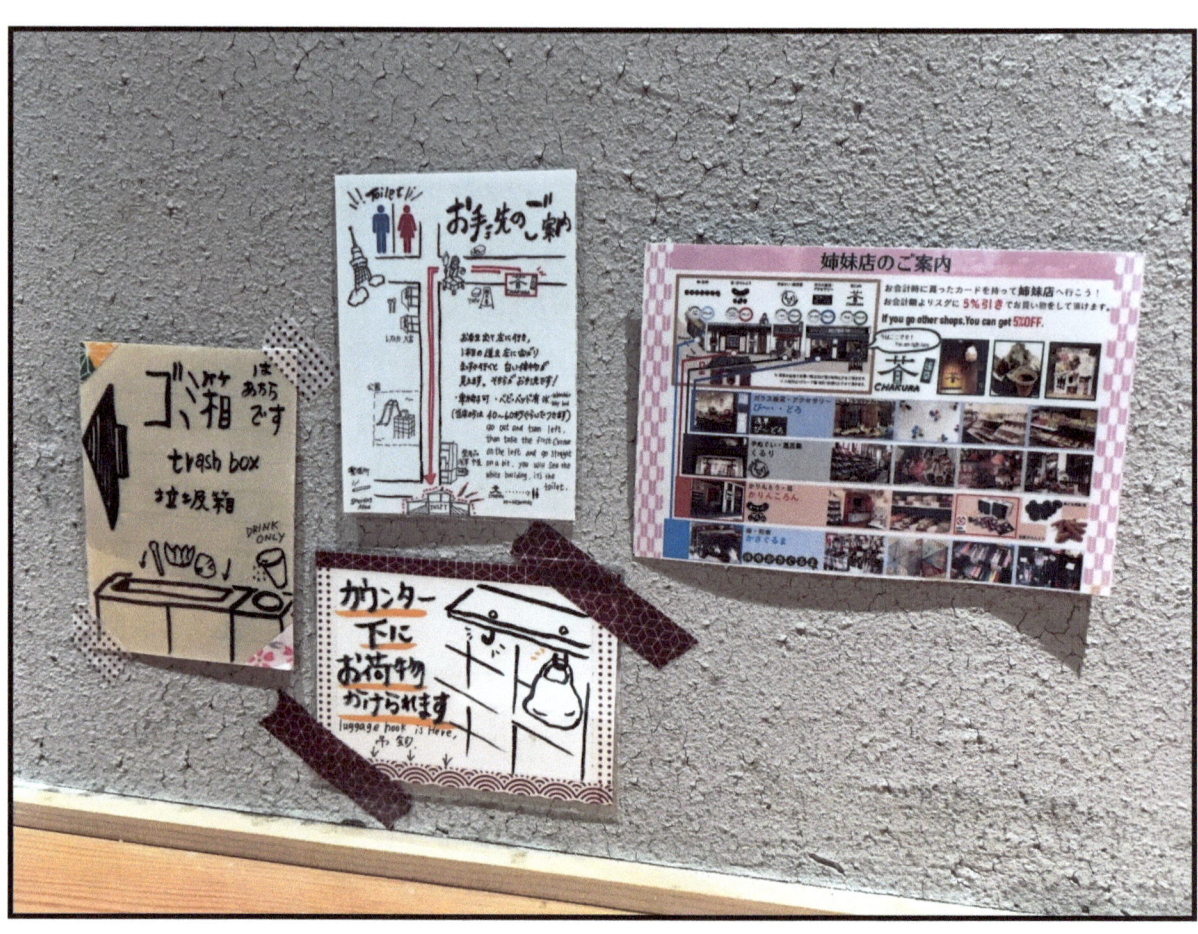

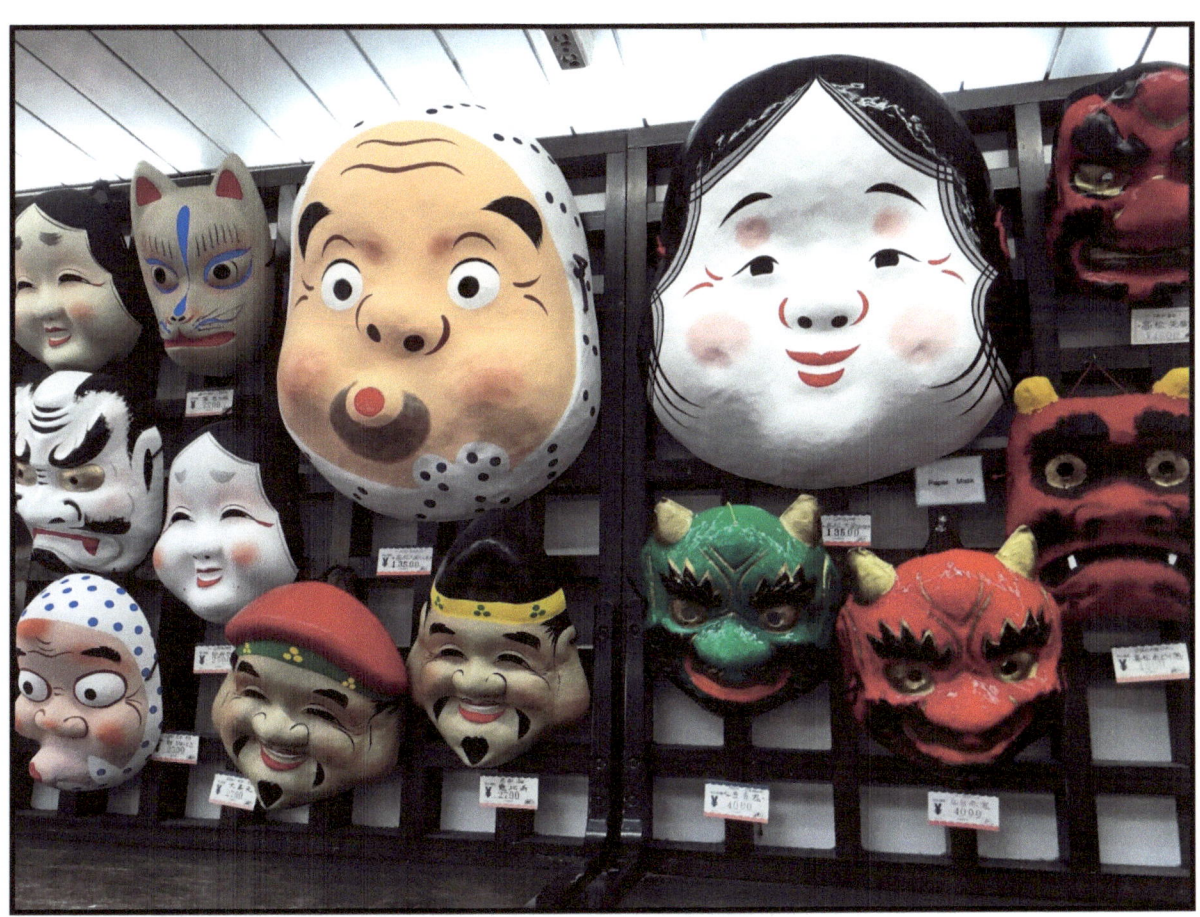

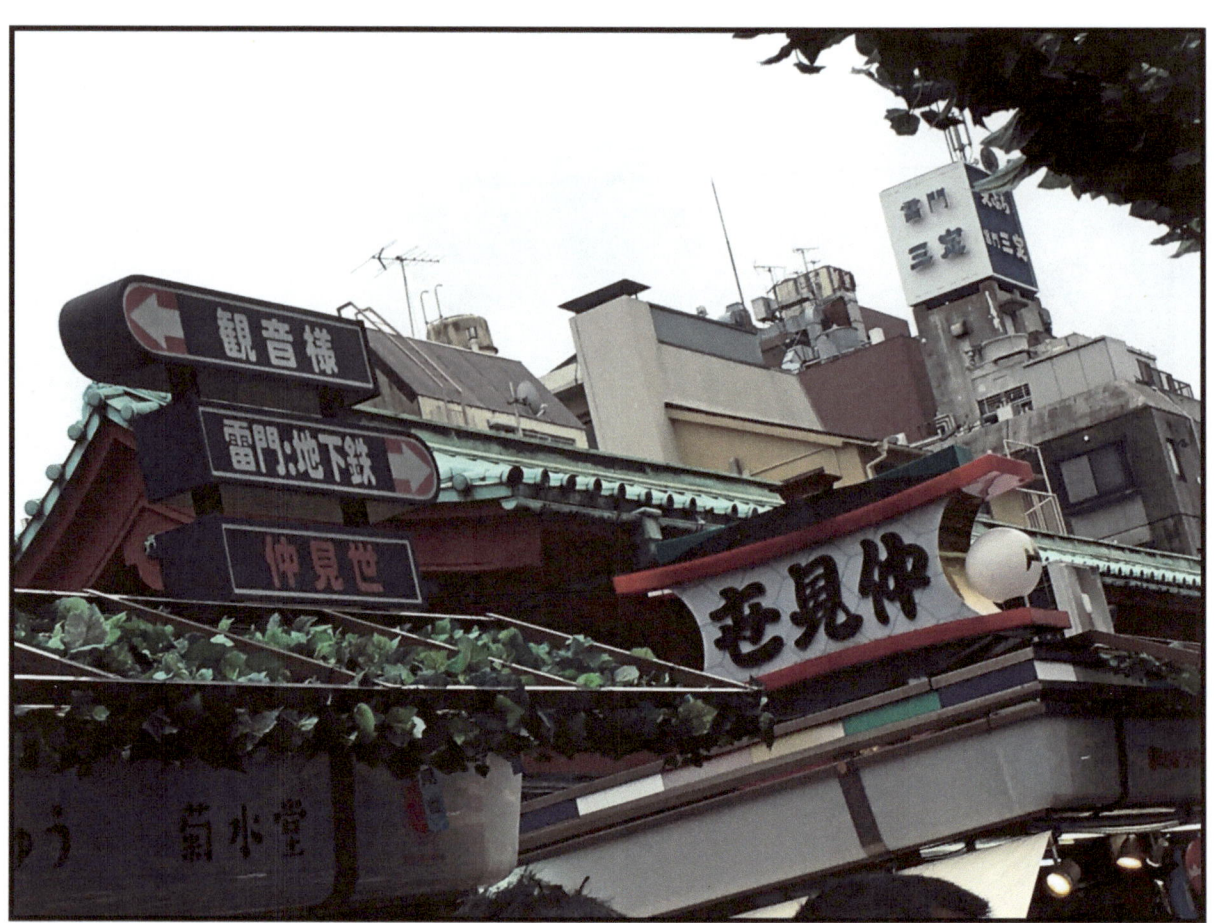

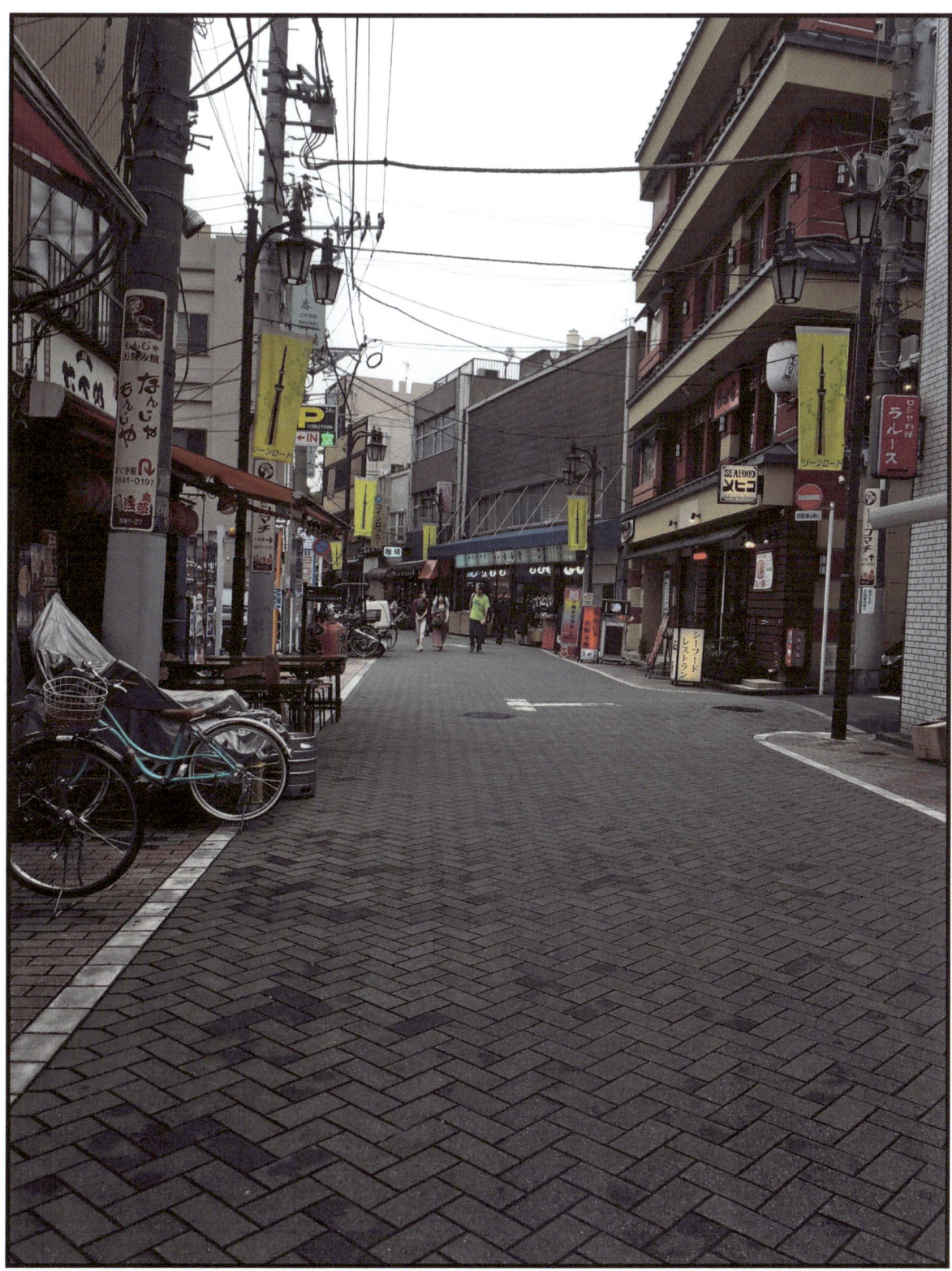

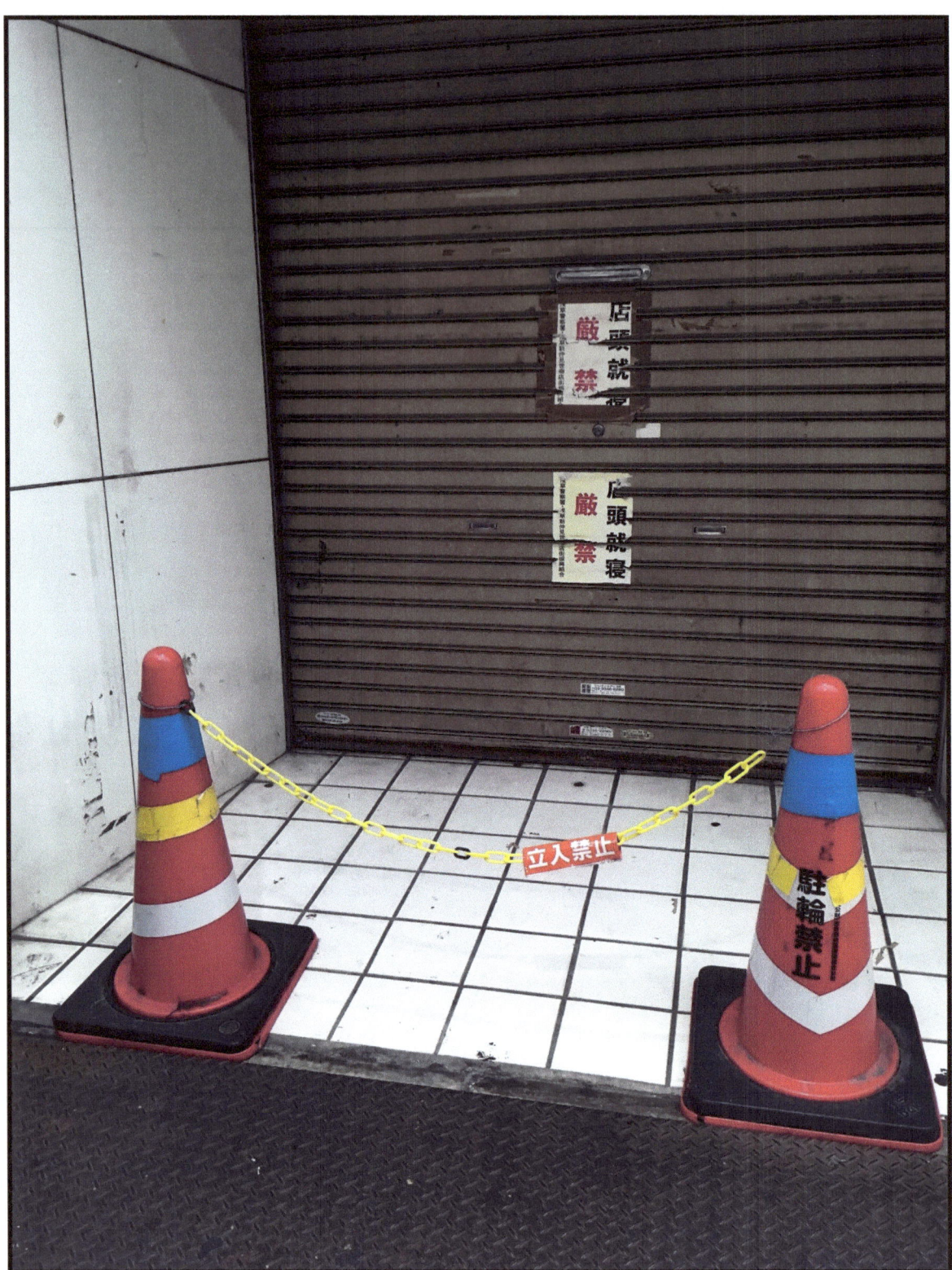

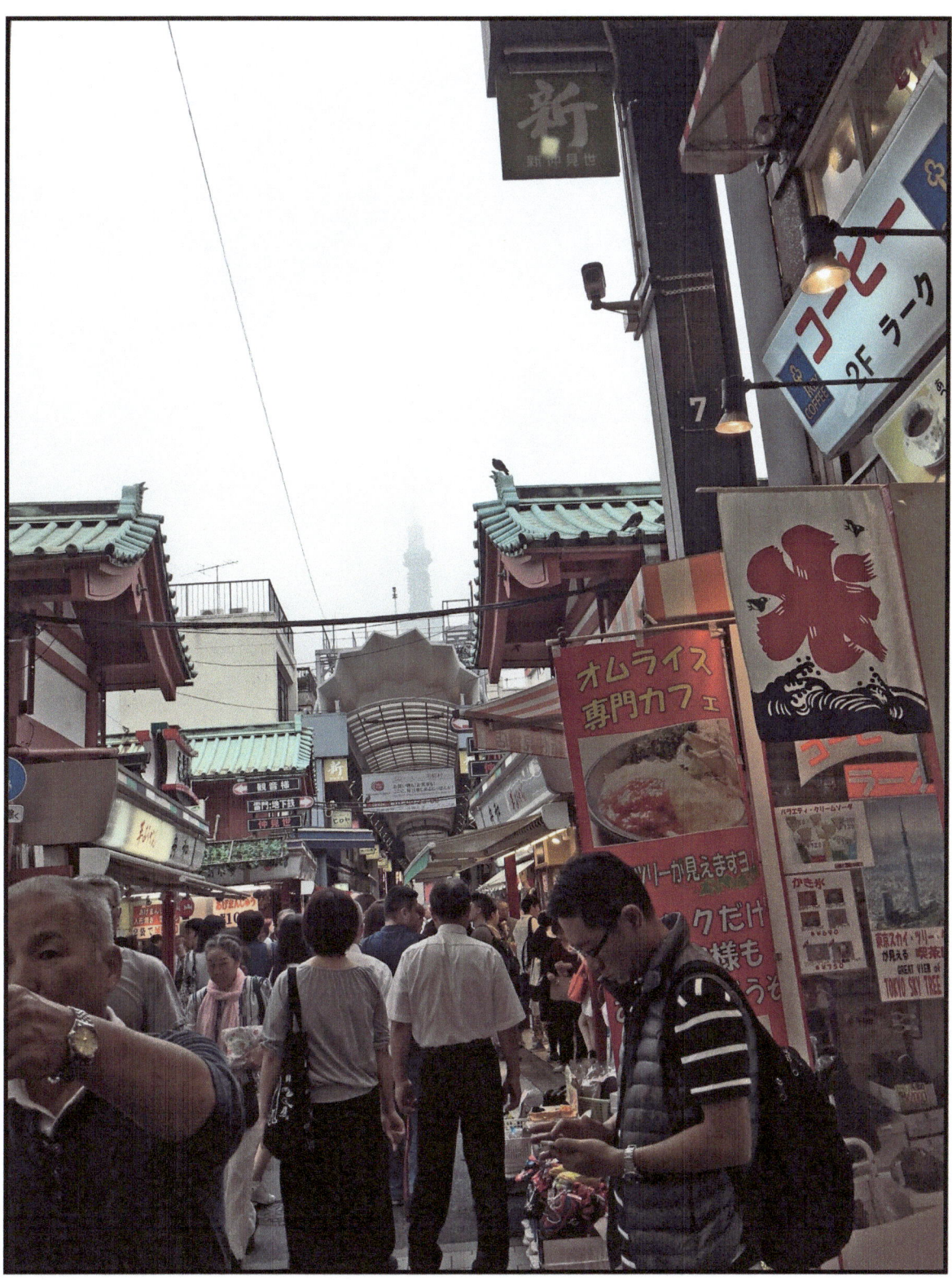

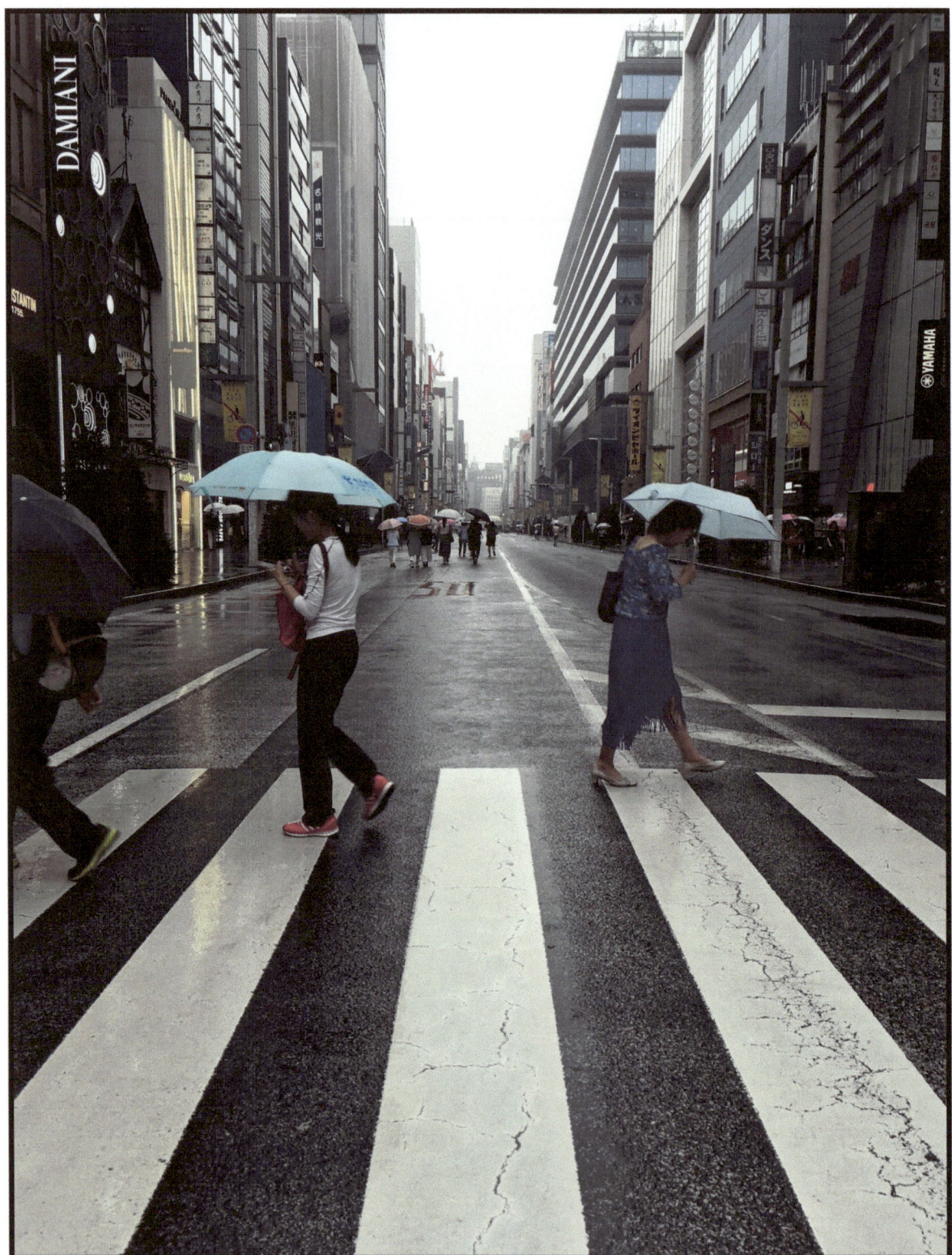

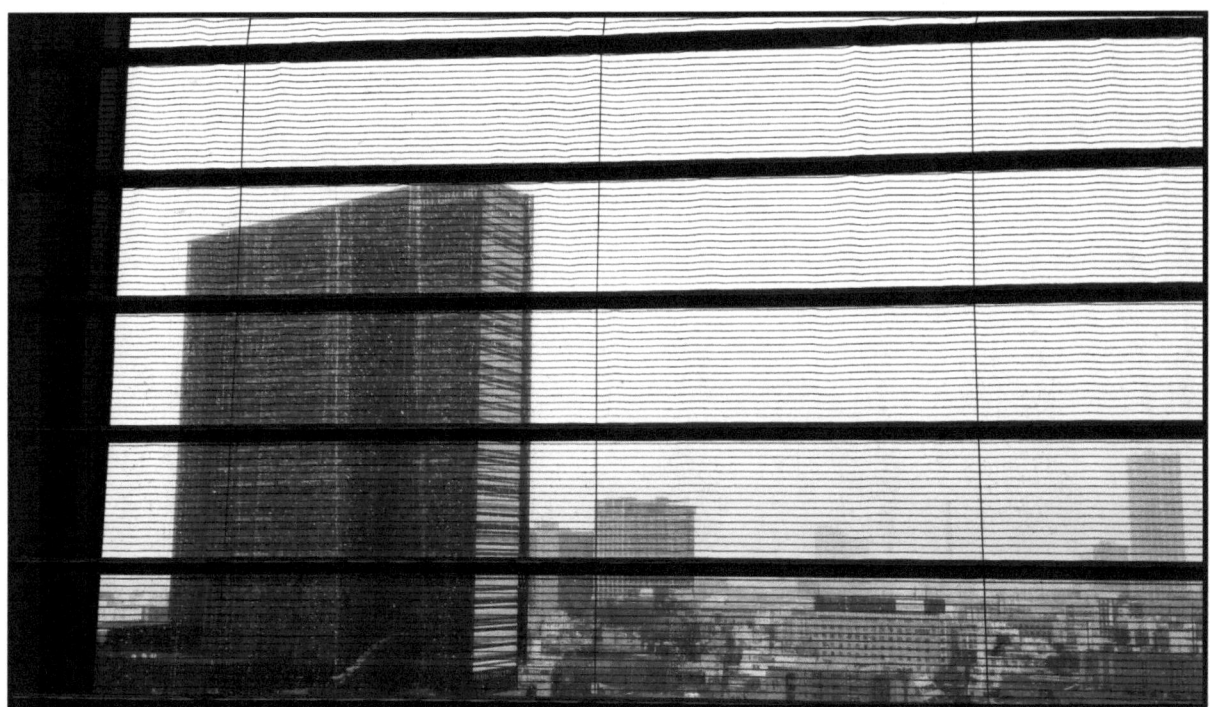

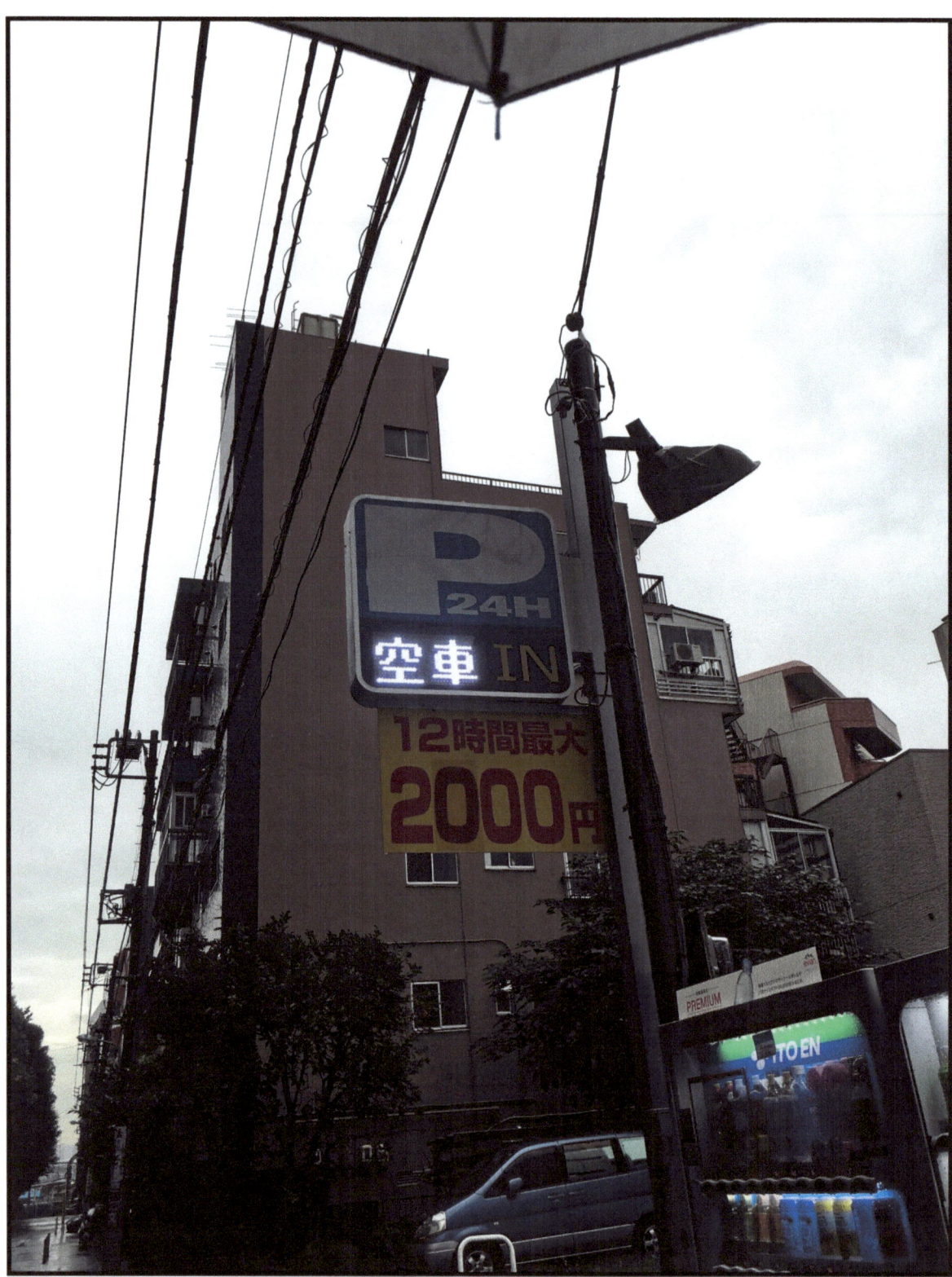

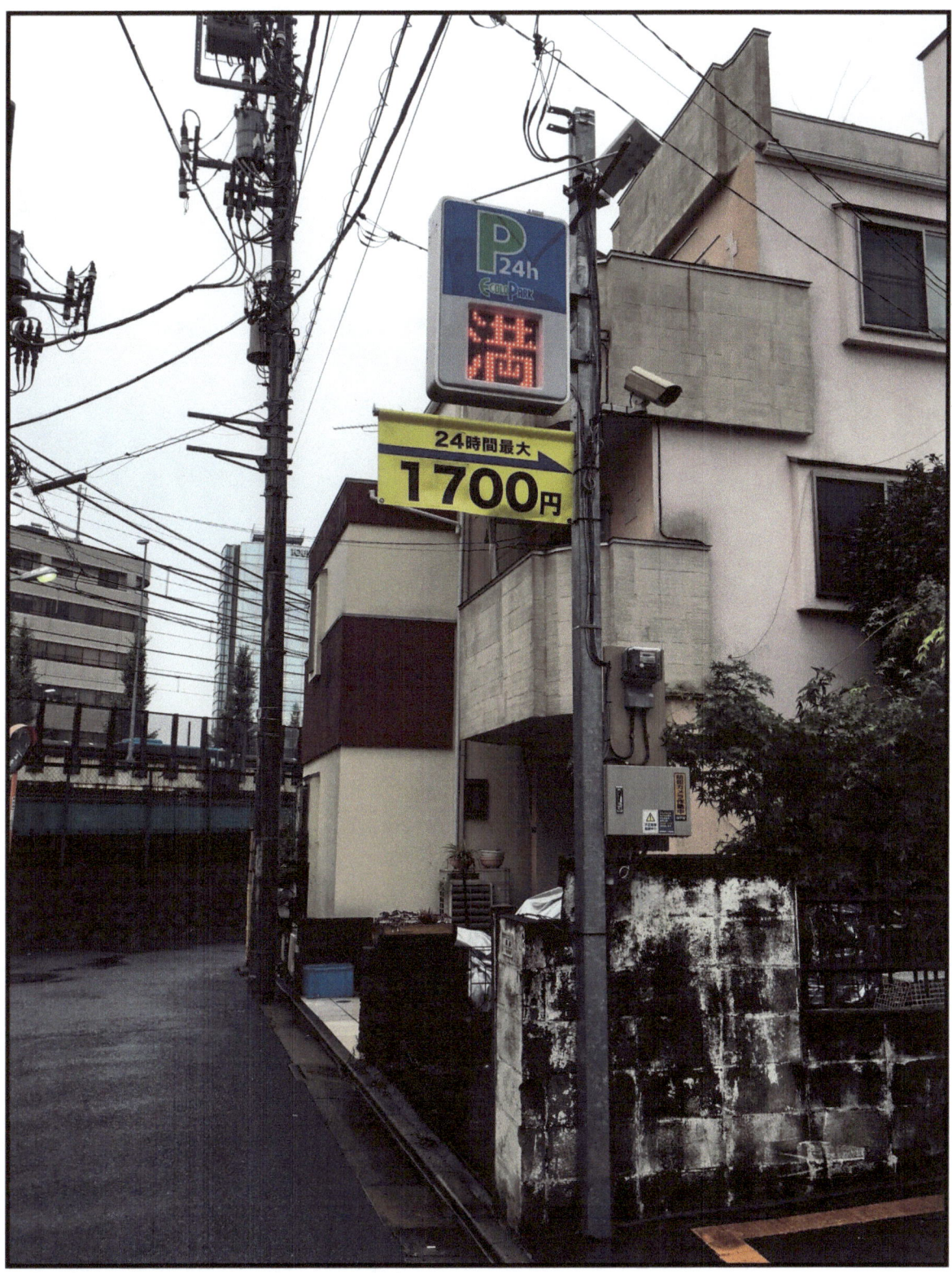

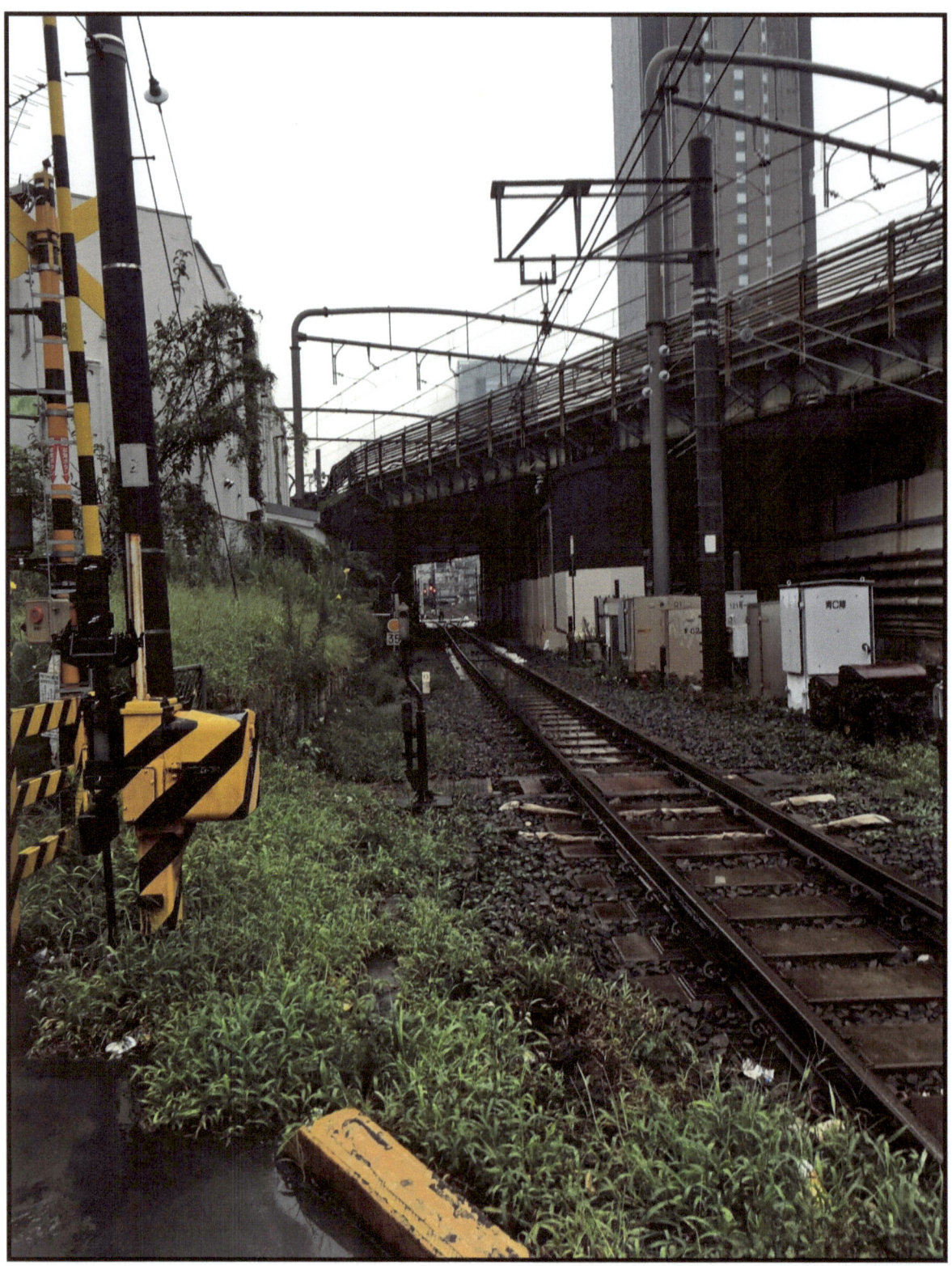

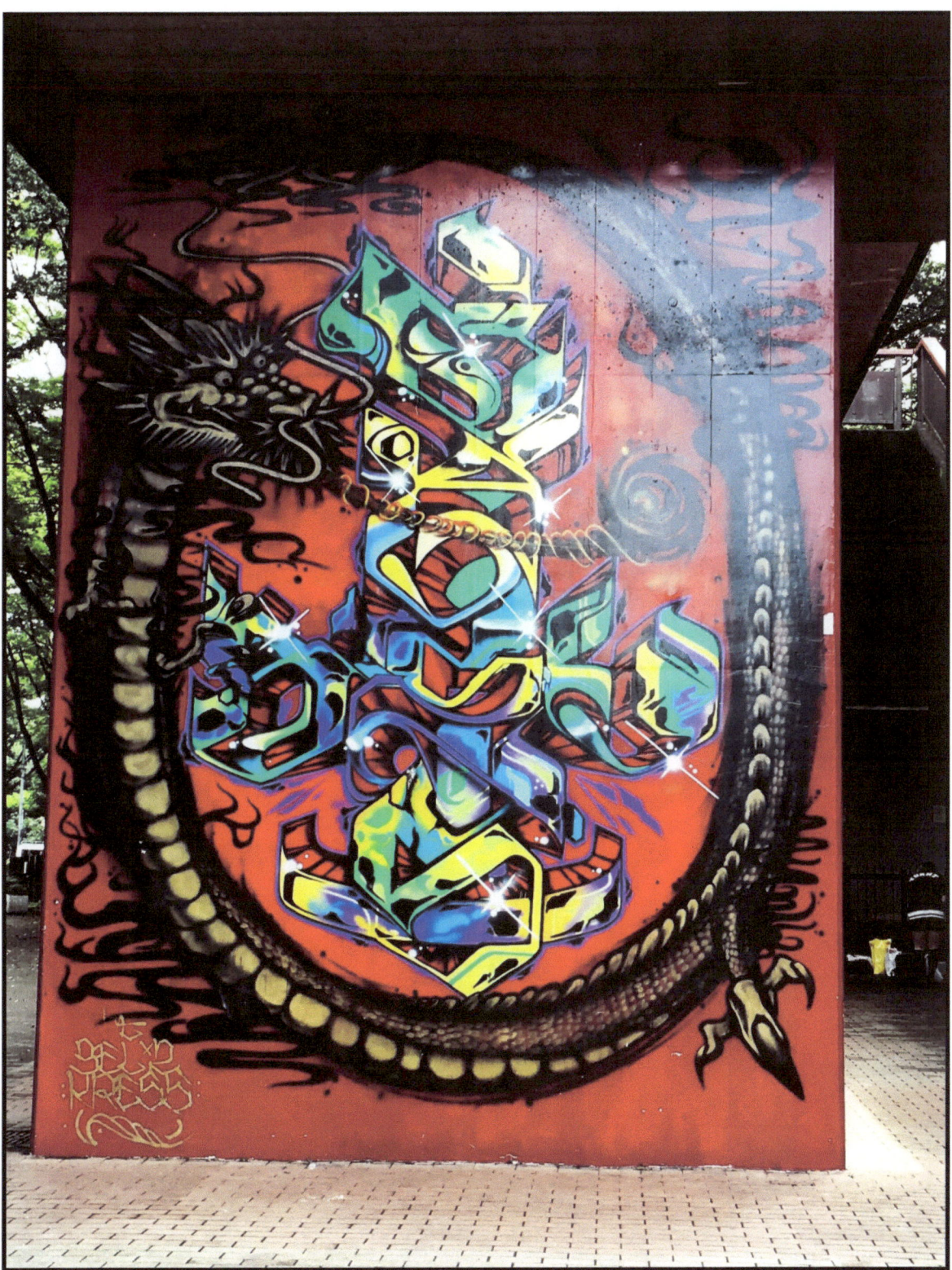

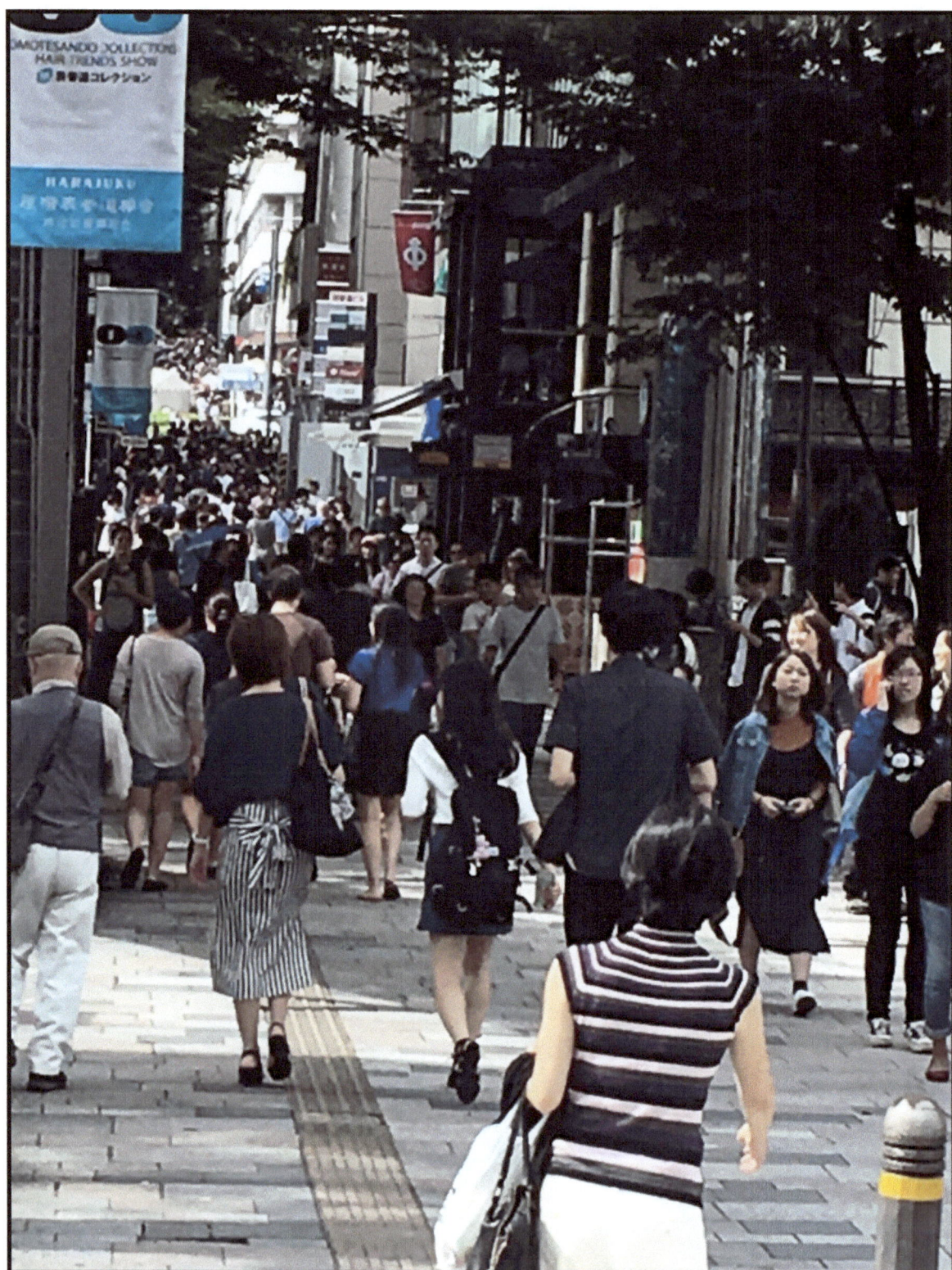

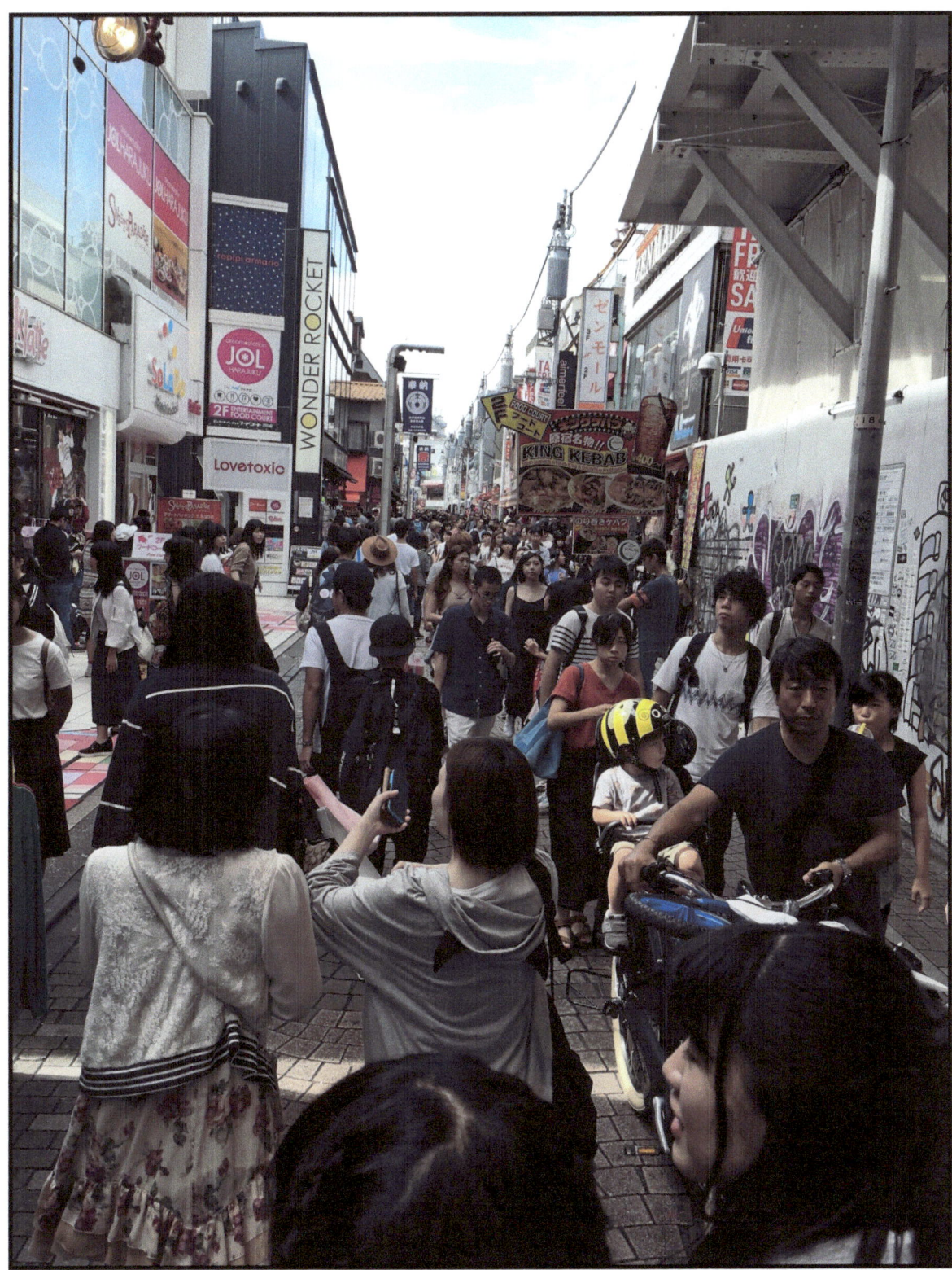

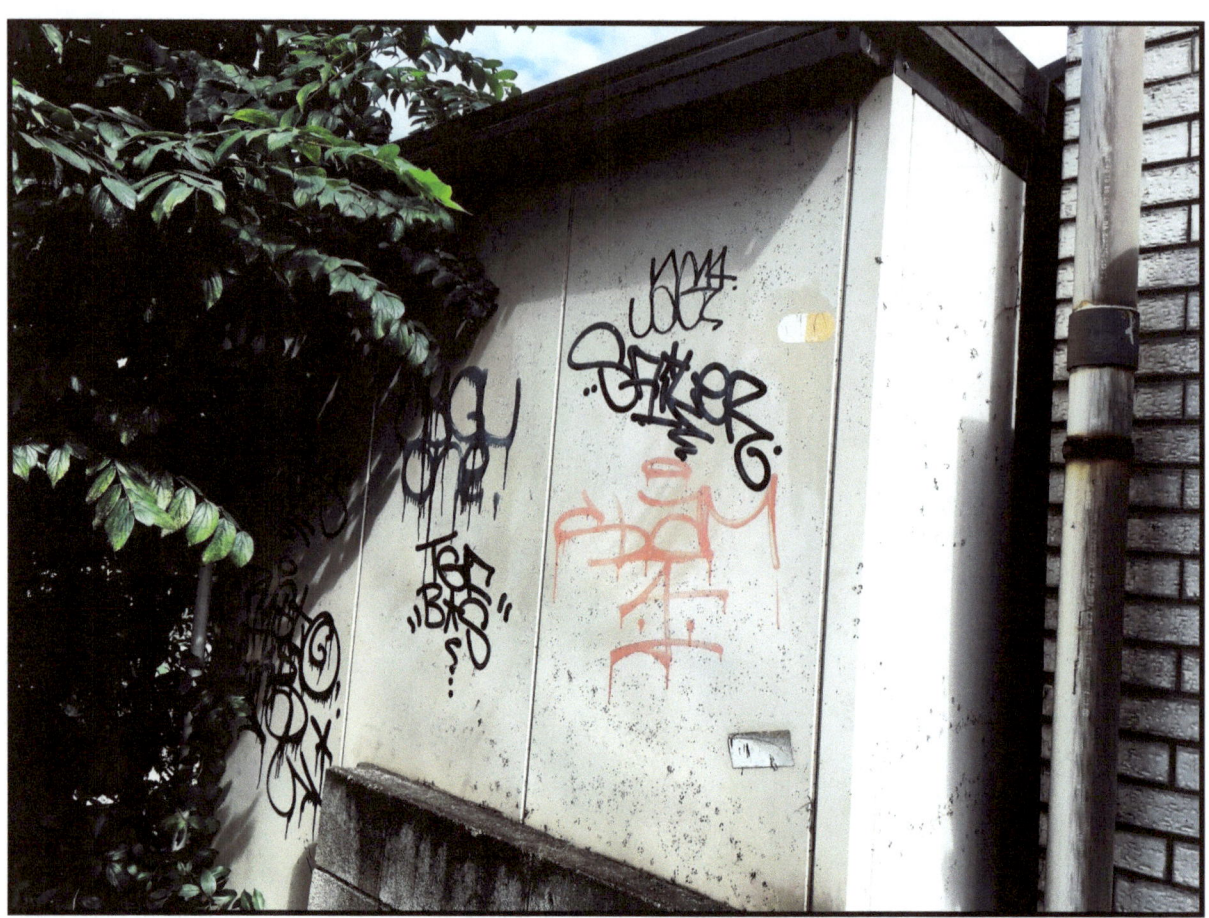

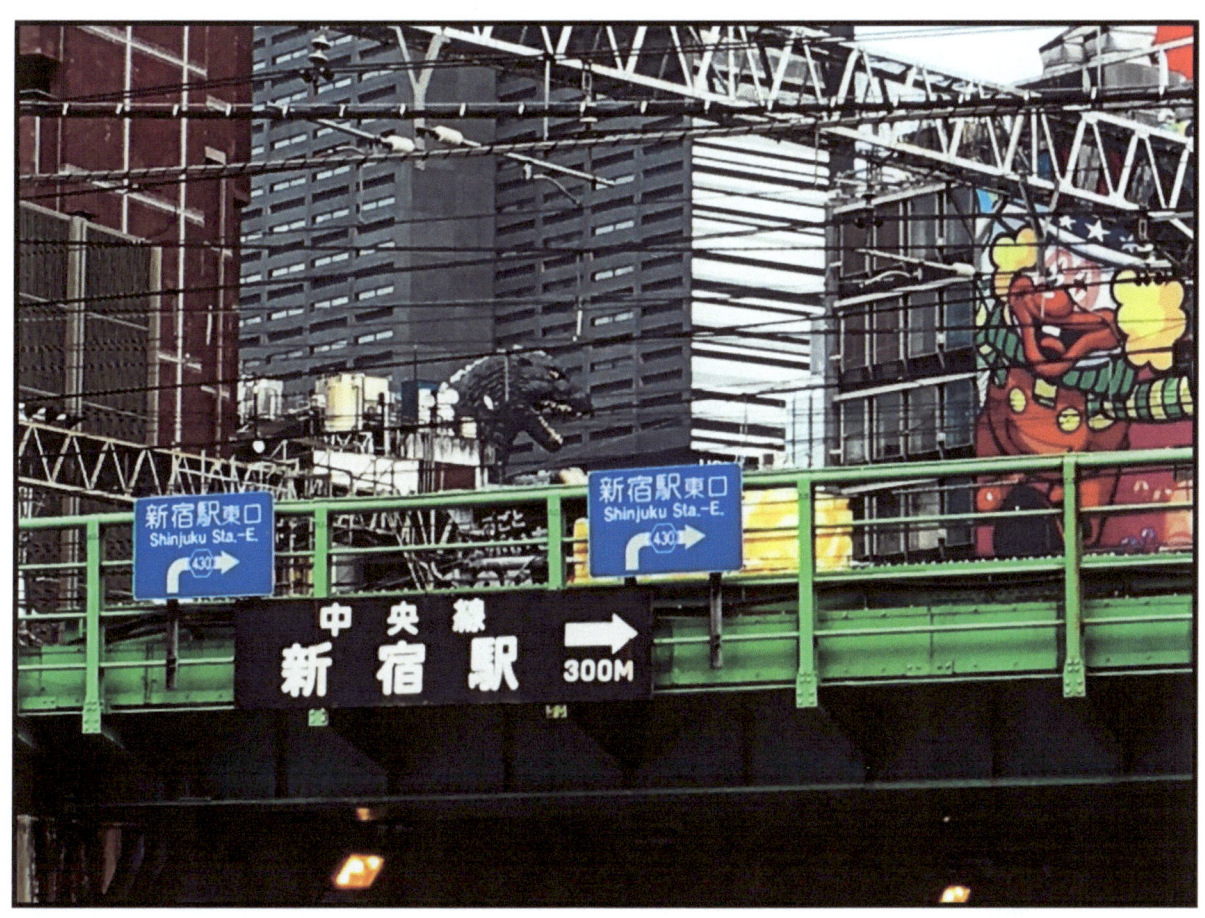

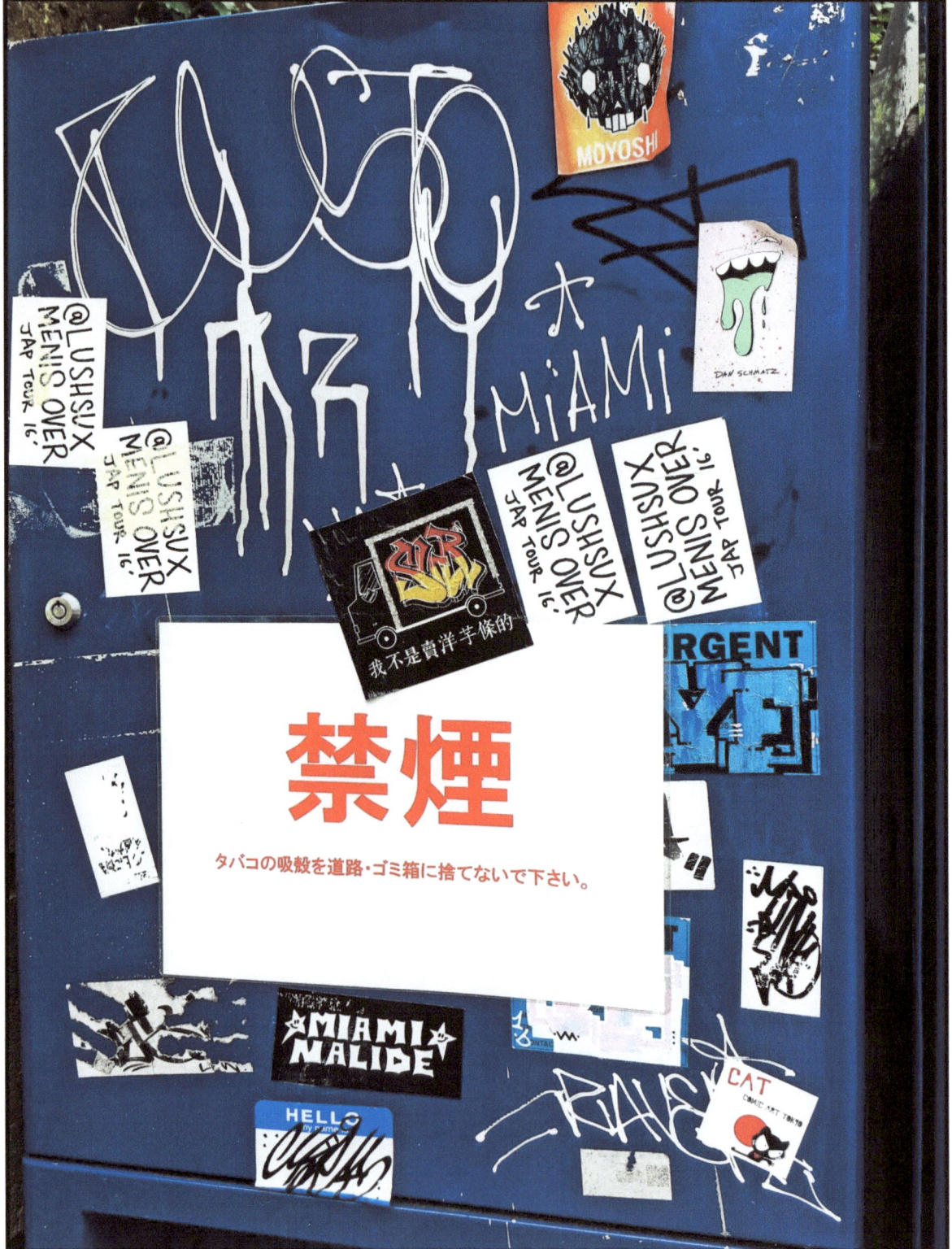

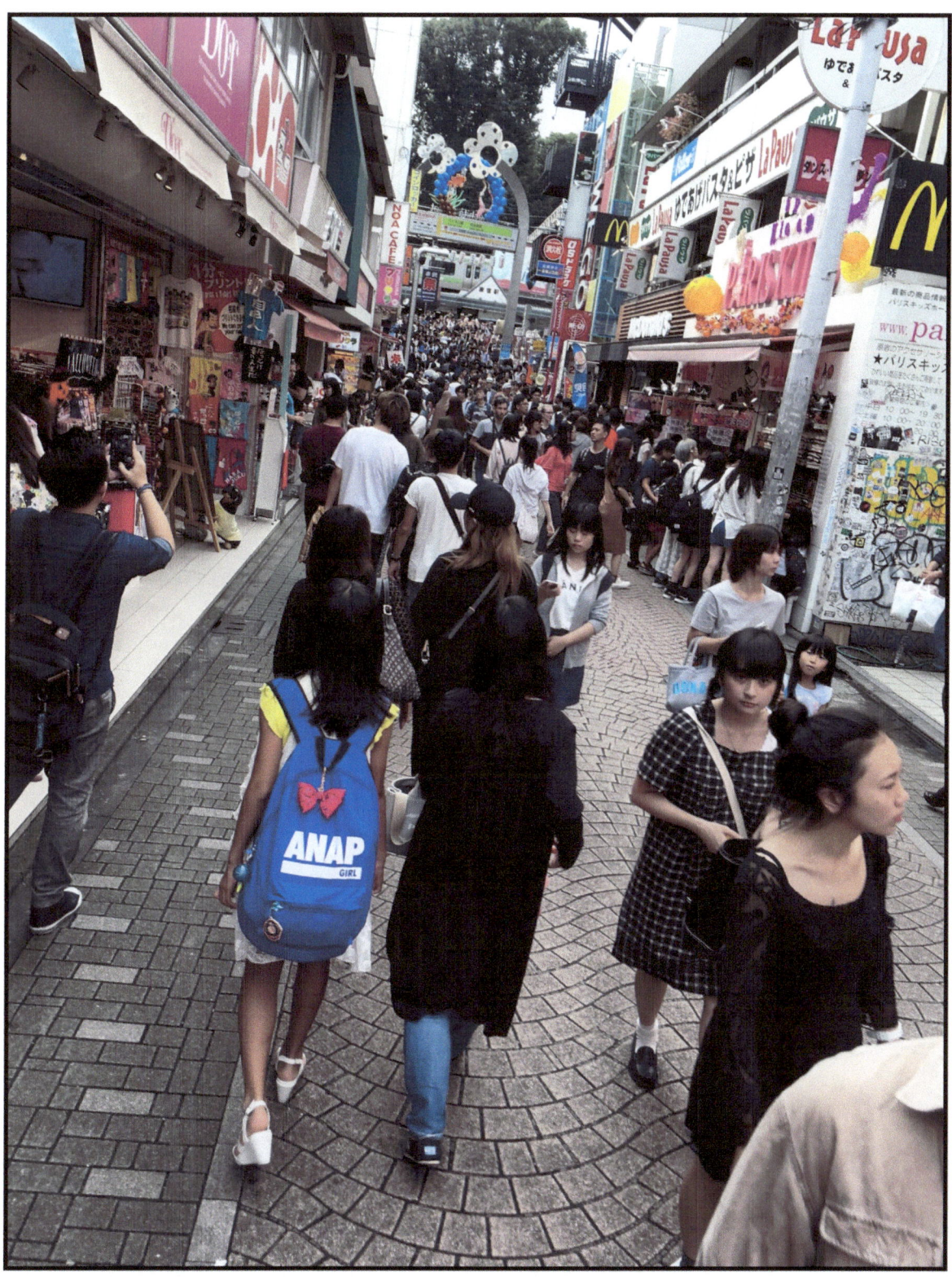

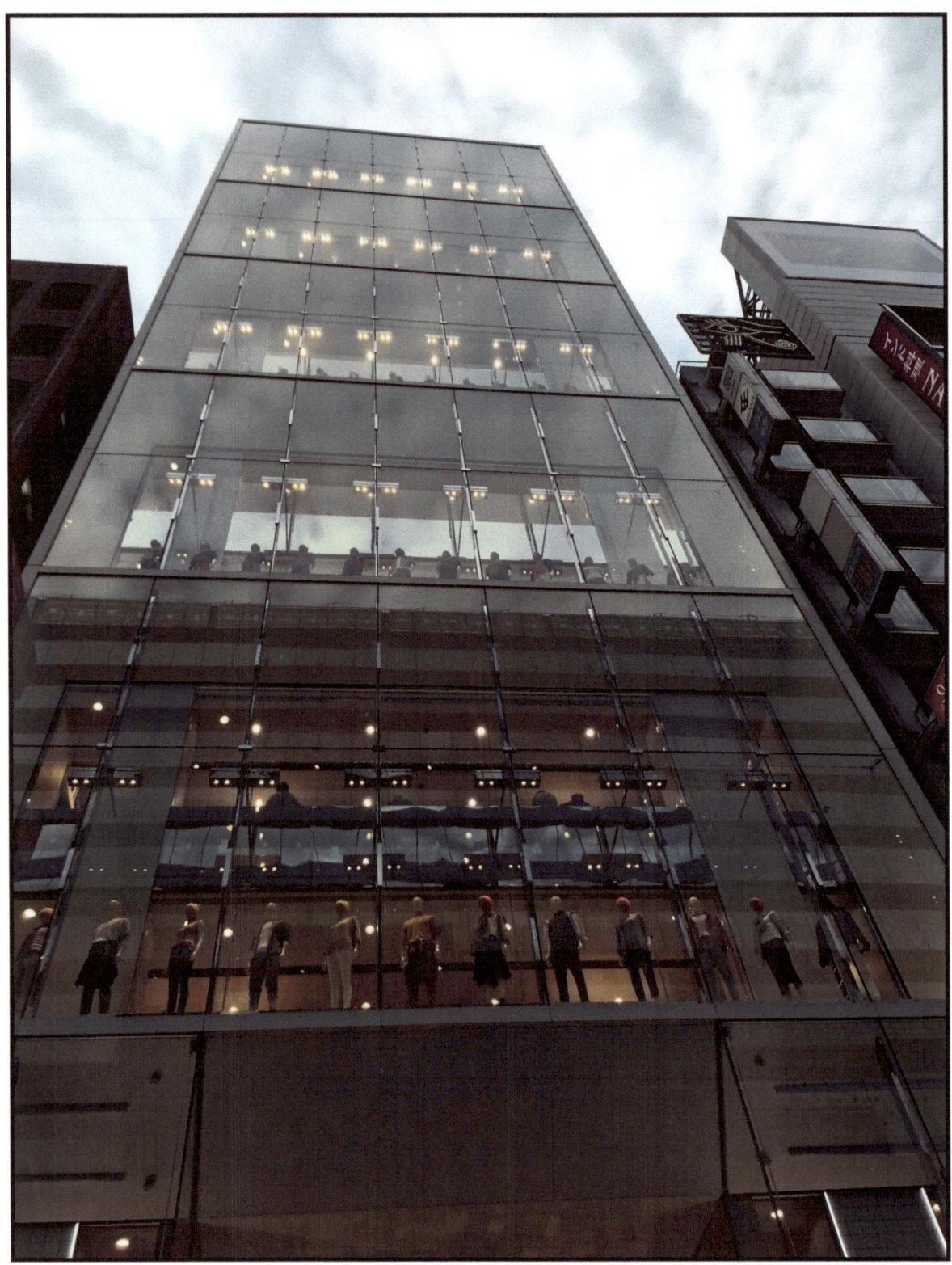

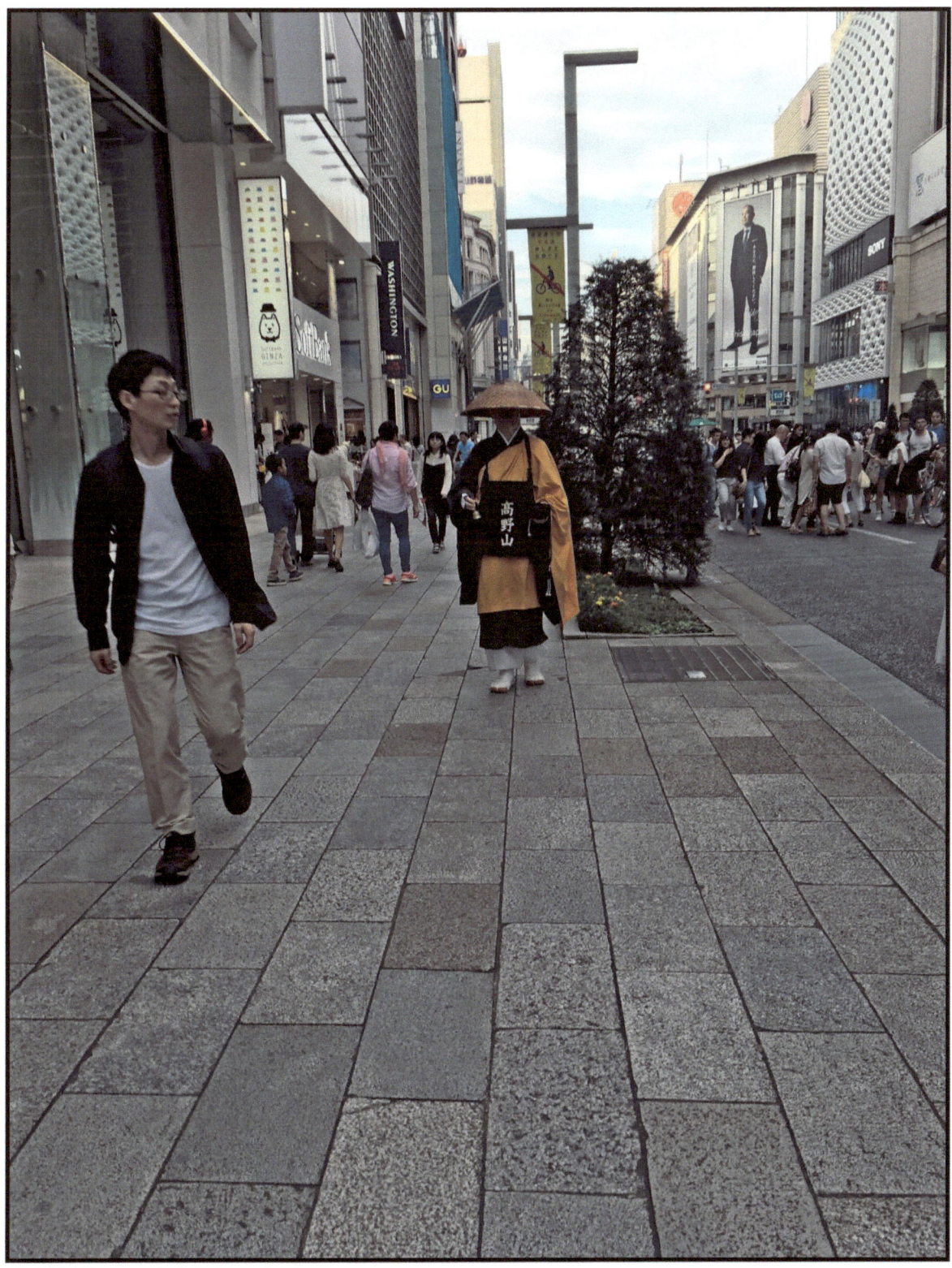

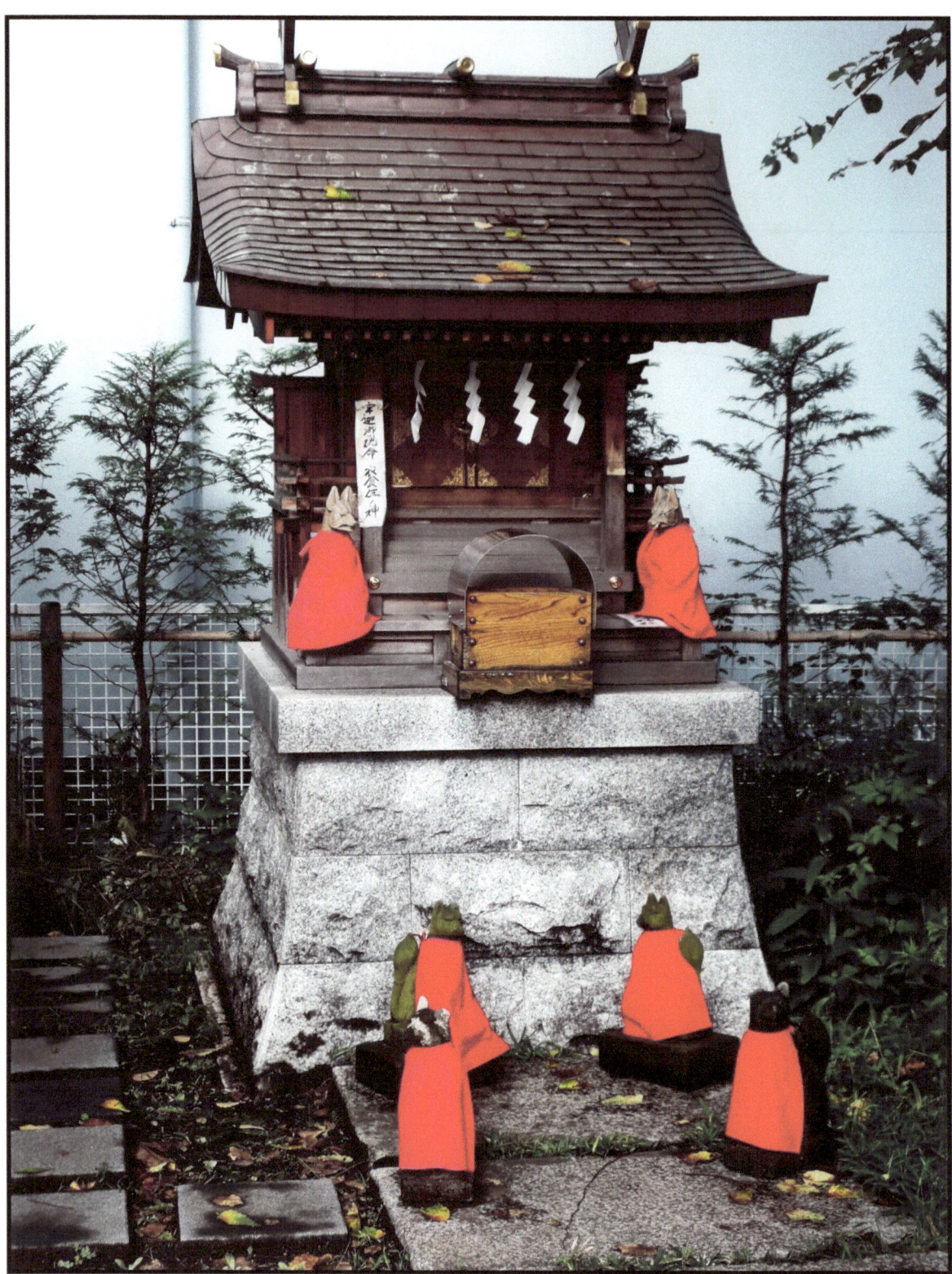

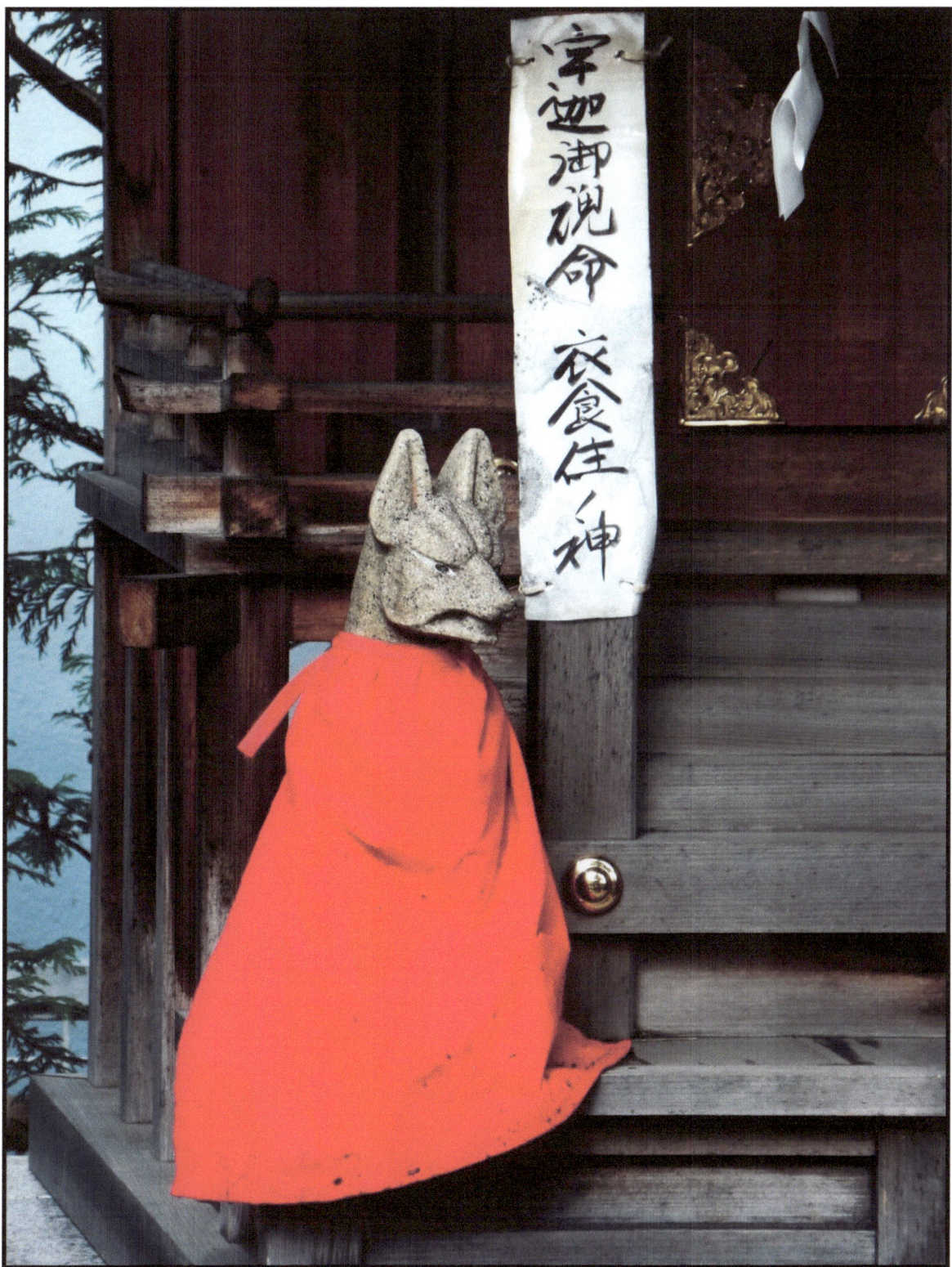

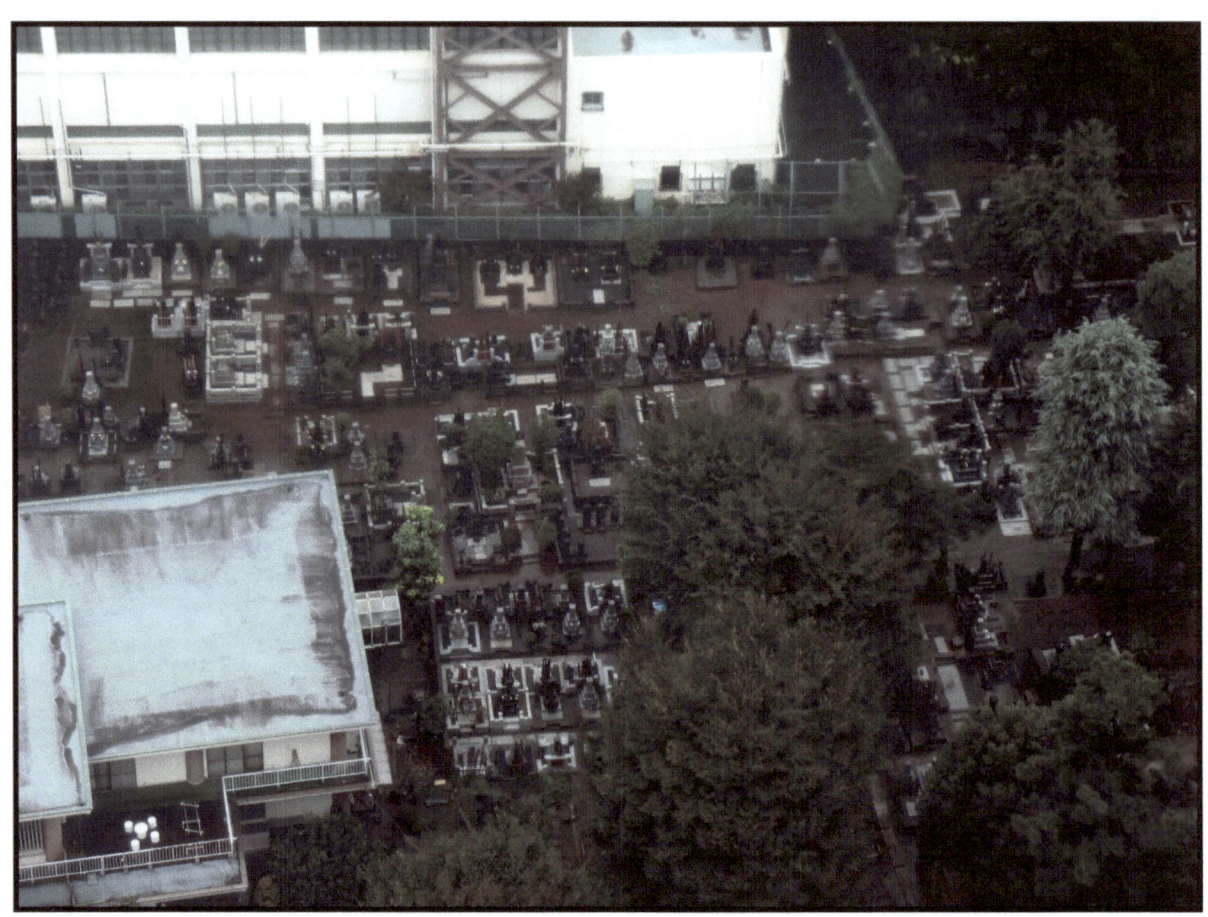

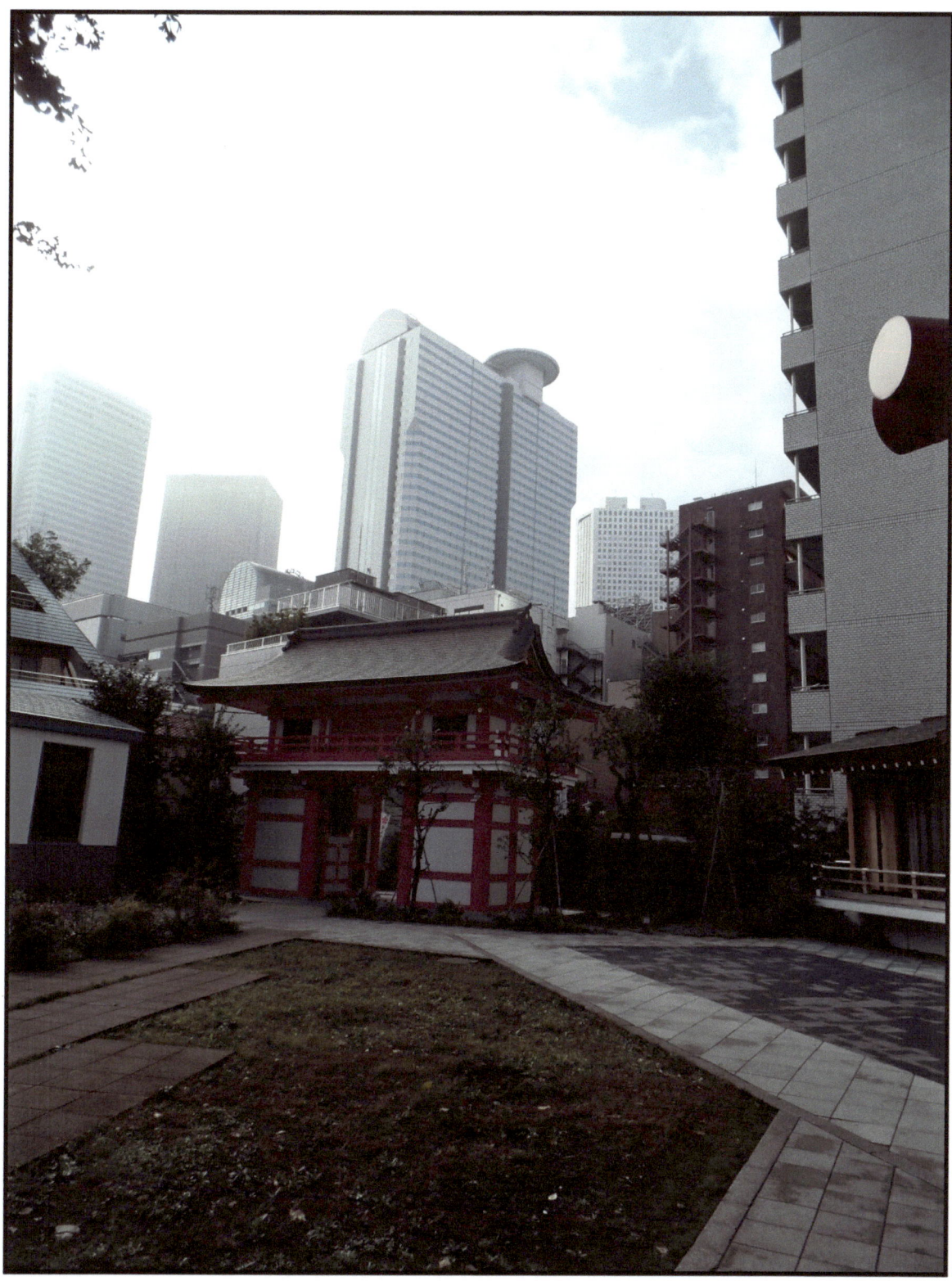

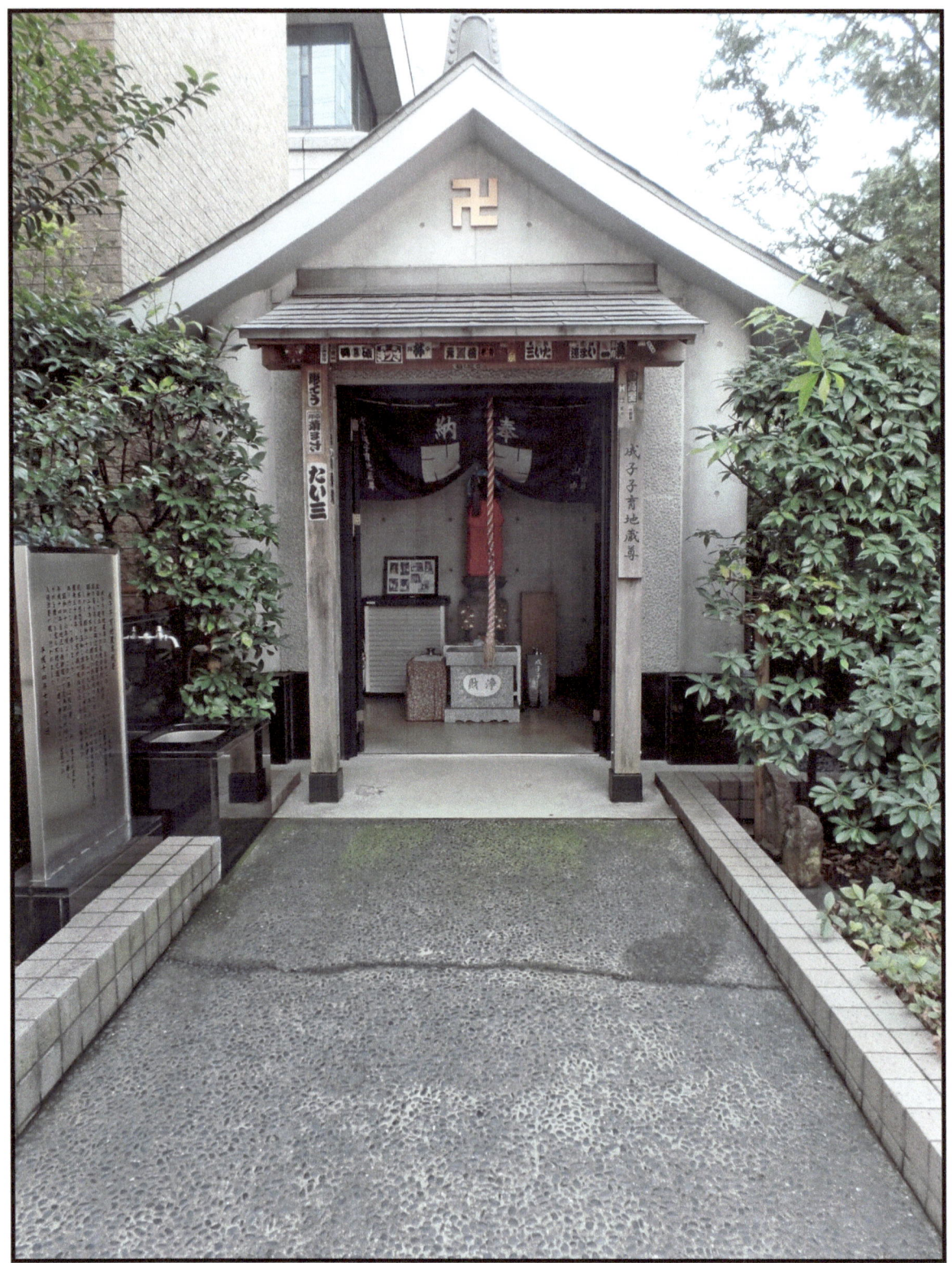

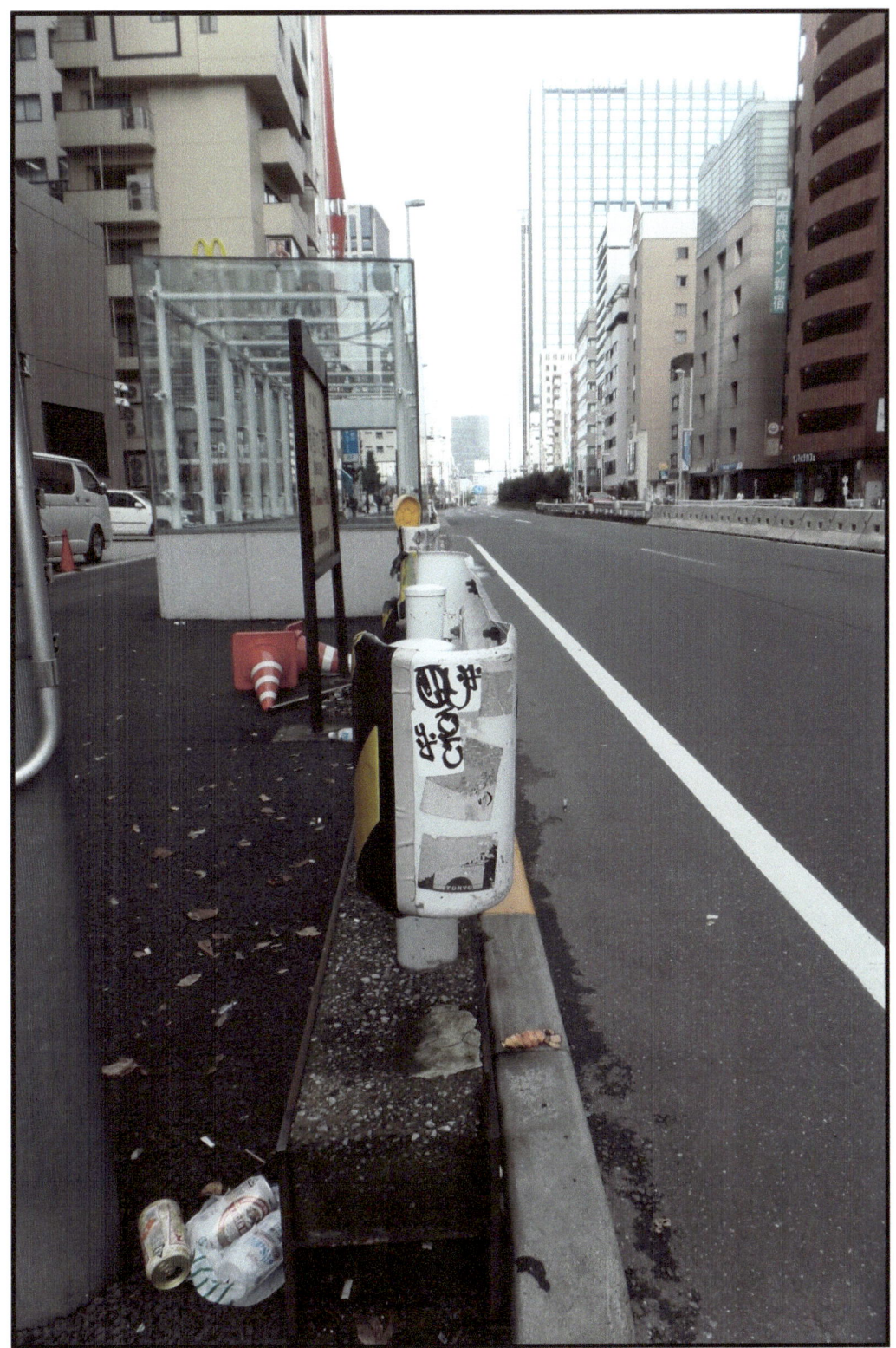

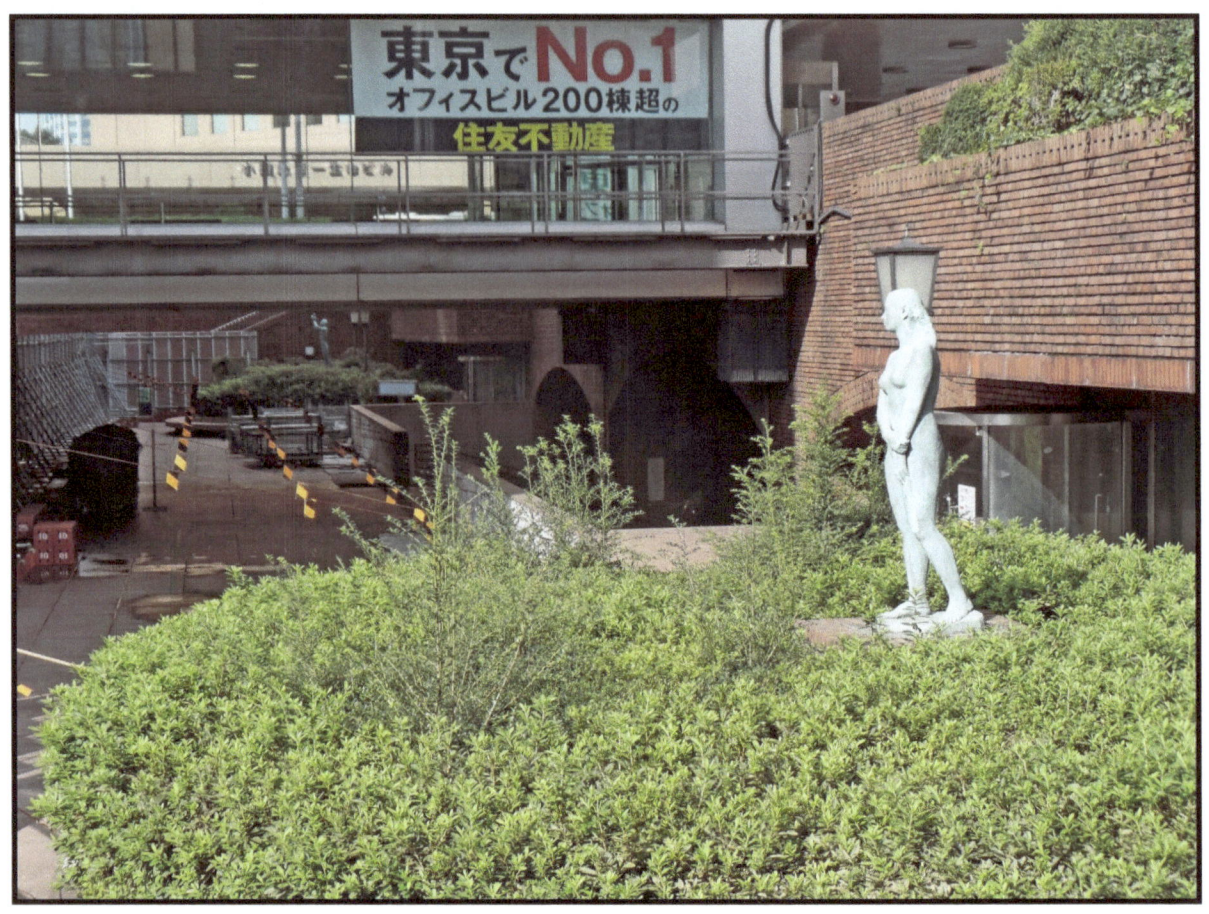

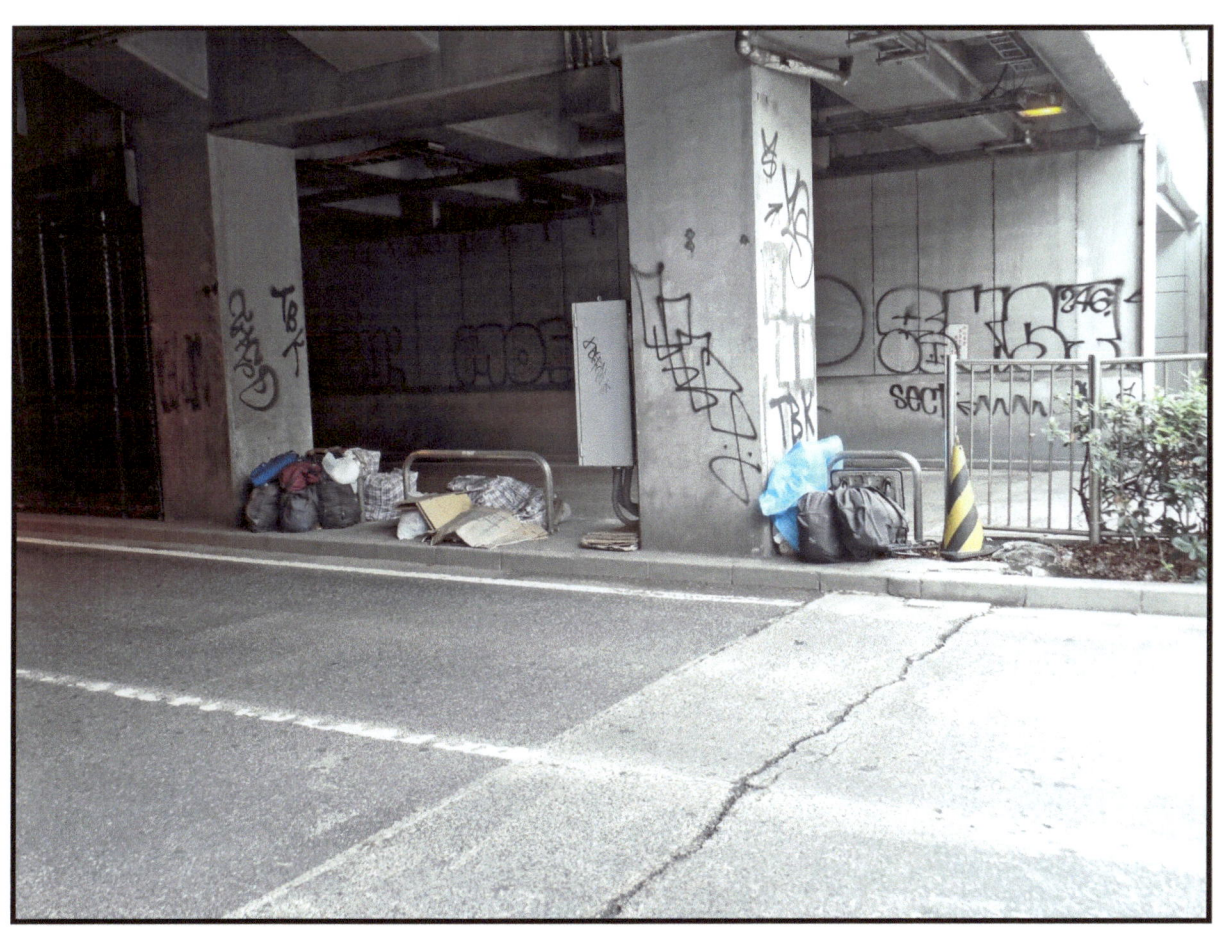

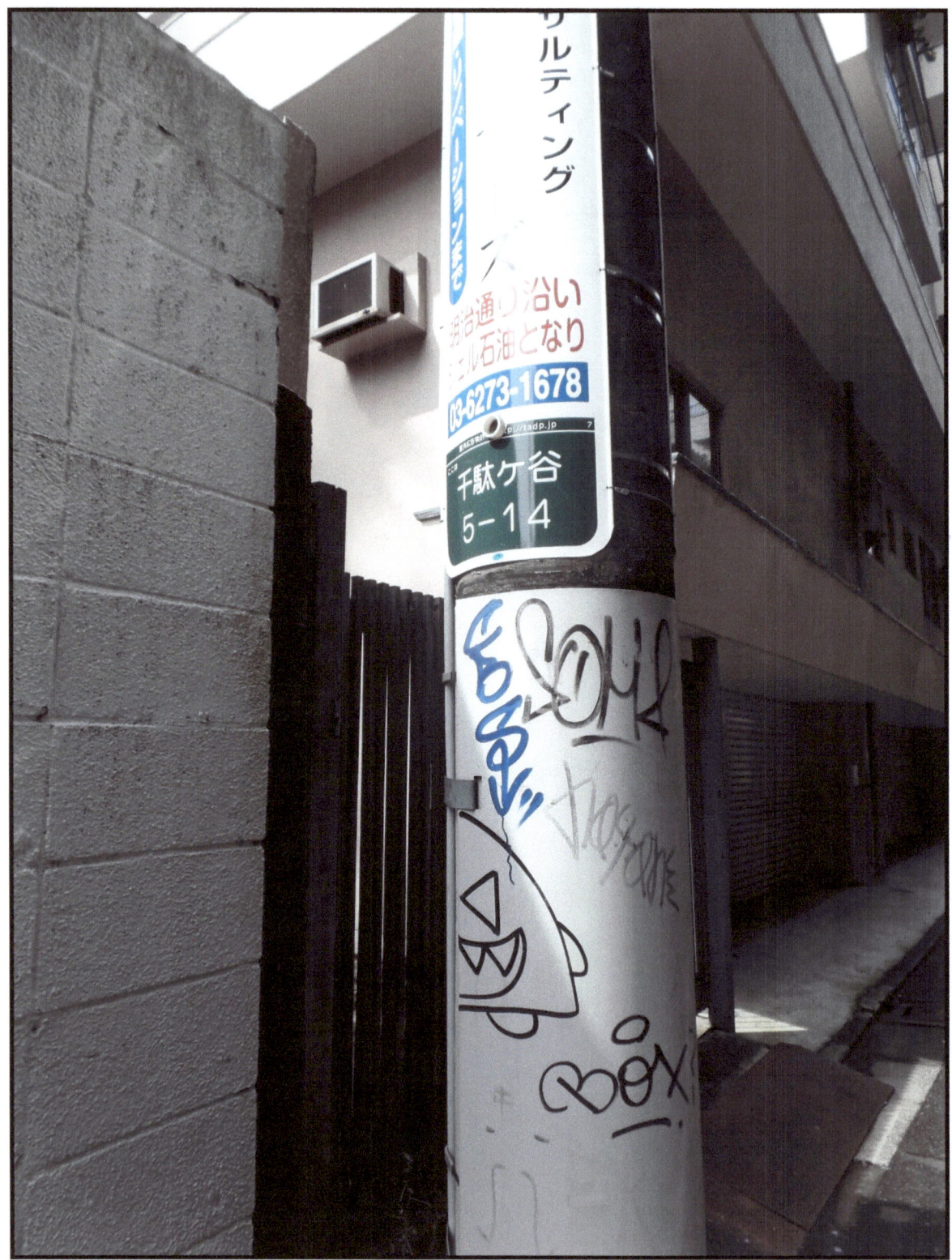

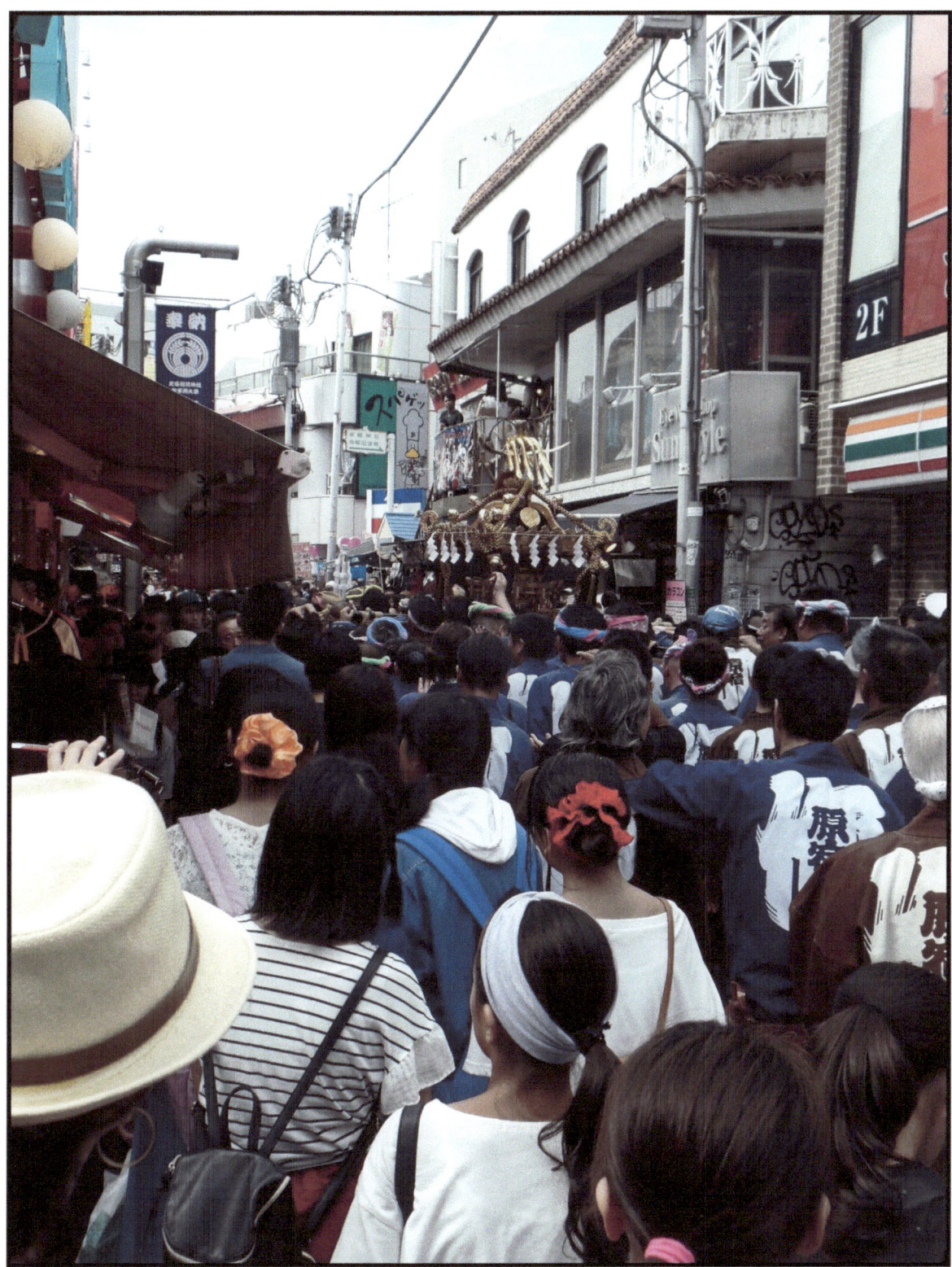

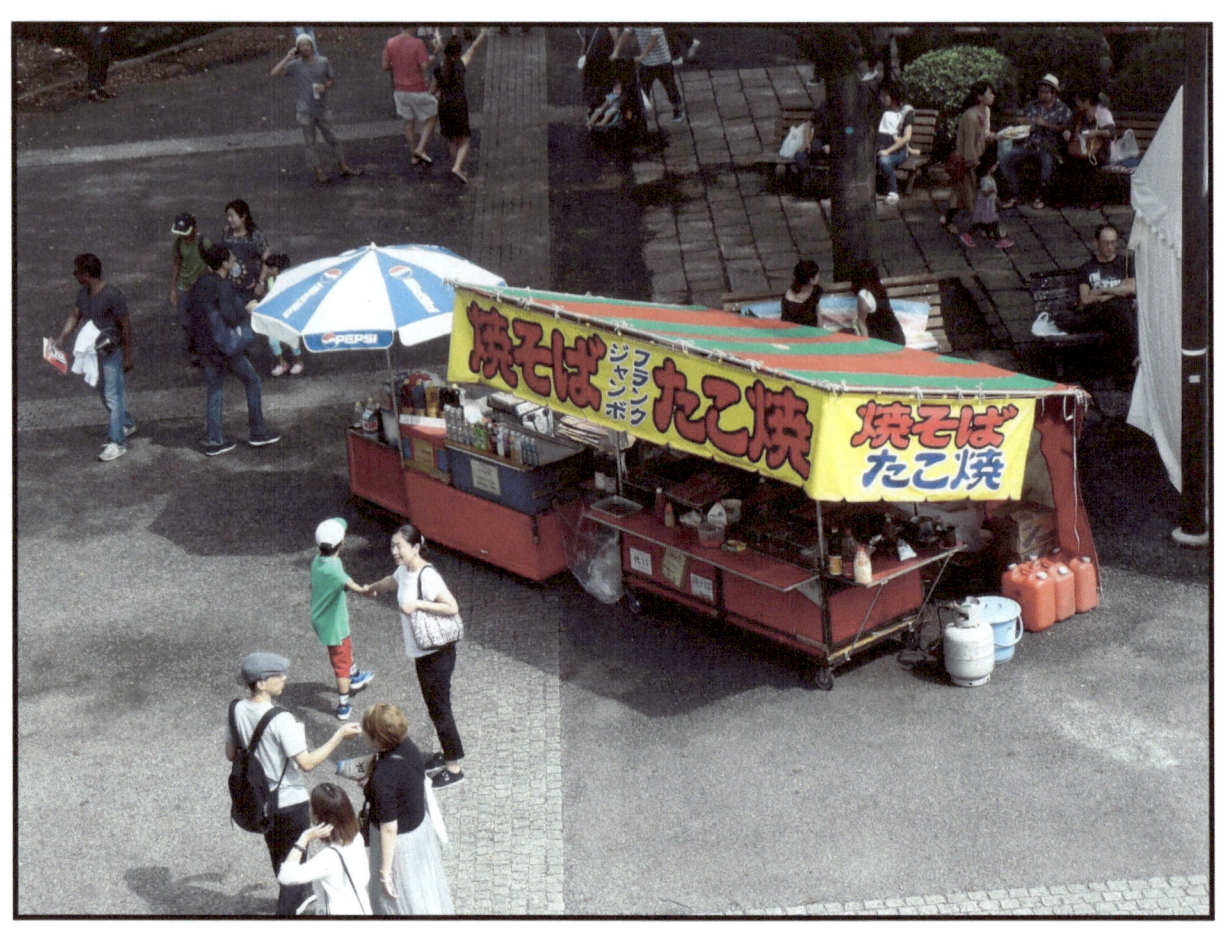

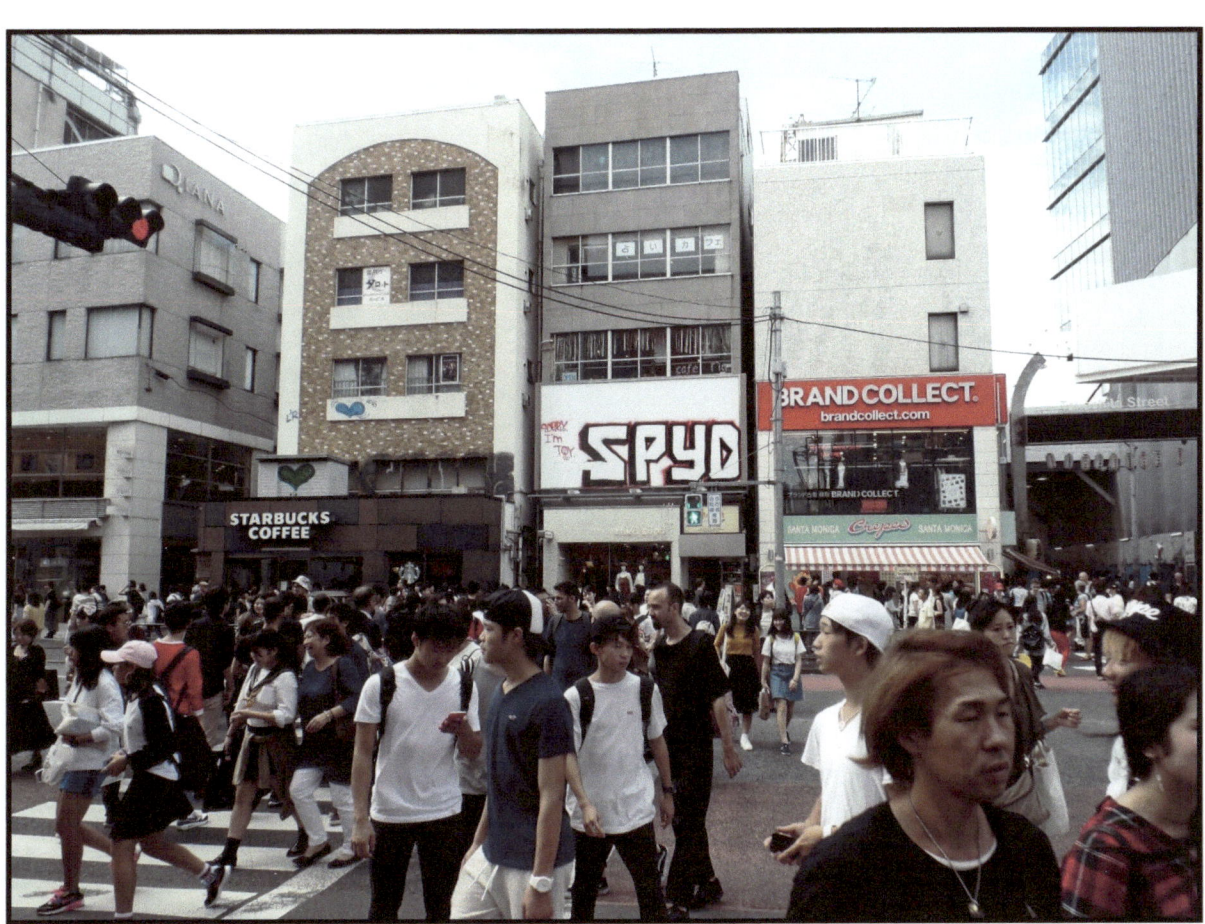

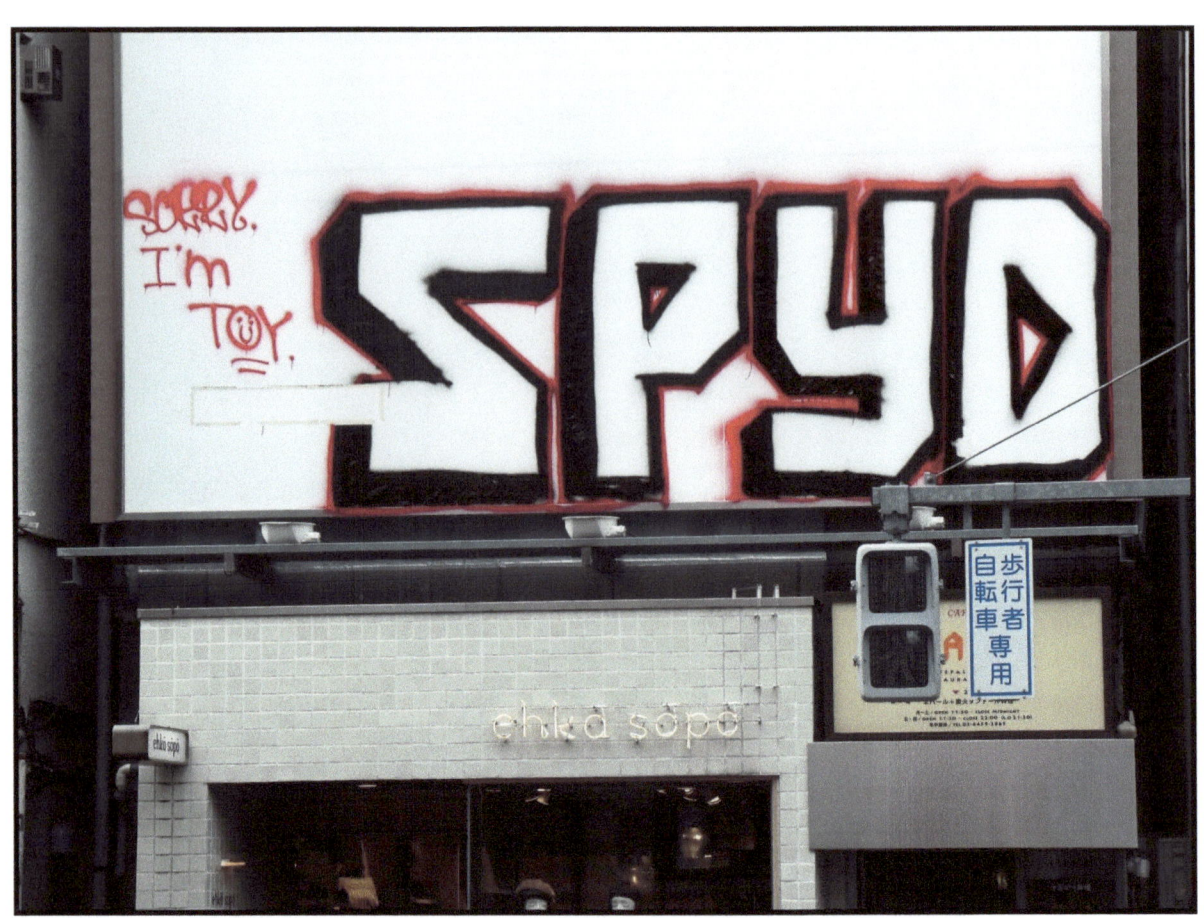

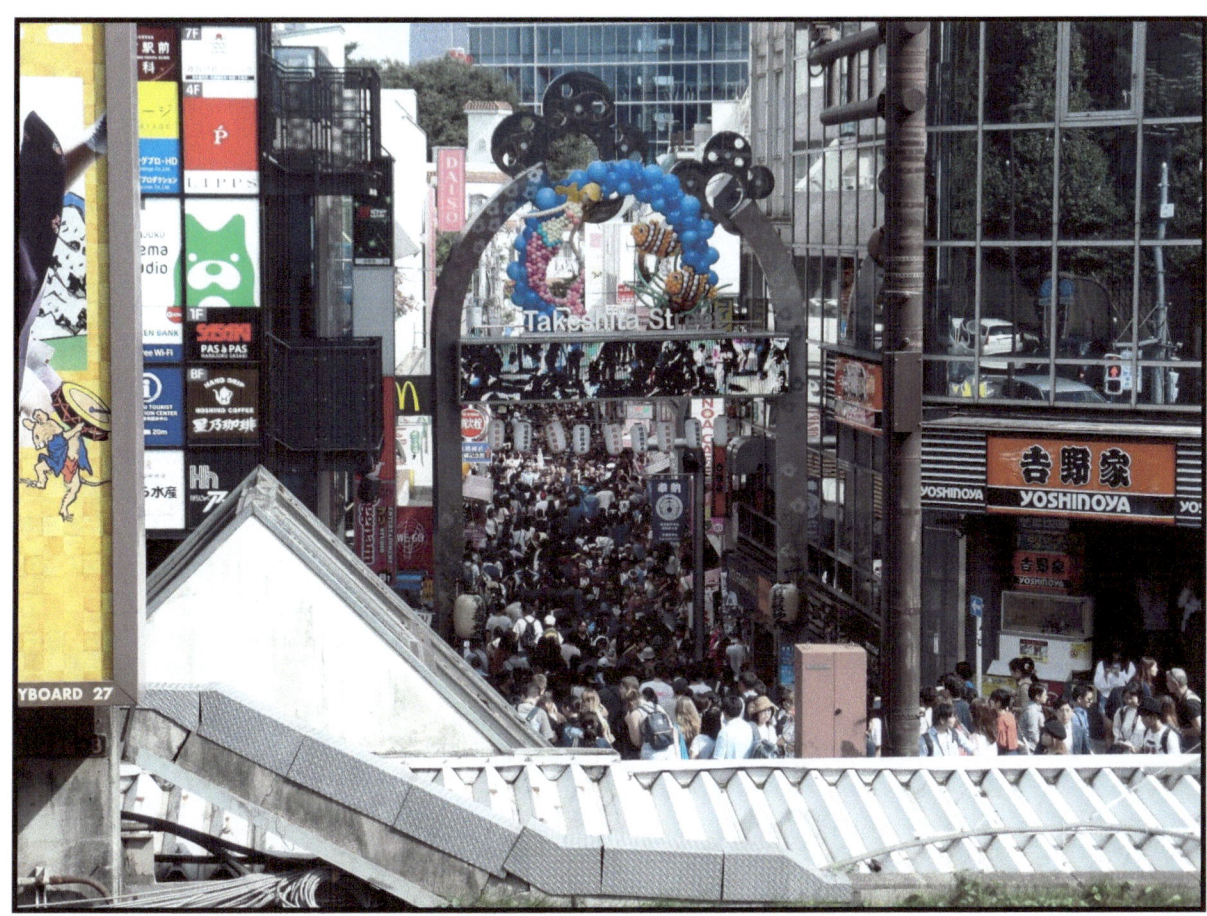

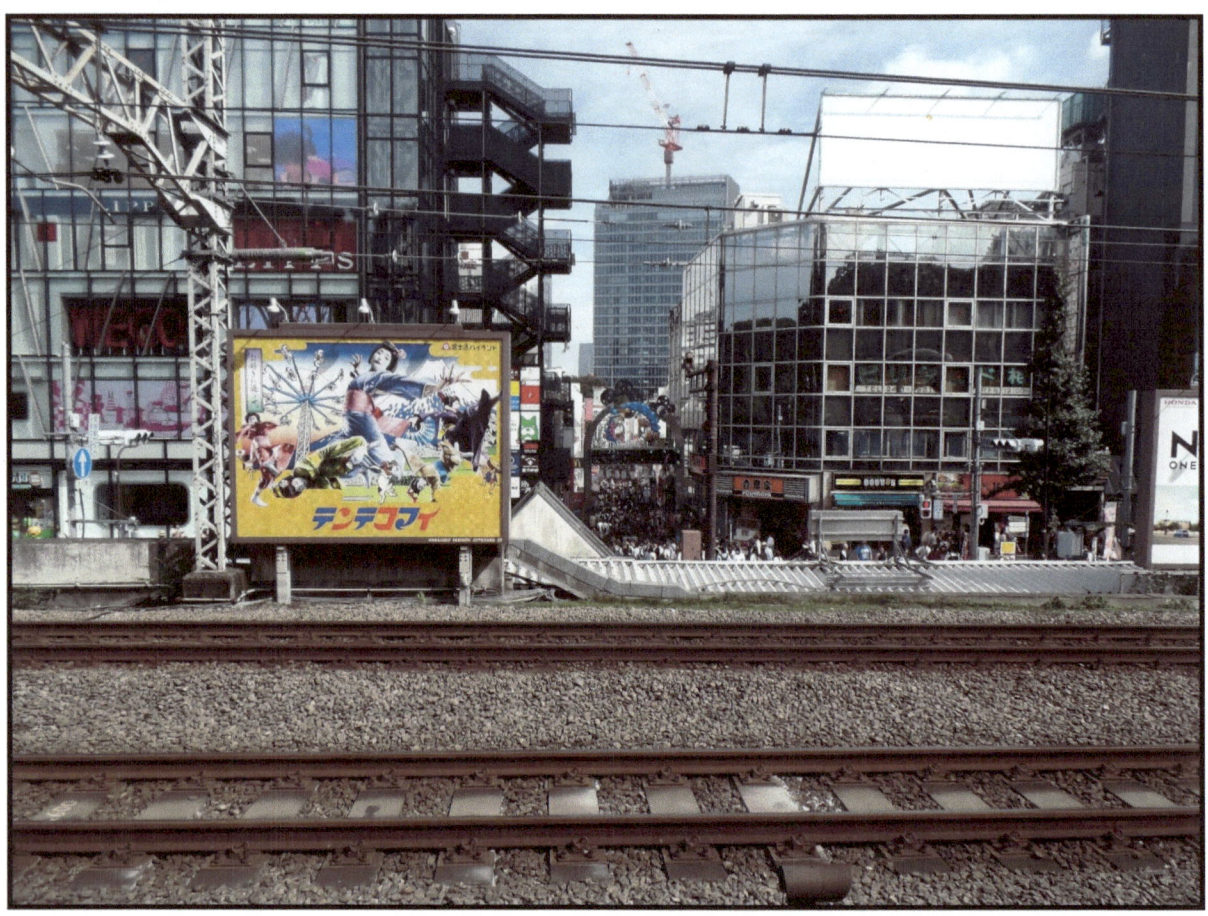

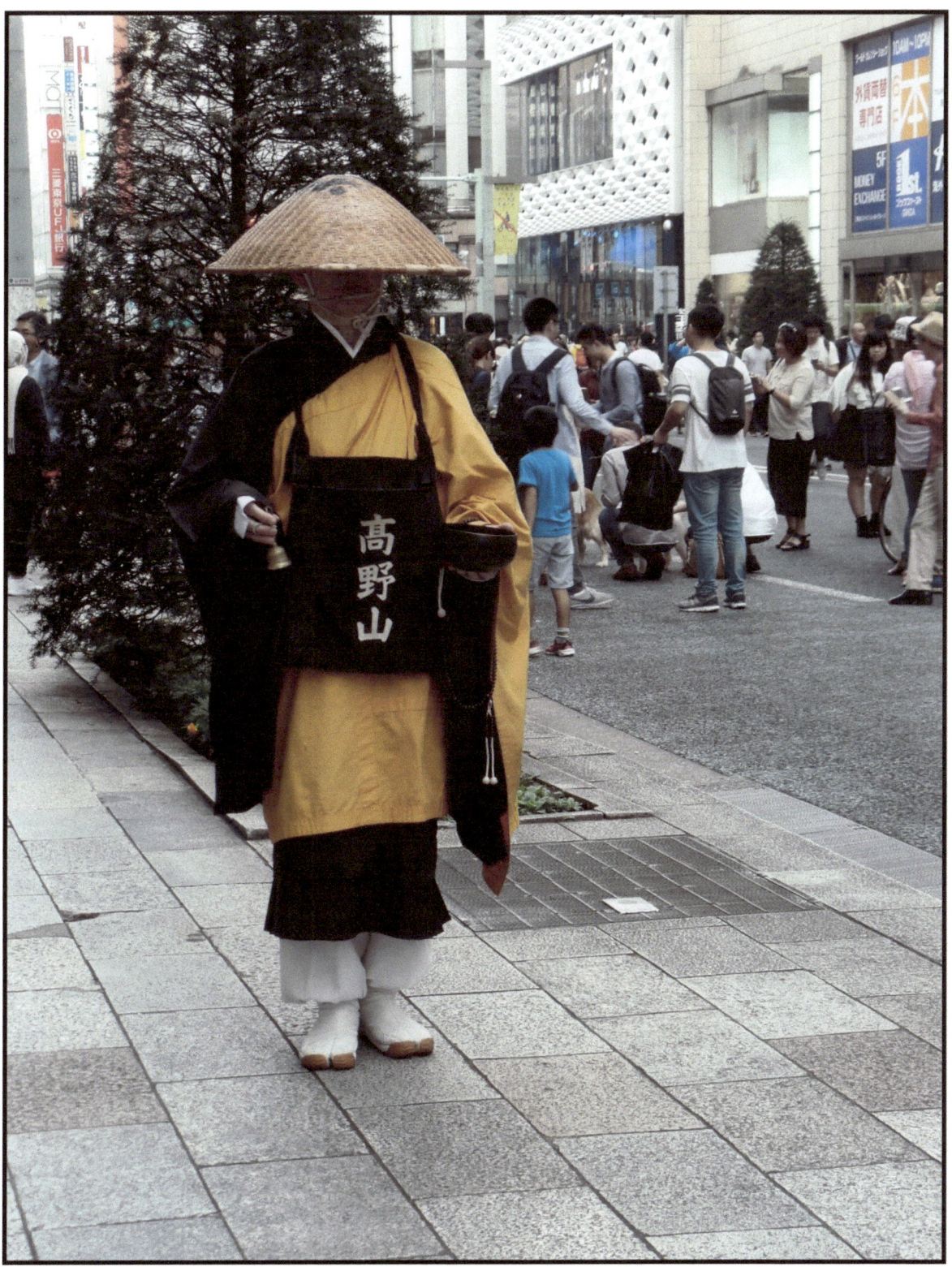

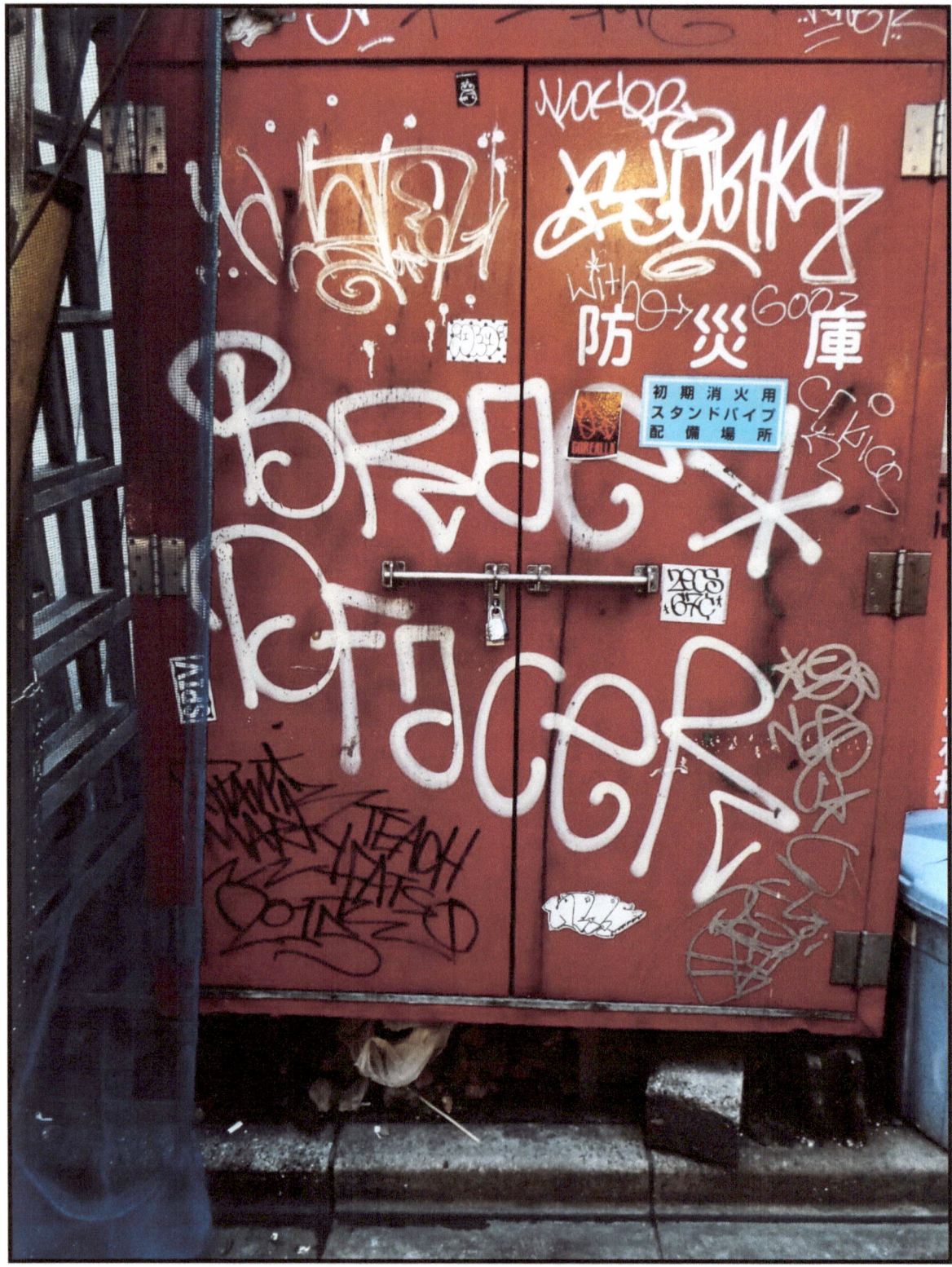

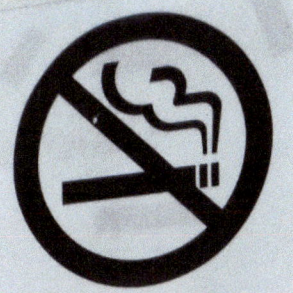

禁煙
No smoking

駐輪禁止

ここに自転車を置くと、撤去されることがあります。
当店では責任はおいかねますので
ご理解、ご協力お願い致します。

シルク三　　　中央通り店

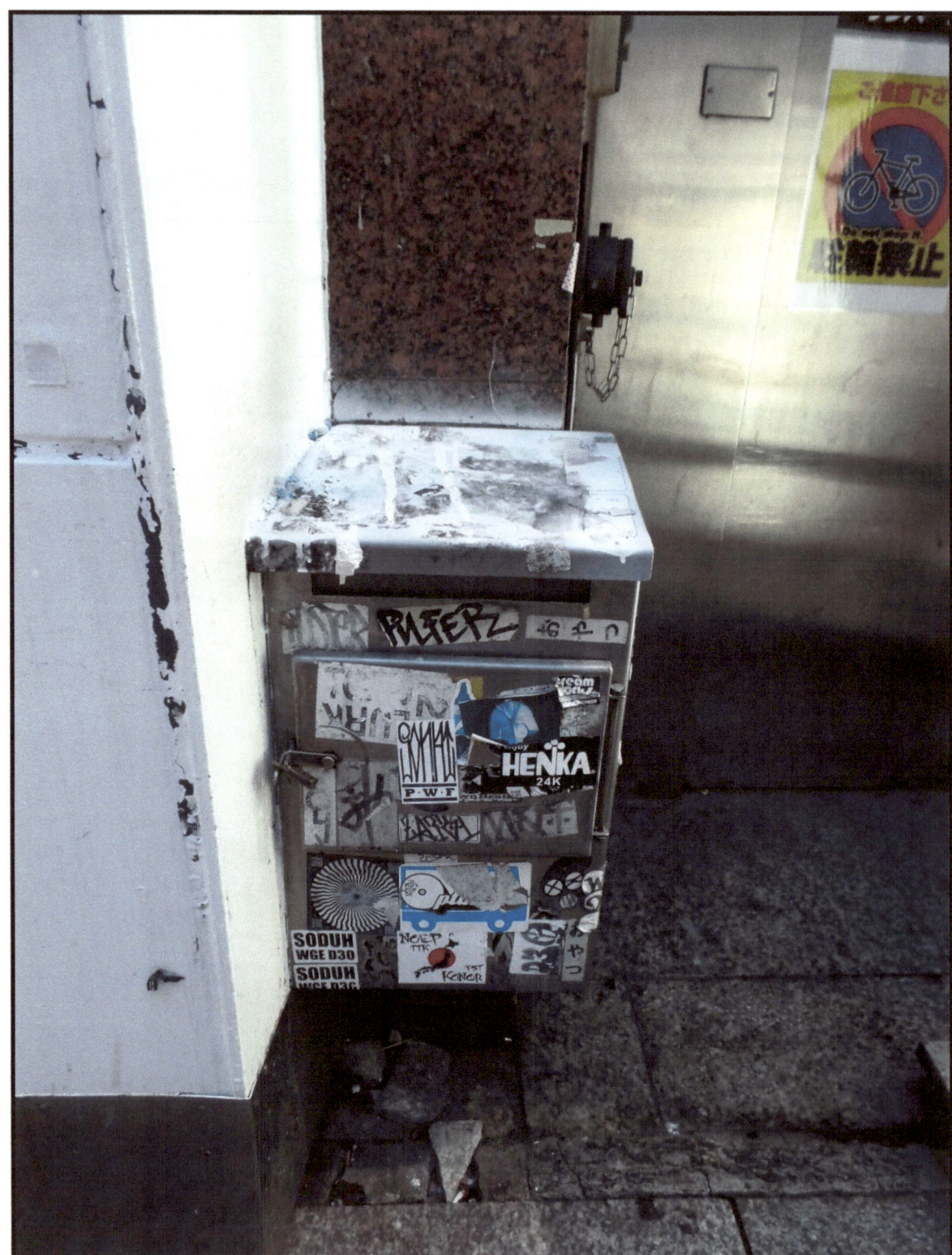

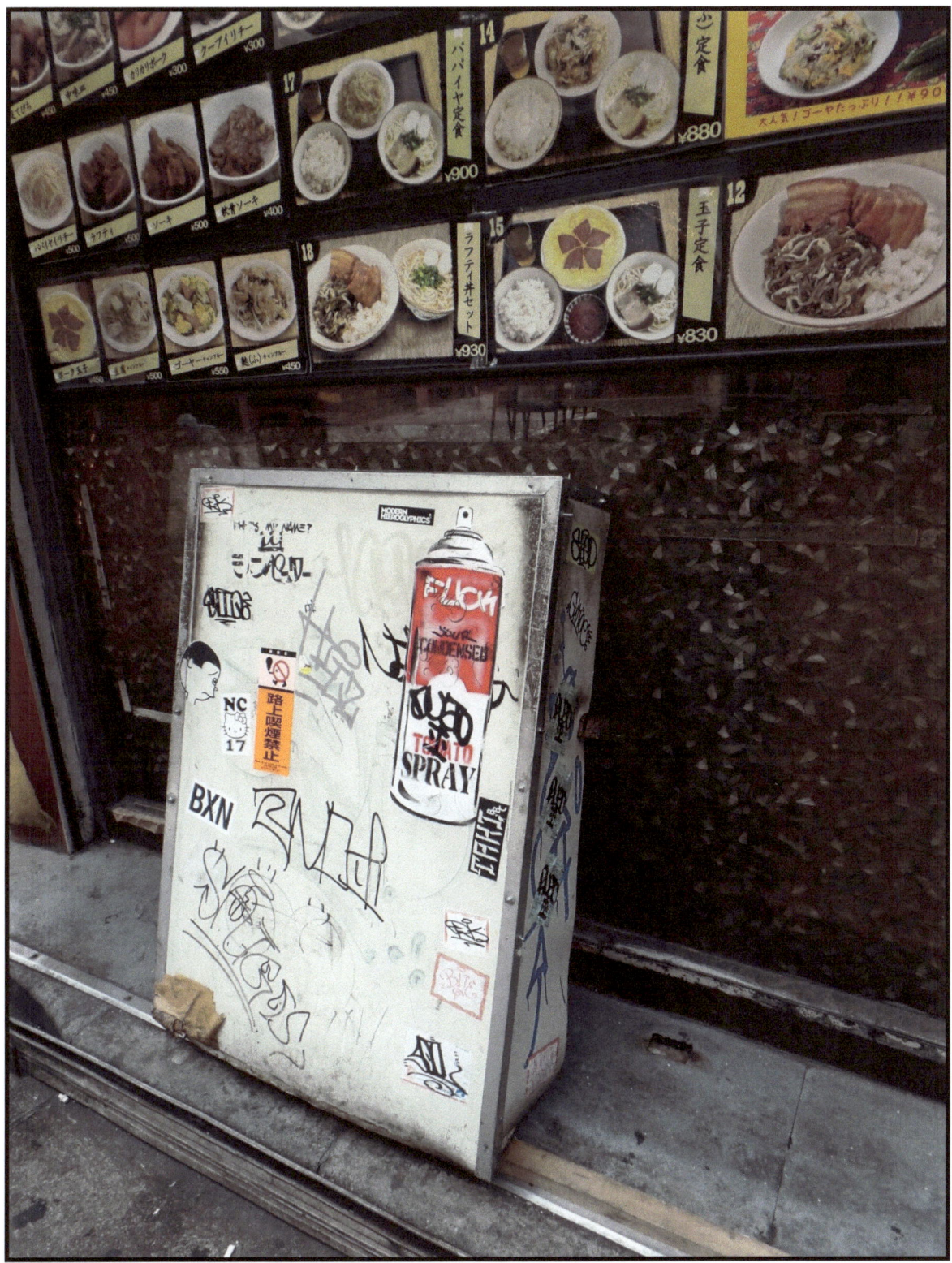

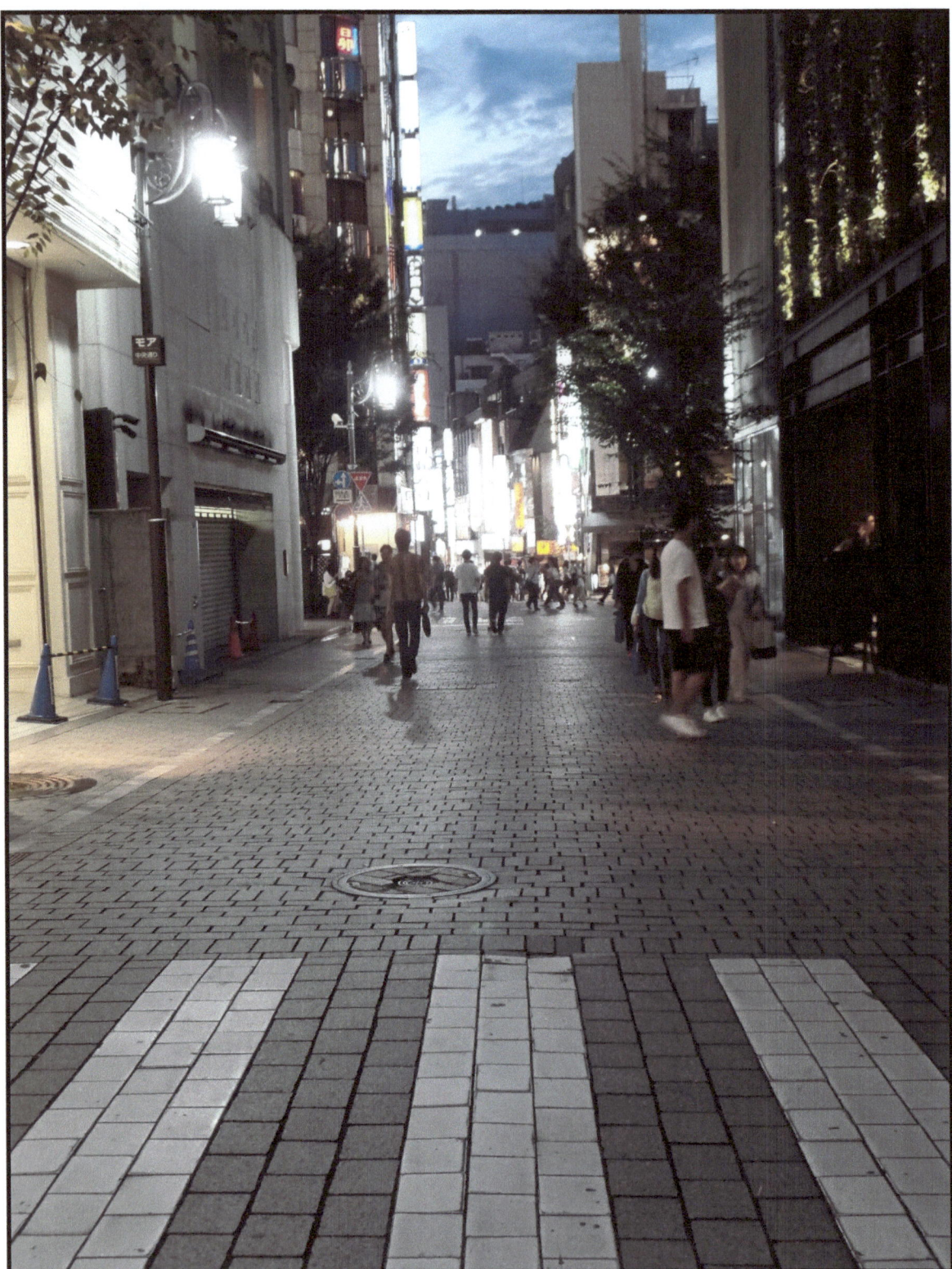

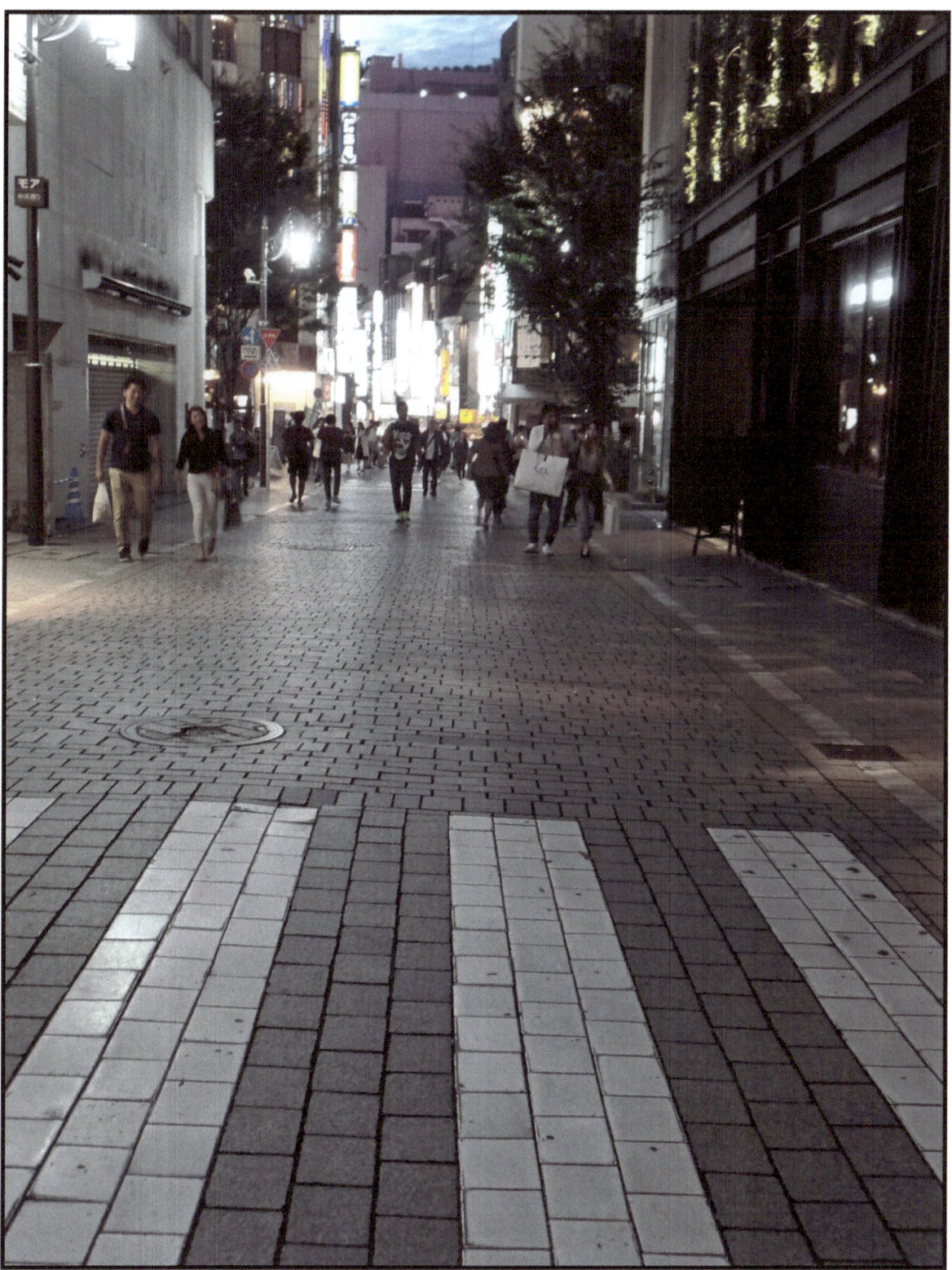

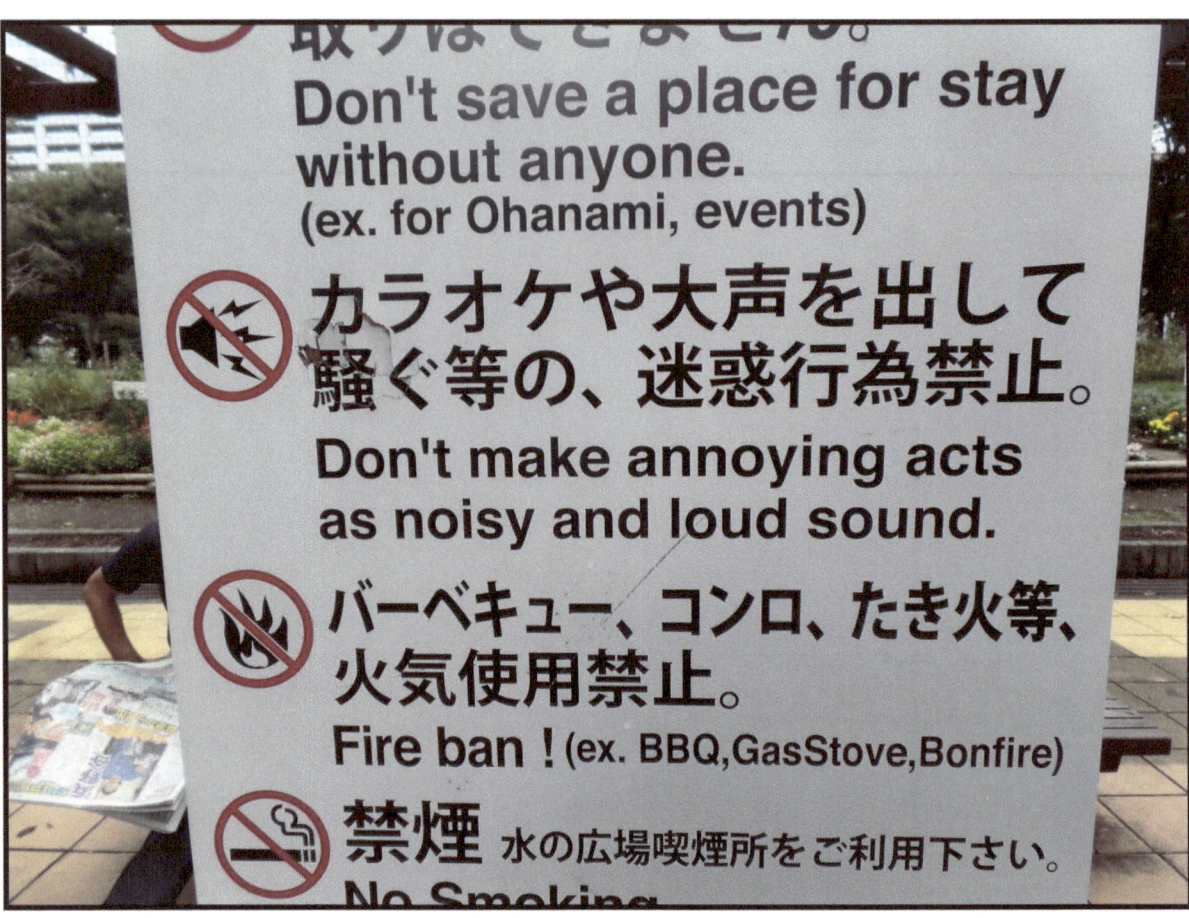

取りはできません。
Don't save a place for stay without anyone.
(ex. for Ohanami, events)

カラオケや大声を出して騒ぐ等の、迷惑行為禁止。
Don't make annoying acts as noisy and loud sound.

バーベキュー、コンロ、たき火等、火気使用禁止。
Fire ban！(ex. BBQ, GasStove, Bonfire)

禁煙 水の広場喫煙所をご利用下さい。
No Smoking

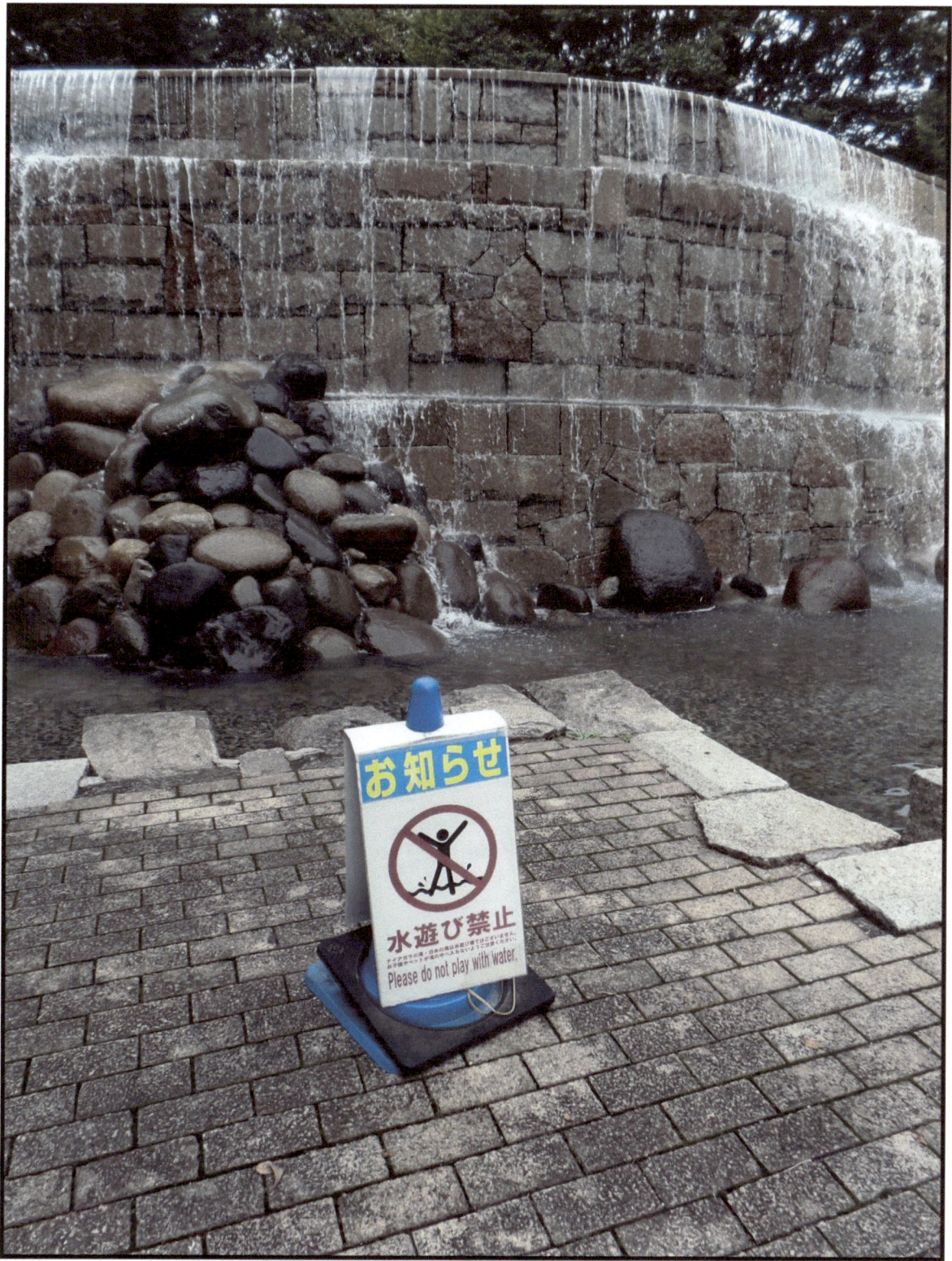

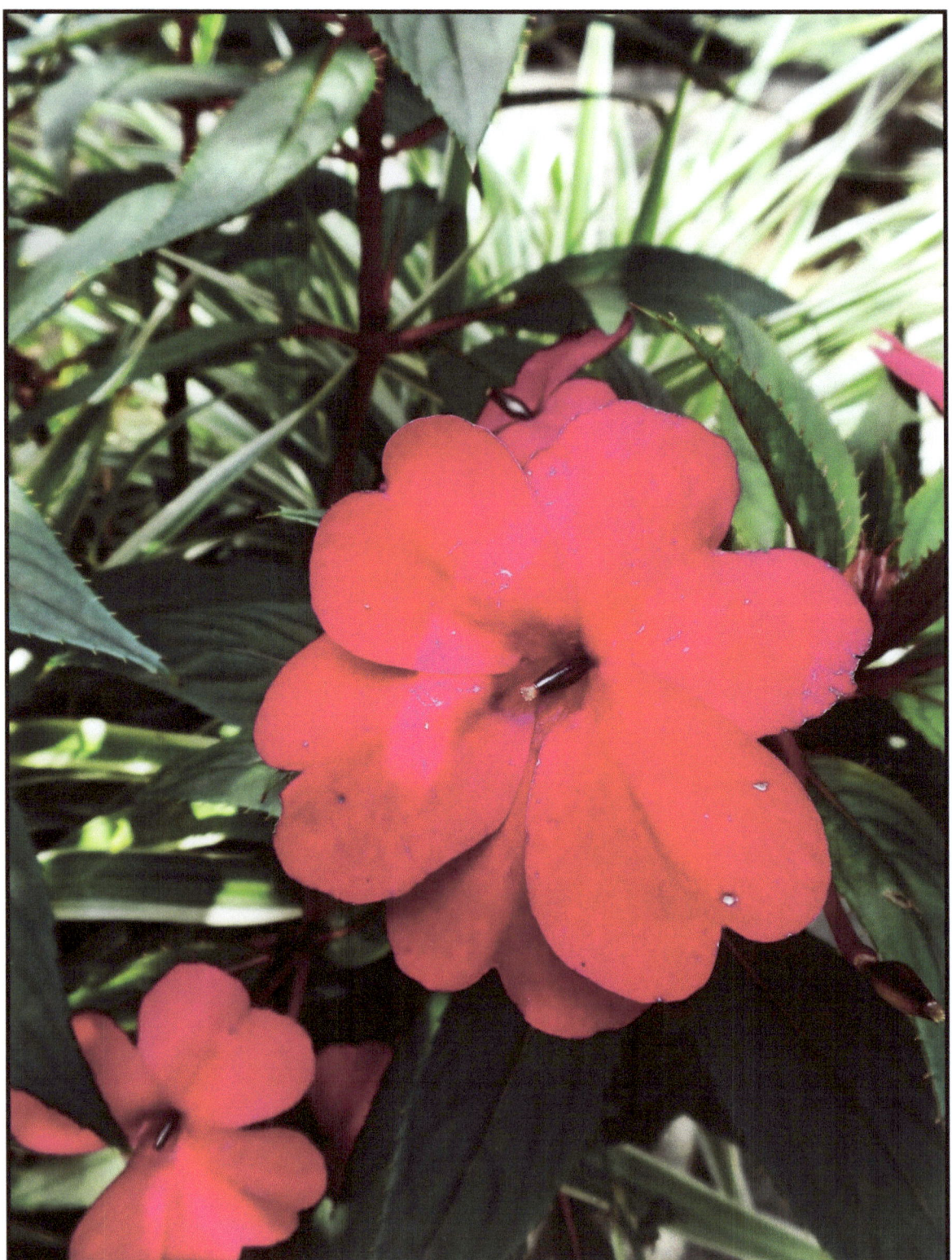

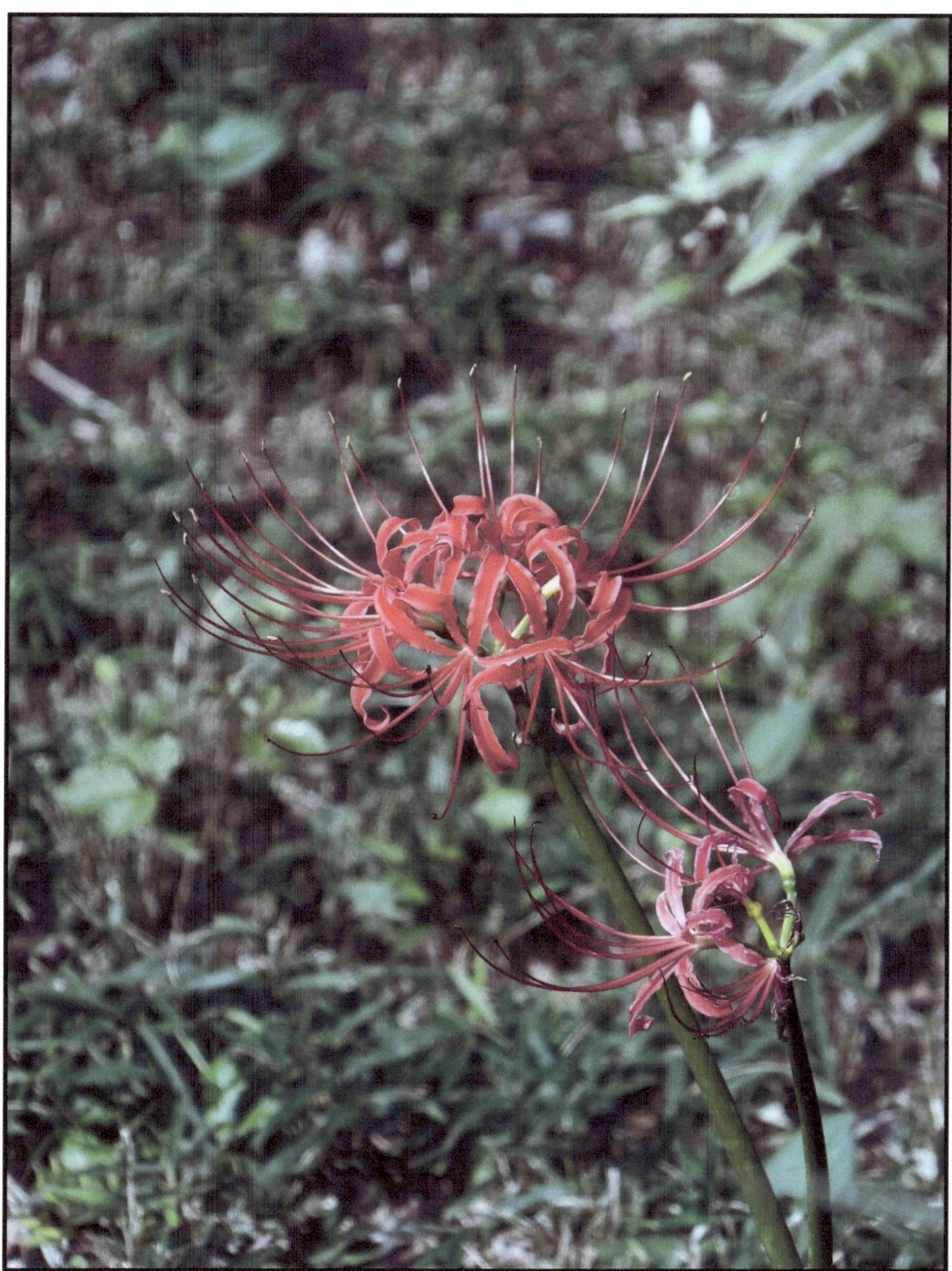

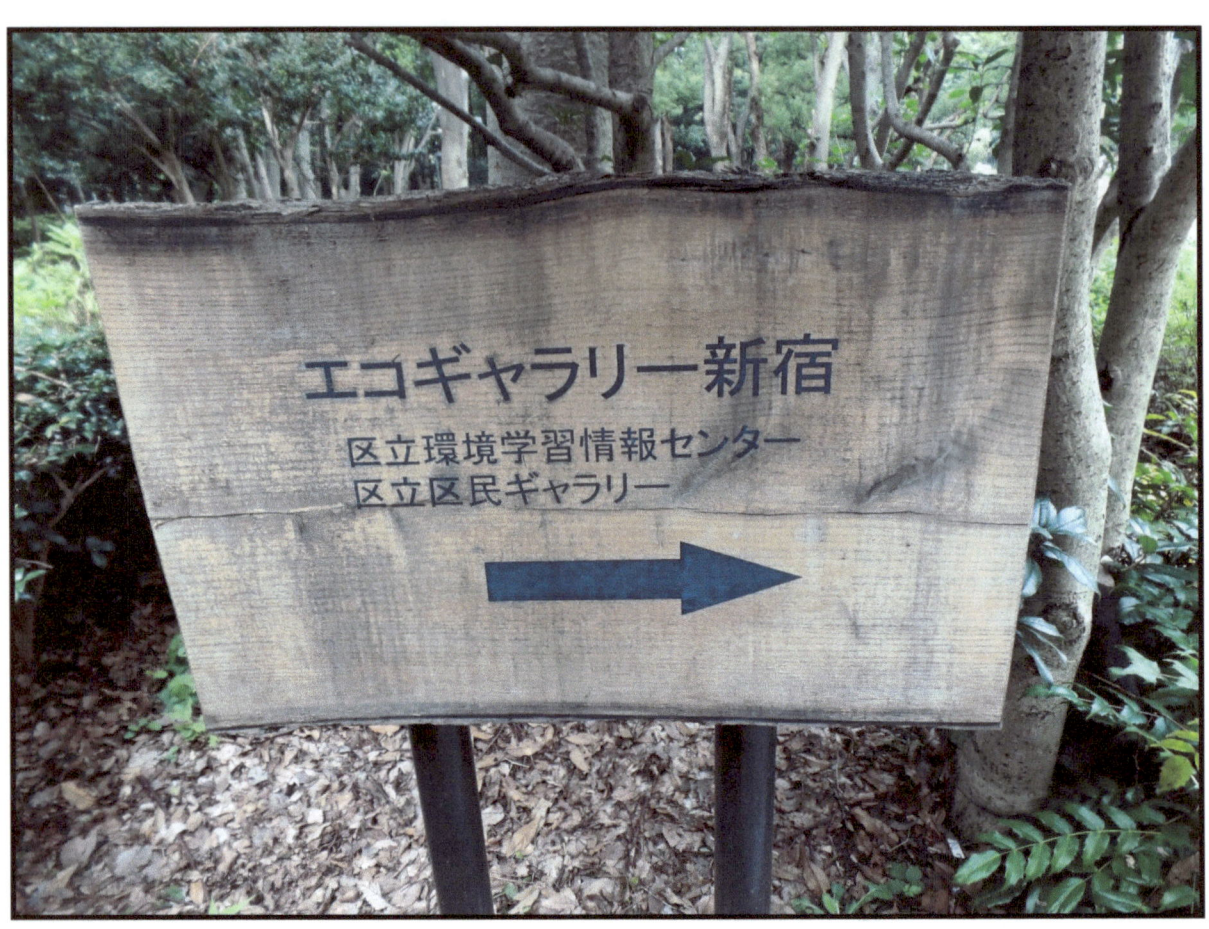

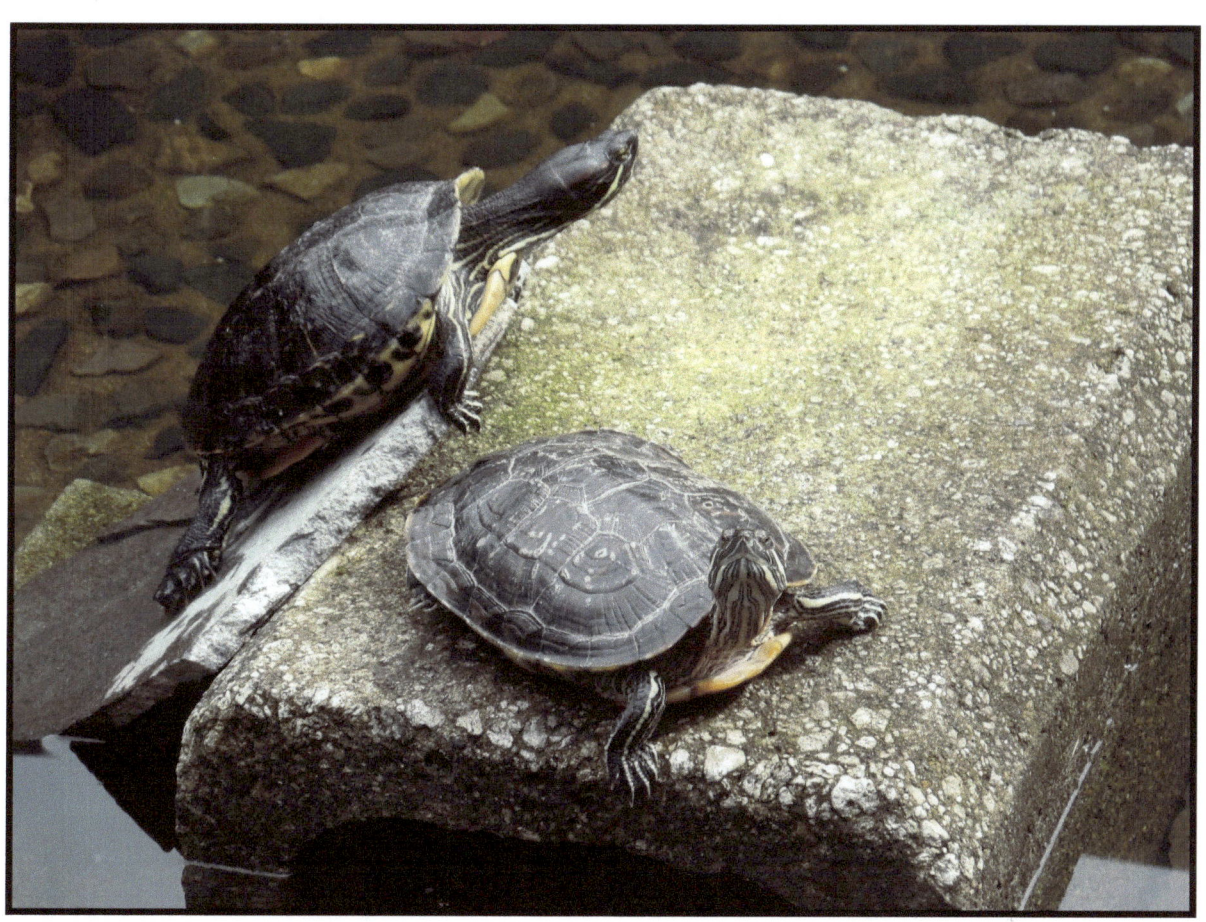

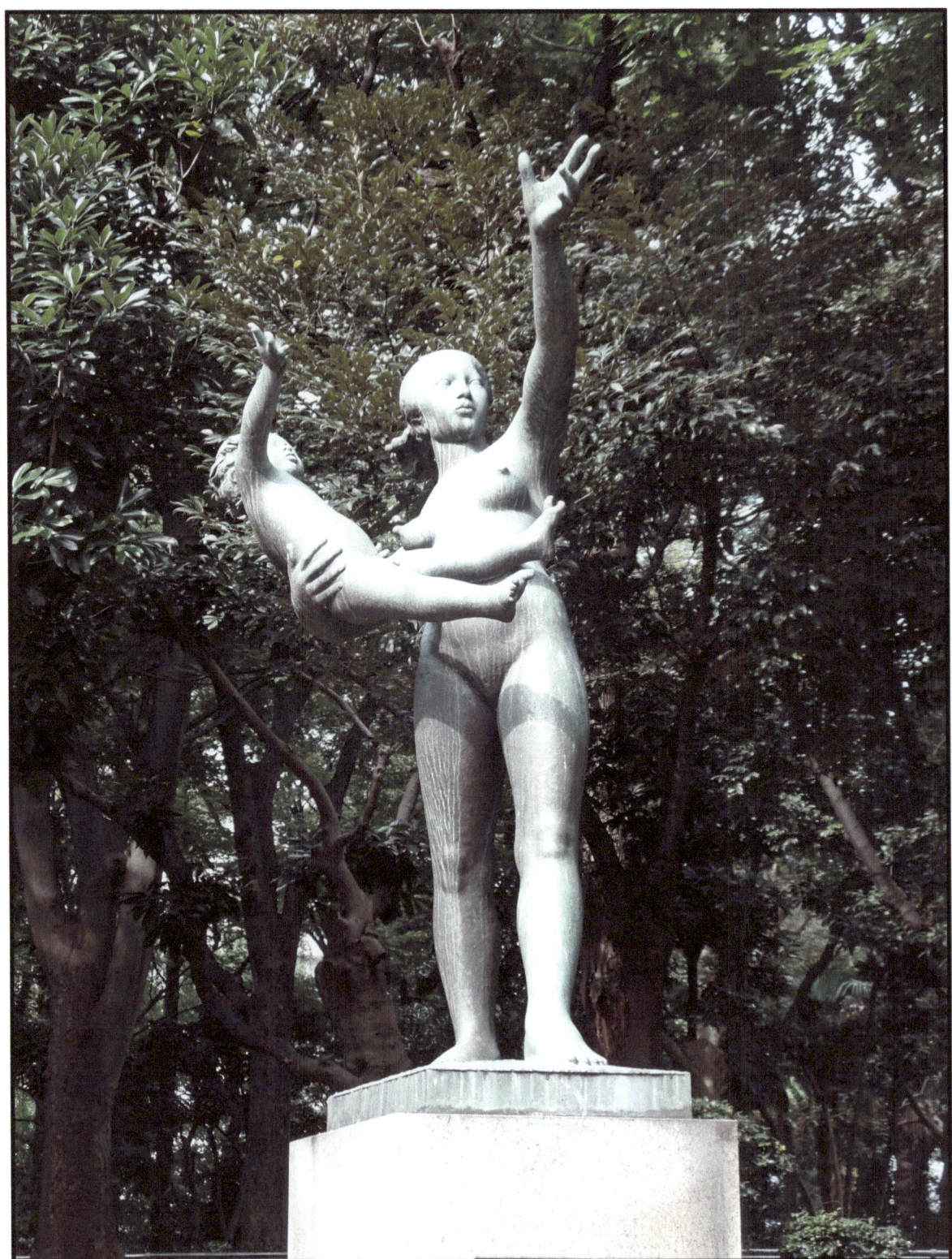

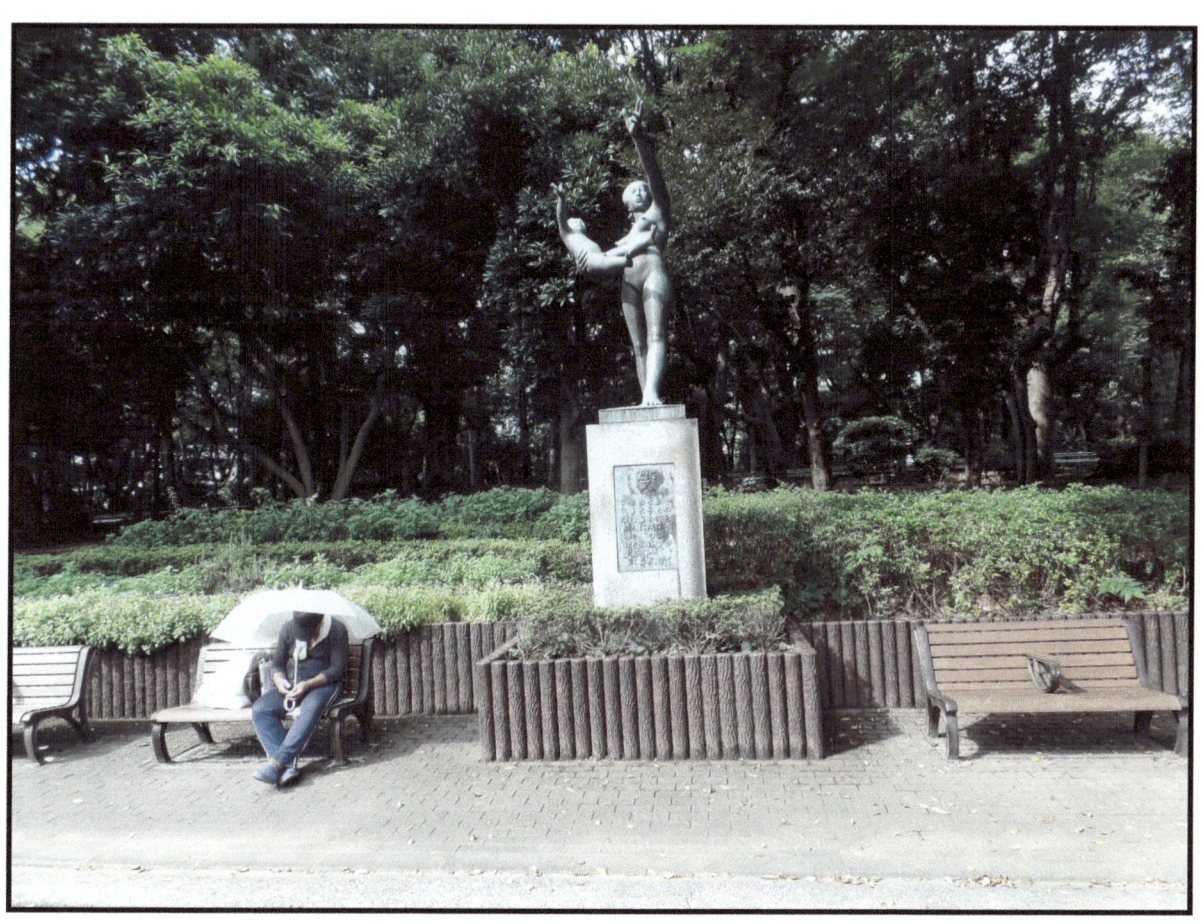

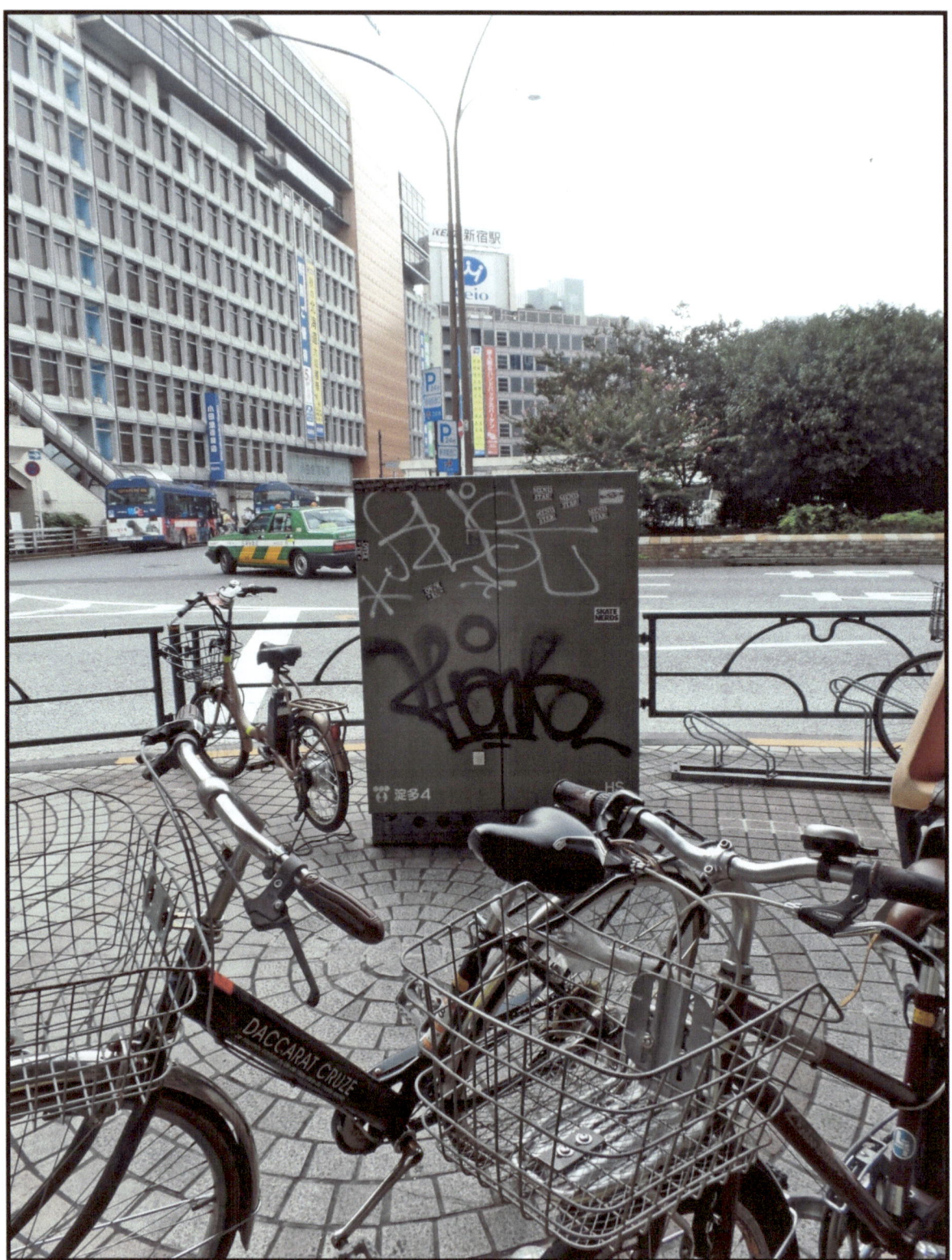

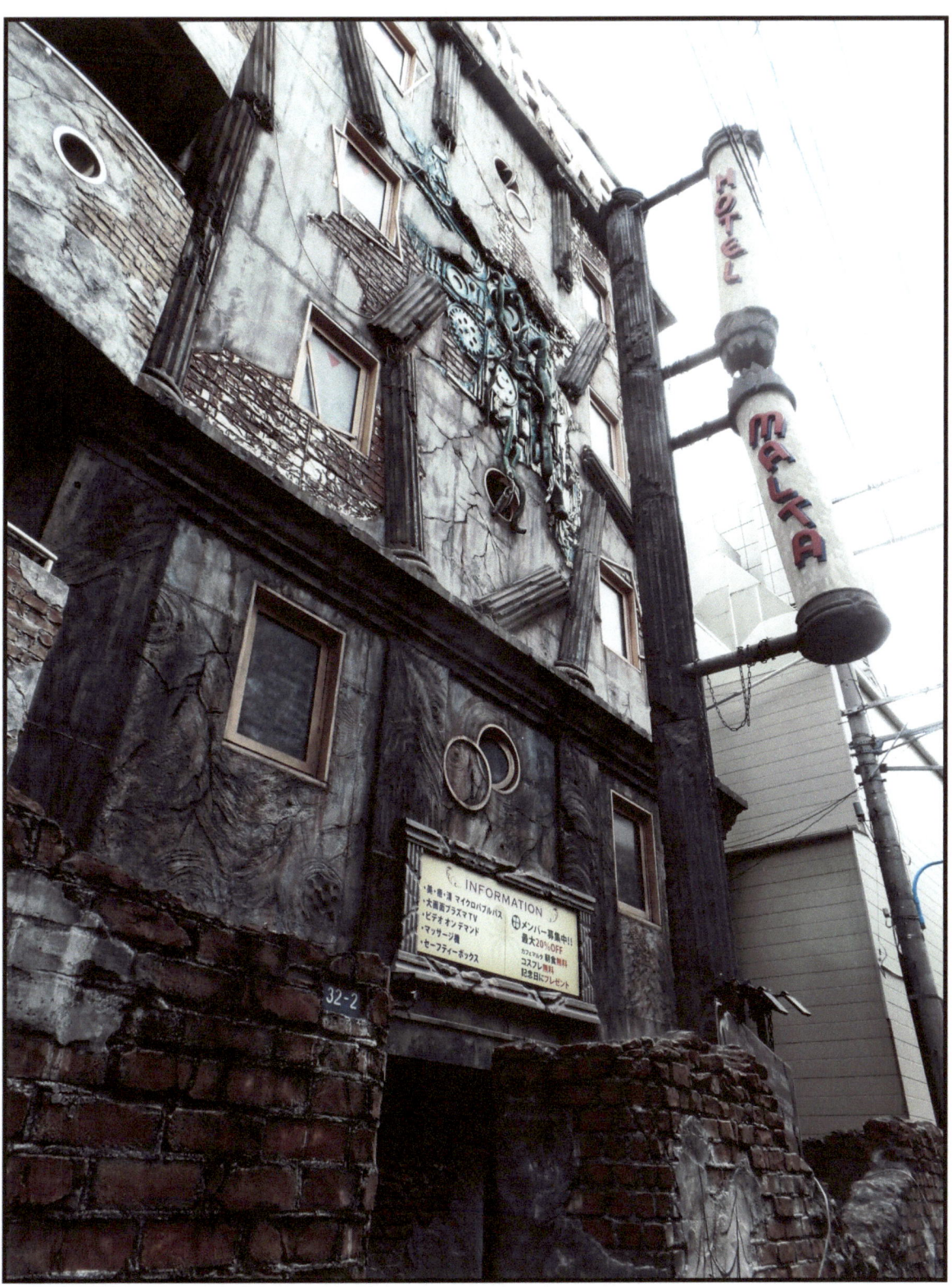

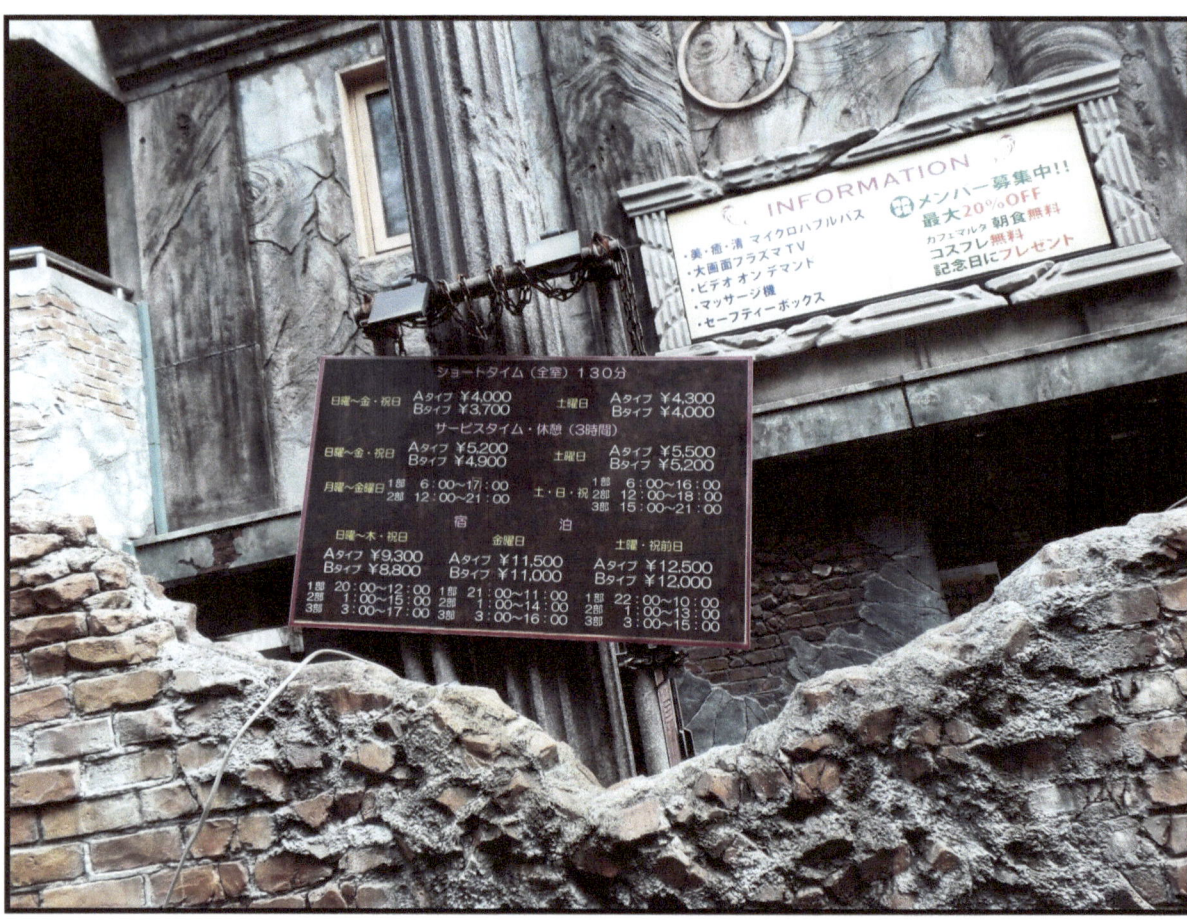

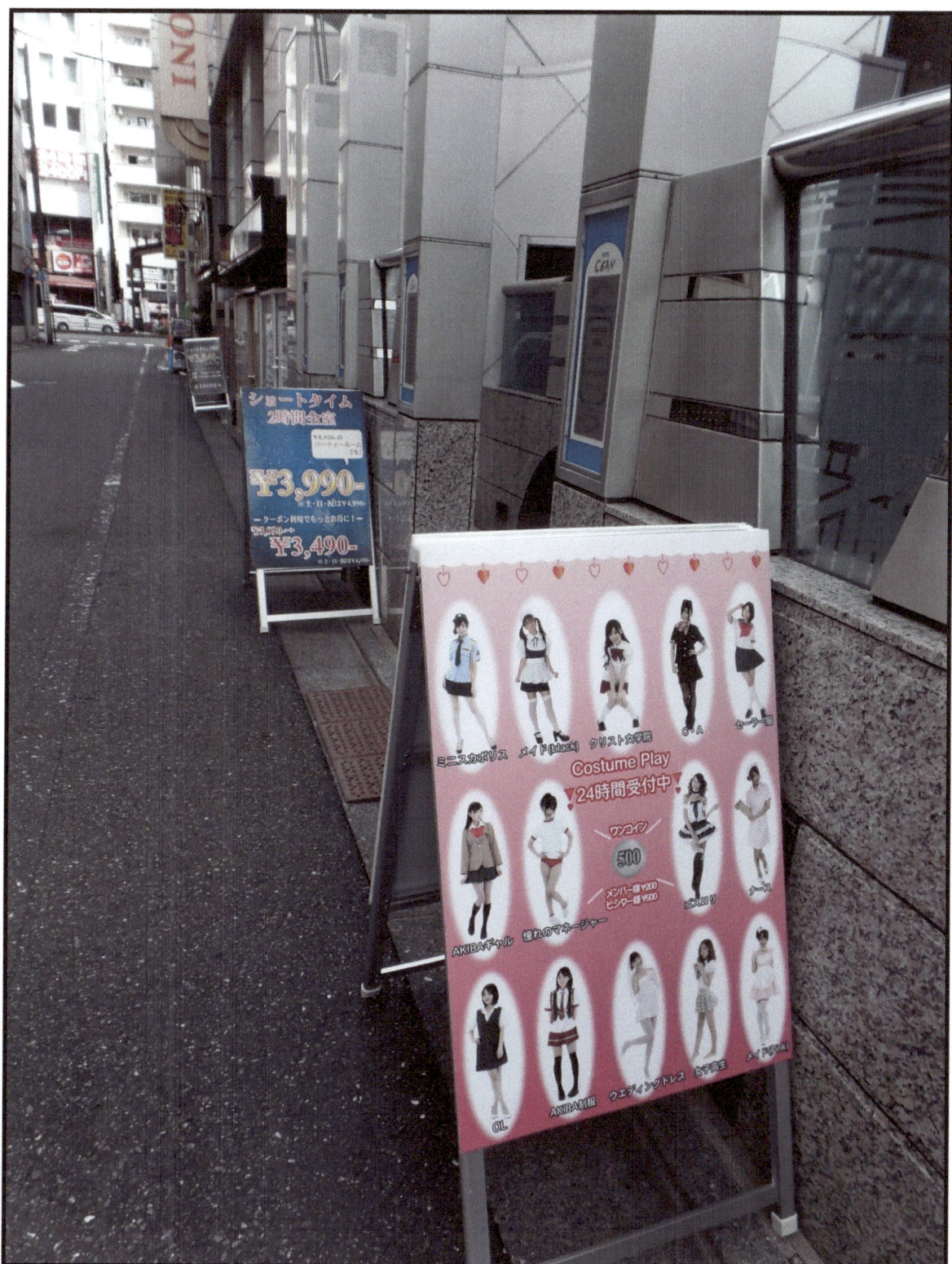

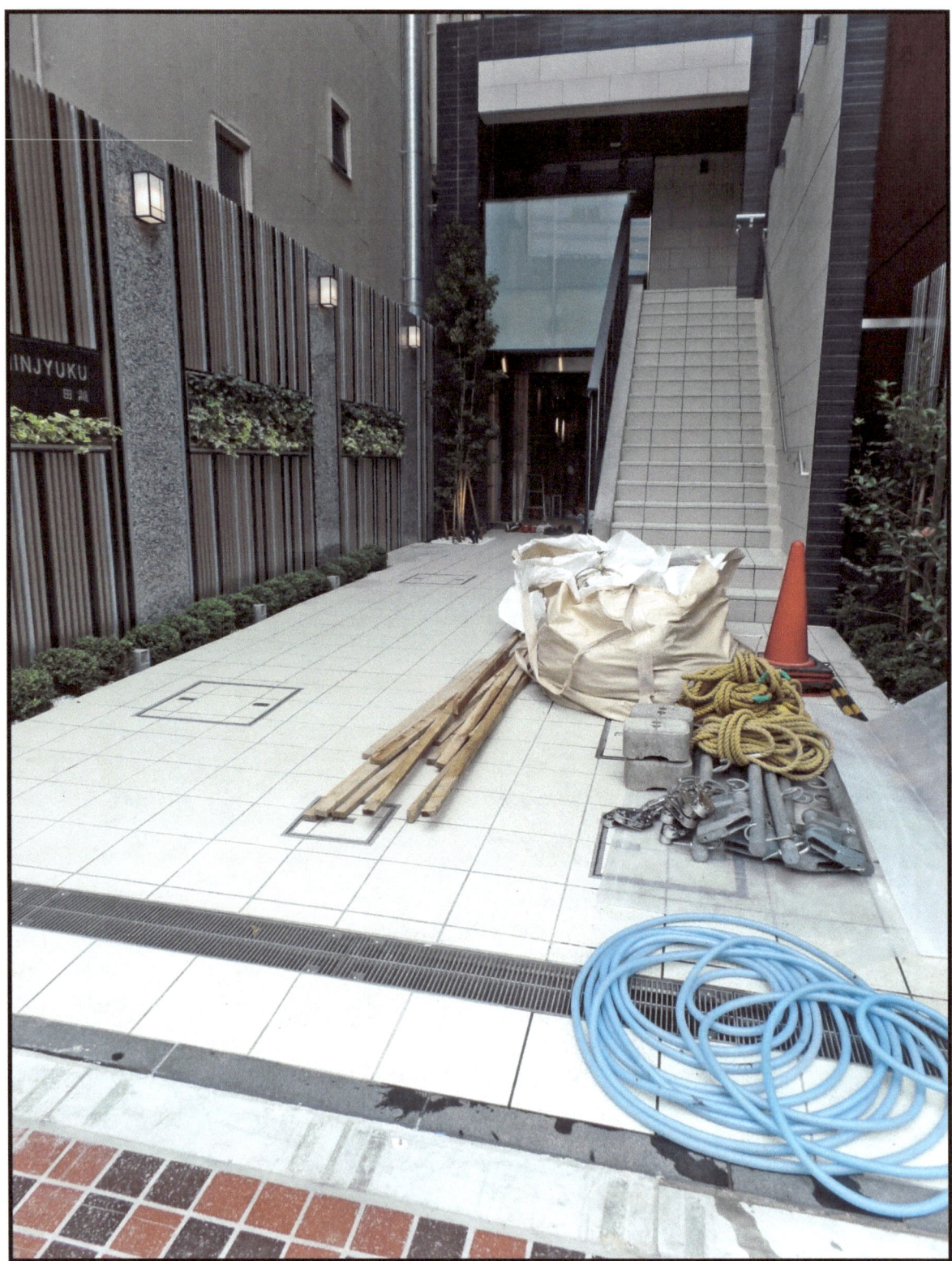